German Poetry
from the Beginnings to 1750

The German Library: Volume 9

Volkmar Sander, General Editor

GERMAN POETRY
from the Beginnings to 1750

Edited by Ingrid Walsøe-Engel

Foreword by George C. Schoolfield

CONTINUUM · NEW YORK

1992
The Continuum Publishing Company
370 Lexington Avenue, New York, NY 10017

The German Library
is published in cooperation with Deutsches Haus,
New York University.
This volume has been supported by a grant from
Robert Bosch Jubiläumsstiftung

Printed in the United States of America

Library of Congress Cataloging-in-Publication Data

German poetry from the beginnings to 1750 / edited by Ingrid Walsøe-
Engel ; foreword by George C. Schoolfield.
    p.   cm. — (The German library ; v. 9)
English and German.
ISBN 0-8264-0337-9 — ISBN 0-8264-0338-7 (pbk.)
    1. German poetry. 2. German poetry—Translations into English.
3. English poetry—Translations from German. I. Walsøe-Engel,
Ingrid. II. Series.
PT1160.E5G38   1991
831.008—dc20   90-26861
                                                                      CIP

Contents

Contents · xiii

Contents · xv

*Indicates extract or abridgment

Foreword

The history of the German lyric is a very long one, and would be longer still, were it not for the almost total disappearance of the pre-Christian poetry of the Germanic tribes. In his *Germania,* written toward the end of the first century A.D., the Roman historian Tacitus describes their heroic songs (chapter 3):

> They recall that Hercules, too, had been among them, and they sing of him as the first of all valiant men when they go into battle. Also, they have certain songs in whose performance, which they call *barditus,* which give fire to their spirits . . . the roughness of the sound and the hollow echo are especially impotant: holding their shields before their mouths, their voices, in the reverberation, swell fuller and more heavily.

The conversion of the Frankish king Clovis I (he had become the leader of his "nation" by murdering his relatives) in 496, while locked in dubious battle with the Alemanni, was a first step in the process of religious change that led, two centuries later, to the great missionary project of the Anglo-Saxon monk, Saint Boniface, in the winning of Hessia, Franconia, Thuringia, and Bavaria for the faith of supernal love, meekness, and human charity. The chopping down of the oak of Donar the thunder god, at Fritzlar in Hessia, was a symbolic start of his task, just as the establishment of the monasteries at Reichenau (724), Murbach (728), and Fulda (744) were its capstones. Boniface had begun his Christian mission under the guardianship of the Frankish king Charles Martel. The latter's grandson, Charles (known to posterity as Charlemagne), saw to it that the pagan Saxons who did not wish to accept baptism were put to the sword. In the so-called Carolingian renaissance that bloomed at Charles's court in Aachen during the monarch's later years (he died in 814), his scholars made some effort to retrieve remnants of pagan song, but none of this material has survived. What we do possess of primitive German verse has come to us as it were by accident: the fragment of an epic depicting a duel between father and son, "Hildebrand and Hadubrand, between two armies," preserved in a manuscript from Kassel of the eighth or ninth century and two spells, in a Frankish dialect, discovered in 1841 in a tenth-century manuscript stashed away in the library of the cathedral chapter at Merseburg in Saxony.

That heathen traces of extraordinary power could be woven into the Christian framework, however, is indicated by the *Muspilli,* with its partly pagan theme, the destruction of the world by fire, and its more or less Christian content, in which the Antichrist does battle with Elijah. The verbal dress of the poem is still the alliterative Germanic verse form (as in the "Lay of Hildebrand" and the "Merseburg Charms"). The long line falls into two halves, each containing two heavy syllables; three of the four stressed syllables in the total line alliterate with one another, that is, they begin with the same sound. It is the verse form, of course, of the Anglo-Saxon *Beowulf* and *The Battle of Maldon,* and it survived in English as late as William Langland's *Piers Plowman* in the fourteenth century ("For trewthe telleth that love is triacle of heven"). This gentler sentiment has a kind of foreshadowing, in Germany, in the almost playful "Weingartner Travel Blessing." Found at a cloister in Upper Swabia, the little prayer has an apparently childlike quality that seems beneficent, even today.

The German documents just named are all in an early form of the language (existing in a number of quite distinct dialects) called Old High German, distinguished by its great richness of vowel sounds and its morphological complexity. A slow phonetic and grammatical simplification resulted in Middle High German, a language far easier to comprehend than its forebear. (The analogy with Anglo-Saxon and Middle English lies close to hand: the former to be penetrated only with special training, the latter accessible to the patient modern reader, provided he or she is given footnotes.) The border area between Old High and Middle High German is represented, in the present volume, by excerpts from the *Carmina Burana,* a name well-known to American concert audiences, thanks to the suite for soloists, chorus, and orchestra by Carl Orff. The

Carmina Burana take their title, once more, from the place where
their principal manuscript was found, the abbey of Benediktbeuern
in Upper Bavaria; the vast majority of the songs in the collection—
products of wandering scholars *(vagantes)* and members of the
clergy—are in rhymed medieval Latin, so that in form (but surely
not in content) they resemble contemporary church hymns. A hand-
ful of the songs, nonetheless, are in the vernacular; some of these,
with a characteristically erotic theme, have been included here.
Notably, these German *Carmina* do not have the patina of learned-
ness of many of the Latin texts; instead, they are unornamented, and
thus quite in keeping with other surviving German poems of the
time, such as the ever-appealing "Dû bist mîn, ich bin dîn," a poem
preserved in a girl's (feigned?) Latin letter to her lover. In the
antiquarian nineteenth century, such poems, or their immediate
descendants, were collected by the philologists Karl Lachmann and
Moritz Haupt under the pleasantly poetic title of *Des Minnesangs
Frühling (The Springtide of Minnesong)*, first published in 1857
and repeatedly revised and augmented. This springtide is generally
reckoned to have lasted from the middle to the final decade of the
twelfth century. Several of the poets who constitute it (insofar as they
are named) seem to have come from Upper and Lower Austria and
Bavaria, and were thus, as has often been noted, geographically at a
considerable remove from the contemporaneous poetry, clever and
complex, of the Provençal troubadours and the Northern French
trouveres. Der von Kürenberg, the author of the famous falcon song,
came from these Danubian parts as did Dietmar von Aist; Meinloh
von Sevelingen may have been a member of a family of *truchsesse*
(lord high stewards) of the dukes of Dillingen, on the border between Swabia and Bavaria. But Friedrich von Hausen can be more
fully identified as the scion of a clan of lesser nobility from the
Rhine-Main region, who died during the Third Crusade, as a vassal
of the emperor-to-be Heinrich (VI), son of Friedrich Barbarossa. The
crusade, against Saladin, who had just retaken Jerusalem, was fairly
ill-fated: Barbarossa drowned in a river in Asia Minor; Philipp of
France went home after having starved out the city of Acre, in uneasy
conjunction with Richard the Lion-Hearted; and Richard himself,
making his way back from the Holy Land, was arrested and held in
prison at Dürnstein on the Danube by Leopold V of Babenberg,
margrave of Austria. (Unable to control his tongue, Richard had

insulted the margrave as they served together against the Saracens.) According to the familiar story, Richard was found in durance vile by the troubadour Blondel de Nesle, who sang half of one of his songs at the foot of the castle's wall; from his cell, Richard answered him with the second half.

If Richard, or his faithful Blondel, could have understood German, they might have listened to the relatively simple minnesongs by the natives of the region, with their open emotions, and the equally natural hope, expressed in their words, of attaining the object of the singer's affections. (As a matter of fact, not only the men but also the women of the Kürenberger and Dietmar von Aist seem beset with sexual longings, and express them.) It is likelier, though, that the more sophisticated and patterned lyrics of Friedrich von Hausen or of Heinrich von Veldeke would have made the greater appeal to the royal prisoner and his troubadour. It seems that von Hausen and von Veldeke met at the splendid festival Friedrich Barbarossa held in Mainz at Whitsuntide, 1184, and there exchanged ideas about a newer, more modern way of writing erotic song. For these and other representatives of the German minnesong, now entering its "classical" age, the composition of love poetry became, in its way, a highly artificial undertaking, based on what—to present-day eyes and feelings—can be an equally artificial emotional constellation. The center of this pattern was the *Frauendienst,* the service of the lady, which entailed a constant devotion—indeed, a reverence—for the altogether unattainable woman, the wife of the singer's lord. It was a literary (and sometimes real) practice made all the more difficult, and unbelievable, by the presence, at least in many of the songs, of the *huoter* and *merkaer,* the watchers and spies or (we might say) snoops, who were attentive to every possible misstep of the singer, even though the singer's songs of unrequited adoration were evidently to be sung before a courtly audience, in a kind of open secret. The causes for the birth and burgeoning of this fragile but vigorous literary and social artifice are many, and have been much discussed by scholarship over the decades. One factor often named is that many, or a majority, of the minnesingers were so-called *ministeriales,* literally "servers," members of the lower nobility, who, as agents of a lord or a prince, often had posts as subaltern military leaders, stewards, or estate managers. They paid a kind of tribute to (or slyly reacted against) their liege by the *Minnedienst,* the love service: the English word *minstrel*, from the Latin root *ministerialis* by way of Old French *menestrel*, is part of the same word-complex. It has also been argued that through this lofty and platonic practice the singer spiritually enriched or ennobled himself. For sources of the cult, scholarship has pointed to similar patterns in the Arabic poetry of Spain, which then was transferred through the troubadours to Germany, to the Mariolatry of Latin religious poetry, to the effect—even thou Ovid had plainly physical aims in mind—of the Roman poet's *Ars amandi* (The art of loving). An interesting subsidiary element in the *Minnedienst* is, of course, its supposed refinement of rough manners and rougher morals; singers and their listeners were expected not to behave in an unseemly fashion, and certainly not to sing frankly about the love of the flesh, Frau Venus, as Tannhäuser is said to have done in the battle of the singers on the Wartburg. Performer and audience were to learn the cardinal virtues of *diu maze* (emotional moderation) and to train themselves in *diu zuht* (discipline) and *diu staete* (faithfulness).

The golden age of the German minnesong is generally reckoned to fall into the forty years from the reign of Heinrich VI (1190–97)—eight strophes from his imperial hand are preserved—to approximately 1230, by which time the emperor Friedrich II, Barbarossa's grandson and Heinrich's son, had shifted his attention and his permanent residence to Apulia and Sicily. Called the *stupor mundi,* "the wonder of the world," Friedrich lived on until the precise middle of the century. Following his reign an already neglected Germany entered a sort of anarchy, the Great Interregnum, to which not even the election of Rudolf of Habsburg as German king in 1273 could bring an effective end. Walter von der Vogelweide, the greatest of the minnesingers and a keen commentator on contemporary events, had predicted the coming decline. Now, if German poetry of the glorious time (and of the glorious emperors) just past had stayed within the limits, emotional and thematic, of the *Minnedienst,* the corpus would have suffered, surely, from monotony—although, within the tight corset of strict *Minnelied,* poets such as Heinrich von Morungen could achieve miracles of self-analysis and psychological depth. Instead, the poetry of the golden age, which contains the courtly epics of Harmann von Aue, Wolfram von Eschenbach, and Gottfried von Strassburg, who introduced a Parnassus of Minnesong into his *Tristan und Isolde* showed a remarkable variety. There were, naturally enough, crusading songs (under which rubric we should understand less inspiratory marching numbers than laments of the singer at being absent from his lady's service); songs of fear about the country's fate while the Hohenstaufen empire went toward its dissolution (as in Walther's case); and songs of grief at the loss of a beloved. (These were sometimes, it should be noted, occasional poetry, as in the epicedium that Reinmar von Hagenau wrote on order for the widow of the Babenberg duke, Leopold V, at Vienna, where Reimar was the court poet). Also, there were poems that by their very nature contradicted the nonpossessive ethos of the love service: for example, Wolfram's songs of uxorious devotion and the *tageliet,* or dawn song, in which Wolfram is again a main representative—see that wonderful song where the dawn, like a giant bird, "strikes his claws through the clouds," awakening the lovers. (The source is the troubadours' *alba,* the *aubade* of the *trouveres.*) In its form, the minnesong likewise seems, on cursory inspection, to be limited: it has two basic types, the strophic *liet,* where each strophe consists of two identical *stollen* and a differing *abgesang,* or epode, a pattern to be repeated in each stanza of the poem, and the *leich,* where the strophes may be of varying sizes and rhymes and metrical schemes. (In the crusading *leich* of Heinrich von Rugge, the longest strophe is sixteen lines, the shortest four.) Yet, here again, the poet's inventiveness often triumphed over the apparently cramped requirements of the one form, the apparent temptation to long-winded looseness of the other.

Very shortly, the practice of *hohe Minne* (lofty love), and its poetic expression, betrayed symptoms of dissolution, and not just in the dawn song and the *tanzliet,* the playful dance song, as represented by Walther's "Under the linden, on the heath": Walther himself complains about *niedere Minne* (lower love), while wondering where decorum has gone. In the dance songs of Neidhart von Reuenthal, born some twenty years after Walther, the courtly world is turned upside down: the social (and sexual) barriers are removed, and the *Minnedienst,* crudely practiced by nobility and farm folk alike, is parodied. (Neidhart would become the super-refined butt of peasant jokes, sometimes scatological, in later medieval literature.) In Steinmar, who may not have been a knight at all, and who lived in the latter part of the thirteenth century, plain realism and plain making-fun of the old courtly world go hand in hand. A realism of a different sort appears in the poems of Swiss minnesingers, springing from a bourgeois culture. A citizen of Zurich, Johannes Hadlaub looked back to a past world of castles, lords, and ladies for his well-to-do audience, while at the same time giving glimpses of town life. He also had a historian's interest in the minnesong; in one of his *Züricher Novellen* from 1876–77, Gottfried Keller tells the tale of Hadlaub's supposed effort, on behalf of his master and patron Rüdiger Manesse, to collect the poems that comprise the great Manesse or Heidelberg Manuscript, with its fanciful illustrations of the classical minnesingers. The Styrian Ulrich von Lichtenstein looked back in a different way, undertaking the grotesque journey— sometimes as a transvestite "Queen Venus"—described in his auto-biographical narrative poem *Frauendienst* as he passed from lady to lady across the eastern and southern marchlands of the empire.

As at its beginning, Austria provided the brightest lights of the minnesong at its end. A native of the Vorarlberg, Hugo von Montfort (1357–1423) demonstrated in his songs that the form was not yet dead. They were directed to each of his three wives. As well, he put the old dawn song to spiritual uses: the watchman, asked if day has come, warns the questioner, the singer, that his time on earth is brief and that he had best remember the "Lord of all Power," and His mother with "twelve stars in her crown." Hugo's great contemporary is Oswald von Wolkenstein, whose South Tyrolean provenience is as sure as Walther von der Vogelweide's is shaky. (Walther's statue, to be sure, adorns the main square of the German-speaking part of Bozen, since 1918, Bolzano.) Oswald, "the man with one eye," put his own long and tumultuous life into what has been called a "lyric autobiography": he traveled widely, as far afield as the Holy Land and Spain and to Avignon, where the schismatic papal residence was about to be shut down. An amorous and political intriguer, Oswald was often imprisoned, on one occasion lured into an ambush by a former mistress. He was an accomplished musician, some of whose song settings have survived. He presented himself with surprising good humor and (as did Walther, Neidhart, and Ulrich von Lichtenstein before him) surprising self-irony. Without doubt, Oswald is a fitting and grand finale to Germany's first major contribution—the minnesong, in all its varieties—to the European lyric.

Simultaneous with the minnesong, and sometimes resembling it, there was another stream of verse, the literature of the *spruch*. The word itself is ambiguous. On the one hand it may refer to poetry of an autobiographical or political-critical nature as practiced by Walther and others, and, as such, was customarily strophic, with fairly complicated rhyme schemes, and was intended to be sung. On the other hand, the term *spruch* was also used to describe verses with a sententious content, in rhyme pairs and without strophic division, meant for verbal (but not musical) performance. A chief representative was "Freidank" (freethinker, so-called because he commented on a large set of moral or behavioral topics), who lived during the golden age; he had taken part in Friedrich II's largely diplomatic crusade to the Holy Land in 1229. Other representatives of this moralizing subgenre were "der wilde Alexander," "der Marner" (who is said to have been murdered, in his old age, for his frankness), and "Frauenlob" (Praise of woman) who despite his much-publicized feud with another versifier, called "Der Regenbogen" (The rainbow) over the relative appropriateness of the terms *wîp* (woman) and *frouwe* (lady), was not in a strict sense a minnesinger but a somewhat pedantic teacher of morality who clad his pronouncements in a dark and would-be learned dress.

Farther down the artistic and social ladder than the genuine minnesingers, these essentially gnomic versifiers are notable as links between minnesong and mastersong. "Frauenlob" in particular was honored by the mastersingers, a group familiar to a modern public through Wagner's *Die Meistersinger von Nürnberg*, just as the minnesingers are known through Wagner's *Tannhäuser*. In the popular mind, the mastersingers, whose first "chamber" appeared in the Augsburg around 1450, have come to stand for German lyric poetry of the sixteenth century. Their arid, epigonic activity flourished principally in the prosperous cities of southern Germany, in Nuremberg above all. They continued to employ the tripart strophe of the minnesingers, their songs were set to music, and their rules of composition and performance were stern, as every listener to Wagner's *Meistersinger* knows full well. These rules, together with a sketch of the poetic guild's history, were set down in 1571 by an artisan named Adam Puschmann, from Görlitz in Lusatia, in his *Gründlicher Bericht des deutschen Meistersangs* (Thorough report of German mastersong). A journeyman-tailor, Puschmann spent six years in Nuremberg, and there became an adept of Hans Sachs, surely the most famous mastersinger of all. The verse by Sachs that lives today, however, is far simpler and more direct than the numbers he wrote to perform for his unimaginative fellow "masters"; the great song with which Sachs greeted the Reformation, "Awake, the day is nearing," adapted by Wagner for the chorus in the final scene of his opera, was meant to stir a broad public.

Here, Sachs belongs not to a moribund tradition from the past but to the vital present, a world in which verse is meant quite simply as propaganda, to arouse and to persuade: Germans must shake off the yoke of Rome. The German language itself had changed: Middle High German had evolved into Early New High German, which had just been given (as it turned out) a kind of standard form, at least for those parts of Germany that would embrace the Lutheran confession. That form was to be found in Martin Luther's bible translation. He made his rendering of the New Testament in 1521 while hiding away, under the protection of Friedrich the Wise of Saxony, on the Wartburg in Thuringia—the very site, once upon a time, of the legendary contest between the minnesingers. Four years earlier, the German Reformation had begun with the posting of the ninety-five theses by the rebellious Augustinian monk, Luther, on the door of the castle church at Wittenberg. The songs of Luther himself bear the clearest witness to the inspiratory and universally understandable intention of verse in the new age, just as does the German-language production of the knight and humanist Ulrich von Hutten. This volatile figure was quite capable of championing, all at once, his dying social class (which descended, often, to sheer highway robbery), the humanism which had come to bloom in Germany in the previous century, and the struggle against Rome—without, however, being much interested in Luther's dogma. The tendentious aggressivity and the deepened spirituality that Lutheranism fostered in its early days were given expression again and again by its many freshly appointed pastors. The Lutheran impulse to hymn-writing, in fact, had not spent itself by the seventeenth century, when such pillars of the now fully institutionalized faith as Martin Rinckart ("Now Thank We All Our God"), Johannes Rist ("Eternity, Thou Thundrous Word"), and Paul Gerhardt ("O Sacred Head, Now Wounded") produced songs that persist, to this day, in American and German hymnals.

At the same time, another kind of German song flourished, largely unnoticed except by the people who made and sang it: the folksong, with its simplicity and its naive and touching emotional tone. It produced such nuggets as the sad ballad of the two royal children, the Christmas song "Es ist ein Ros' entsprungen," the song of erotic longing, "Wenn ich ein Vöglein wär," and the song of a soldier's or journeyman's parting, "Innsbruck, ich muß dich lassen," which last had the exceptional good fortune to be set to music by the court composer of the emperor Maximilian (who reigned on the Reformation's eve). This enormous corpus gained literary respectability only with Johann Gottfried Herder (who gave "Es waren zwei Königskinder" its first printing in the second edition of his anthology *Stimmen der Völker in Liedern* [Voices of the peoples in song, 1807]). Herder's great florilegium, as the title indicates, was international in scope. For the German-language realm alone, Achim von Arnim and Clemens Brentano put together their Romantic anthology *Des Knaben Wunderhorn* (The boy's magic horn, 1806–8), which became an inexhaustible fountainhead of theme and mood for German poets and composers of the nineteenth century, culminating in the two cycles for voice and orchestra of Gustav Mahler, the *Lieder eines fahrenden Gesellen* (Songs of a journeyman, 1883), whose texts are Mahler's own, and the twelve songs from *Des Knaben Wunderhorn* (1889).

The Reformation brought popular social movements with it. In 1525, the German Peasants' Revolt reached its climax; in the same year Thomas Münzer, the self-styled "servant of God against the godless," set up his communistic theocracy in Mühlhausen (Thuringia). These mass stirrings (given voice to the "people" in quite a different sense than in the case of Herder's title) were put down with exceptional cruelty, in the first case by the princes and nobles of the Swabian League, in the second by the freshly baked Lutheran Philipp of Hessia, "the Magnanimous," and his Catholic father-in-law, Georg of Saxony, in both instances with Luther's noisy support. It is one of history's heavy ironies that, a little later on, many of the leaders of the Swabian League entered the Schmalkaldic League, the Protestant confederation that opposed the troops of the emperor Charles V, who was determined to stamp out Protestantism in the empire. After the disastrous battle of Mühlberg in Saxony (1547), Philipp and Johann Friedrich of Saxony (the nephew of

Luther's protector) were taken prisoner; but luck (and fickle allies, including Moritz of Albertine Saxony, Philipp's son-in-law) turned against Charles, and the tired emperor left Germany for the monastery at Juste in Spain, empowering his younger brother Ferdinand to negotiate the Religious Peace of Augsburg (1555). By its formula of *cuius regio, ejus religio,* each ruler of a political entity within the empire was to determine the religion of his subjects, Lutheran or Roman Catholic. (The Reformed Church, or Calvinism, was ignored in the arrangement.)

In the apparently more serene Germany of the years 1555 to 1618, after the tumult of the Reformation had dwindled, one might expect that a secular "renaissance" lyric would appear, treating themes of love and learning with refinement and subtlety, rather as in England under Henry VIII (with Sir Thomas Wyatt) and Elizabeth (with Edmund Spenser and Philip Sidney), or in France, where Charles IX was the patron of Ronsard and his circle, the poets of the Pleiade, or even in Poland, where Jan Kochanowski was favored by king Zygmunt August. This did not happen. As a surrogate, Germany and its adjacent lands saw the bloom of the neo-Latin lyric, whose first great representative was Conrad Celtis (1459–1508). Like many other German humanists, he was the son of humble parents: his father was a winegrower, from Wipfeld near Würzburg in Franconia. Using the meters and poetic forms of antiquity (the Catullan hendecasyllabic, the multiple forms of the Horatian ode, the distich of the Roman elegists), Celtis wrote erotic and cultural-patriotic poetry of a high order and intensity. In one of his *Imaginary Portraits,* Walter Pater paid tribute to the ode with which Celtis had closed his *Ars versificandi* (The art of versification) of 1486, his injunction "to bring Apollo with his lyre to Germany"—in other words, to transfer the spirit and the literary forms of the Greco-Roman past, revived, to northern Europe. (Not a little enviously, Celtis noted in passing that the revivification had long since taken place in Italy.) This literature was to be written in an imitation of classical Latin, not in the despised medieval jargon; and certainly, Celtis would not stoop to the German vernacular of his day, which he correctly judged was not up to the subtle and complex tasks he meant to address. Celtis died in Vienna, an ornament of its university, and riddled with the scourge of the time, venereal disease. His followers were many in the enormously abundant neo-Latin lyric of the sixteenth century. They included Hutten who, in his Latin verse, made savage fun of what he had seen, a jaundiced and irascible observer, at Rome or elsewhere in the Italian peninsula; the biting epigrammatist and writer of socially acute bucolics, Euricius Cordus (1482–1535), to whom Lessing gave an accolade; the "poet-king" of German humanism, Helius Eobanus Hessus (1488–1535), with his heroines modeled on Ovid (feigned love letters in verse, in Hessus's case from the imaginary pens of pious women); the semi-pornographer Simon Lemnius (1511–50) from the Grisons in Switzerland, whose attacks (personal, not confessional) on Luther so annoyed the reformer that, from the Wittenberg pulpit, he demanded—in anticipation of Khomeni—the death of the foul-mouthed upstart; and, in Holland, the early-dead Janus (or Johannes) Secundus (1511–34), the author of *Basia* (Kisses), which Goethe so admired. The elegist Petrus Lotichius Secundus (1528–60) belongs to the next generation: he served as a soldier in the Schmalkaldic War before he went to Montpellier, Avignon, and Italy for medical training as a physician. Returning to a professorship in medicine at Heidelberg, a center of humanistic learning since Celtis's days, he died young, as romantic legend has it in belated result of an aphrodisiac accidentally administered to him in Bologna. The last notable member of this German neo-Latin school was Paul Schede, who took the sobriquet *Melissus,* the "honey-voiced one." A cosmopolitan who had lived in France and England, he was an admirer of Ronsard's art, which he imitated in his own Latin poetry. (His collected Latin works came out in Paris in 1586.) But Schede also wrote verse in German. Once converted to Calvinism, he translated the psalms of Calvin's successor, Théodore de Bèze, and the French proto-Huguenot Clement Marot, into his native tongue, and was appointed director of the Palatina, the great library at Heidelberg, by another Calvinist convert, the Rhenish Palatinate's electoral prince Friedrich IV. Schede also composed some worldly lyrics in the vernacular, including early efforts at a form otherwise almost unknown in sixteenth-century Germany, the sonnet, which on the model of the Italians, Petrarch in particular, flourished in England, France, and Spain.

That Schede's pioneering secular "Renaissance poetry" survives at all (he did not deem it worthy of publication) is due to the zeal of the Heidelberger Julius Wilhelm Zincgref. Friedrich V of the Palatinate—the son-in-law of James I of England—succumbed in 1618 to the lure of the Bohemian throne, tendered by the mutinous Protestant nobles of that imperial crownland. After the defeat of the forces of poor Friedrich, contemptuously called the Winter King, at White Mountain in 1620, in what was the first phase of the Thirty Years' War, the Palatinate had become fair game, and was invaded first by the Spanish troops of Ambrogio Spinola, then by a Bavarian army led by the pious Johann Tserklaes Tilly. Plundering the Calvinist center, Tilly's master, Maximilian of Bavaria, generously gave the Palatina to Pope Gregory XV. Zincgref fled to Strasbourg, and there brought out the collected poems of Martin Opitz, a bright young Silesian he had known briefly in Heidelberg on the eve of its downfall. To these *Teutsche Poemata*, Zincgref subjoined an appendix of other "chosen German poets" in which a few of Schede's poems were included, as well as other verse, by various hands, which seemed to presage, or present, the "renaissance" spirit in German verse. Dissatisfied with what the hapless Zincgref had done, Opitz issued another, much revised edition of his own poems a year later, at Breslau, the capital of Silesia. The place of publication was noteworthy. Once Polish, Silesia had become substantially germanized in the thirteenth century; now largely Protestant, and lying between the imperial-Catholic and Protestant spheres of influence, it became a major battleground of the Thirty Years' War. ("Unhappy Silesia! O wretched fatherland!" another great Silesian poet of the age, Andreas Gryphius, would write.) After the war was over, Silesia fell officially into the empire's and the Counter-Reformation's hands, but the people managed—thanks to stubborn courage and the skillful diplomacy of its city-diplomats—to maintain a modicum of their Lutheran faith and cultural identity. With its writers inspired by the example of Opitz, the so-called father of German poetry, who was compared by his contemporaries with Homer, Virgil, and Ovid, Silesia was easily the most fertile literary region of Germany during the seventeenth century.

Opitz's first poems were in Latin, and he continued to write Latin verse until his death (1639). Yet before he was out of his teens, he had grasped the lamentable fact that Germany did not possess a "modern," an "artistic" literature, despite the richness of its tongue. He suggested remedies first (in 1617) in a Latin treatise called *Aristarchus, sive de contemptu linguae teutonicae* (Aristarchus; or,

concerning scorn for the Teutonic tongue)—we think of Dante's
Latin tract from three centuries before, *De vulgari eloquentia*—and
then expanded his ideas in 1624 with his *Buch von der deutschen
Poeterey* (Book of German poetry), in which he followed in the
footsteps of Du Bellay's *Défense et illustration de la langue française*
(1549–50), Ronsard's *Abrégé de l'art poetique français,* and, perhaps, Sidney's *Apologie for Poetrie* (1598). A principal intention of
Opitz's little book was to do away with the *Knüttelvers* (roughly,
cudgel verse) generally used in the sixteenth century, with its three-
or-four-foot lines, its great permissiveness (it allowed any number of
unaccented syllables to intrude into its basic iambic pattern), and its
tendency to be careless about a congruence between word accent
and metrical stress, which could make words emerge with a comical
misaccentuation. Opitz recommended that lines of verse should be
composed of regular iambs or trochees, and that word-and-verse
stress correspond. Taking the French as a model, he strongly favored
the Alexandrine line, six iambs with a clearly marked caesura,
twelve syllables if the ending (the rhyme word) was masculine,
thirteen if feminine. Spurning the folksong, and its metrical and
linguistic irregularities, Opitz argued for what has been called "an
early baroque classicism": he suggested a limited number of rhetori-
cal (and sound) devices for giving "elegance or adornment" to the
poetic line, he made the differences between genres clear, at least in
some cases (for example, the eclogue and the elegy), he recommended in the strongest terms the use of the sonnet (turning poems
of Ronsard into German as illustrations), and, less strongly, recommended such large forms as the so-called pindaric ode. He was keen
to suggest foreign models, not just Ronsard but the Dutch poet
Daniel Heinsius, whose sonnets and panegyrics he also translated.
(Netherlandic examples were cleverly employed by Opitz; if the
Dutch, in their closely related tongue, could write the new poetry,
Germans could surely emulate them.) Nor was he forgetful of the
classical and neoclassical tradition: for the elegy, he listed the "masters," Ovid, Propertius, Tibullus, Jacopo Sannazaro (the Latin-and-
Italian poet of the late fifteenth century), Janus Secundus, and
Lotichius Secundus. Above all, he plumped for the nobility or even
the divine nature of the poet's calling—but added, of course, in his
how-to-do-it book, that the art of writing elegant poetry had to be

learned, albeit "this glorious science" would require inspiration as well.

By means of this pamphlet, and his own copious verse, much reprinted during and after his lifetime, Opitz opened the sluices for a flood of poetry, and of poetic handbooks. One manual after another was produced in the course of the century, all more detailed and better organized than Opitz's, but none as stimulating; and the writing of sonnets (as well as reams of other verse, often occasional, in Alexandrines) became a cottage industry in Germany. It must be noted that the production of verse according to the Opitzean model was a Protestant phenomenon. The Catholic Counter-Reformation did not encourage literary creation for any worldly sake. The rather few Catholic poets writing in the vernacular perforce chose exclusively and sometimes saccharinely devotional topics (the Jesuit Friedrich von Spee his *Trutz-Nachtigall,* the convert-novelist Grimmelshausen his nightingale song, the convert-priest Angelus Silesius and the actor-turned-Capuchin Laurentius von Schnüffis their allegorical pastorals). Interestingly, the Jesuit Jacob Balde (1604–68) could escape, on occasion, the religious mold, through his deft and subtle political and philosophical comments, but he made these in his Latin odes and *silvae* (poems of mixed content). Balde's German verse is crude; like almost all Catholic vernacular verse of the time, it is meant to appeal to a mass public, or congregation—and Balde's German, like that of his fellow believers, has not had the benefit of training in the powerful language of the Luther bible. Modern observers have proposed that the "baroque art" of Protestant Germany was essentially a "word art," that of Catholic Germany, with its handsome churches and cloisters, an "image art."

The Lutheran emphasis on the importance of the word of God, as represented in Holy Scripture, had a kind of secular outlet—again, limited to the Protestant sections of Germany—in the so-called language societies, which had the purpose of keeping the German tongue pure and supple (by seventeenth-century standards), and of seeing to it that the laws of rhetoric and genre were properly applied. Also, these societies, in which princes, noblemen, scholars, clergymen, and Germany's few professional writers met (or at least corresponded), served to bolster Opitz's belief in the importance of the poetic vocation, and gave practitioners of the literary art the sense of belonging to a larger entity, the equivalent of the res publica litteraria of the humanists. Of the societies, the first and most prestigious was the "Fruchtbringende Gesellschaft" (Fruit-bringing society) of Prince Ludwig von Anhalt-Köthen, with its headquarters at Weimar. Others were the "Aufrichtige Gesellschaft von der Tannen" (Upright society of the fir) in Strasbourg, distinguished more by the patriotism of its program than the poetic gifts of its members; the "Teutschgesinnte Genossenschaft" (German-minded fellowship) in Hamburg, founded by the man of letters Philipp von Zesen, and with a ladies' auxiliary; the rival "Elbschwanenorden" (Order of the Elbe swan) in Lübeck, founded by Zesen's nemesis, the pastor Johannes Rist (who depicted Zesen in his plays as a silly dandy); and the more compact "Pegnesischer Blumenorden" (the Pegnitz flower order) of Nuremberg, on the Pegnitz River, which—in its gifted members, Harsdörffer, Klaj, Birken—gave German verse some of the musicality Opitz may have neglected, introducing the dactyl and the anapest that Opitz had forbidden. (In his poetics, Zesen was the spokesman of even greater metrical variety.) Other local or regional schools developed as well: imitators of Opitz in wealthy Danzig (now the Polish Gdansk) and in his native Silesia; the gentle group of poets at Königsberg (now the Russian Kaliningrad) in East Prussia, who, gathered around Simon Dach, had a kind of sweet naiveté, and called their little club, the "Musical Pumpkin Hut" (the pumpkin, as in the book of Jonah, was an emblem of the transitoriness of human existence); and the more sophisticated poets of the Middle German (Leipzig-Dresden) academy-court axis (the ebullient Schirmer, eventually a librarian at Dresden, the equally lively Stieler, who, after the youthful sins of his song collection *Die Geharnschte Venus* [Venus in arms] became a respected lexicographer).

Of course, there were the outsiders, too: the Swabian Georg Rudolf Weckherlin, a migrant to England, with his superb erotic poetry (directed, evidently, to his English wife, Elizabeth Raworth), and Paul Fleming, a member of a trade-and-diplomatic mission sent by the ambitious duke of Holstein-Glückstadt to Muscovy and Persia, a poet whose strong personal note can smack, for Anglophone readers, of the Elizabethan and Jacobean lyric. Weckherlin's *Geistliche und Weltliche Gedichte* came out in Amsterdam in 1641 (revised and expanded in 1648), a year later Fleming's collected poems appeared posthumously at Hamburg. It can be argued that with their collections, and the appearance, at about the same time of the sonnets and odes of Andreas Gryphius, the German lyric of the seventeenth century had quickly reached its zenith, to be followed in short order by the epigrammatic art, variously lay or mystic, of the Silesians Fredrich von Logau, Angelus Silesius (most of whose often paradoxical epigrams were written before his conversion), and Daniel von Czepko, and the sonnets and spiritual songs of the Lutheran refugee from Lower Austria, Catharina Regina von Greiffenberg. (In her brilliant use of emblems, Greiffenberg has few rivals in the century, and might be called its greatest woman poet—were it not for Sibylle Schwarz, with her adolescent ardor: German poetry would not see another prodigy of her rank until the debut of "Loris" in 1891—the seventeen-year-old Hugo von Hofmannsthal.)

During the century's second half, poetic oddities appeared: the compulsive and exquisite eroticism of Hofmann von Hofmannswaldau, the tormented *concetti* of Daniel Casper von Lohenstein, the crazy religious fanaticism of Quirin Kuhlmann—to which list another Silesian could be added, although examples of his work do not appear in the present volume: Hans Aßmann von Abschatz, with his renderings, after the Italian Adimiri, of sonnets about peculiar sorts of beauty (for example "The Lovely Hunchback" and "The Lovely Big Nose") and his "Wintergreen of German Heroes," in part a catalogue, overwhelming in its sound (like Kuhlmann's repetition of the word *Triumph*), of the names of Silesian noble families. Curiously, the Silesian tradition came to stand, at its end, for literary concupiscence if not perversity. From 1695 until 1727 a Silesian poetaster, Benjamin Neukirch, brought out the seven volumes of *Des Herrn von Hofmannswaldau und anderer Deutschen auserlesene und bisher ungedruckte Gedichte* (Selected and hitherto unprinted poems of Mr. von Hofmannswaldau and other German poets), in which items of Hofmannswaldau were included that the Breslau patrician would not have wanted published during his lifetime, as well as verse—sometimes of a magnificently scabrous sort— by the late Lohenstein and other, lesser names. And, shortly before the final volumes of the Neukirch series appeared, the works of still another Silesian, recently dead, were issued, Johann Christian Günther, a poet for whom love was not mechanical and carefully orchestrated lust, but suffering: Günther looked ahead, some fifty years, to the Goethe of Sturm und Drang.

The poetry of the seventeenth century (or the baroque) fell quickly into disrepute. The late Silesians, especially, were reviled for their Marinism as for their lubricity. They became the whipping boys of the powerful rationalist critic Gottsched, and his influence was so strong that the entire baroque corpus came to be largely ignored, save for some lip service paid to Opitz, Fleming, and Gryphius. Günther kept his reputation as much for the unhappy story of his life as for his art. During the nineteenth century, German scholarship collected and admired the minnesong, while the "age of bombast" stayed pretty well in limbo. It was only in the 1920s that criticism came to appreciate the literature of the seventeenth century on its own terms: religiously and erotically both intense and artificial, constantly engaging in excessive ornament and rhetoric, delighting in the grandiloquent verbal gesture, even at the approach of death, as in the "Dying Song" of a baroque grandee, Anton Ulrich von Braunschweig-Wolfenbüttel.

An exhausted reaction against baroque excess and maximalism set in, fostered in a new and sensible climate. (At least one poetic form was exhausted too: the sonnet would lie fallow until it was rediscovered, on the basis of romance models, by Gottfried August Bürger in the 1790s.) Nature, which had never figured very large in the baroque scheme of things (save for the stylized *locus amoenus* and the persistent adduction of Horace's Bandusian spring), caught the attention of poets both by means of its wonders, and through the presence of God in all His creation, large or small. A playful and, as it were, measured sophistication asserted itself in anacreontic and rococo poetry, which was graceful and witty, and influenced by French models (Gresset, Piron, Moncrif, "Gentil-Bernard," the Abbé de Bernis). Yet its German practitioners were certainly much less naughty than, for example, the Piron who wrote *Le Cantique à Priape*. Their poems are (more or less) respectable jests, exchanged between the members of a small circle, centered around the staid Saxon university town of Halle, where a number of them had studied. Their mostly imaginary eroticism is to be taken much less seriously than their very real friendships, and their cultivation—as provincial and bourgeois equivalents of Lord Chesterfield—of a tolerant, "Horatian" attitude, i.e., the Roman poet regarded as the arbiter of gentle pleasure and a sensible attitude toward life. It is no accident that the two figures of antiquity toward whom these polished versifiers looked, Anacreon and Horace, are both wise, well along in years, and fond of their cups—in moderation.

The members of the Halle circle attracted altogether earnest admirers, for example the Prussian officer Ewald von Kleist, author of the "Ode to the Prussian Army," who died of wounds after Friedrich the Great's defeat at Kunersdorf. A strong current of patriotism, as of sober piety, had long run parallel to the rococo mode (with its ribbons, shepherdesses, and zephyrs). Ramler taught at the cadet school in Berlin, and showed his love of country by the very title of his popular anthology *Lieder der Deutschen* (Songs of the Germans). These *poetae minores* and their colleagues pursued mostly admirable aims, but possessed only limited imaginations. Suddenly though, a bonafide genius was able to bring all the disparate strains of the mid-century together, and transform them. The reader will see how, in "The Lake of Zurich" Friedrich Gottlob Klopstock infuses the rococo picnic, and the cult of friendship, with a sense of the grandeur and mystery of nature. Today it may be difficult for a German audience, let alone an American one, to appreciate the strengths of Klopstock's lyric poetry: his often-strained diction and his fondness for complex Horatian strophes (or equally complex metrical and strophic patterns of his own devising) are barriers, as is his tendency toward what may best be described as unflagging exaltation. We may smile, too, at his occasional over-glorification of his Danish patrons, at the sometimes lachrymose idealization of his beloveds, and at his manufacture of cultural myths. (This is especially noticeable in his "bard poetry," in which he conjures up a scrambled vision of the ancient German past, blithely mingling the Celtic concept of the bard with the Teutonic *barditus* of Tacitus.) One must, however, admire the great range of his topics, the inventiveness and unconventionality of his language, his emotional sensitivity and overriding love of humanity, with which he combined an exceptional visionary gift. Unlike some other seers, he was concerned about the lot of his fellow men. At a climactic point Goethe's *Die Leiden des jungen Werthers (The Sufferings of Young Werther)*, the protagonist's beloved Lotte goes to a window after a rainstorm, looks out, puts her hand on her heart, and, her eyes full of tears, says "Klopstock!" Werther and the public of Goethe's day knew that she alluded to Klopstock's "Die Frühlingsfeier" (The celebration of spring). A century later, and more, Klopstock still had his devotees. Mahler used his ode "Die Auferstehung" (The resurrection) for the finale of the Second Symphony, and Rilke found, in Klopstock, a guide toward his own late poetry, the *Duino Elegies* and the *Sonnets to Orpheus*.

GEORGE C. SCHOOLFIELD

Introduction

In compiling this anthology, it occurred to me that an anthologist and a gardener have much in common, for an anthology is but a collection of the flowers of verse, a display of lyric blooms and poetic shrubbery, reflecting not only the preferences of the horticulturalist, but also the availability of suitable seedlings and beneficent climatic conditions. And so it is that some readers may lament the absence of their favorite flowers amidst the colorful display, or wonder at the lush intensity in certain periods, but I ask those readers to consider that this particular garden of verse was planted entirely with translated blossoms, and they are often hard to find, although well worth the effort.

My task was to compile, within strict spatial limits, a representative selection of nine centuries of German verse in English translation, from spells and travel blessings in the tenth century to the complex odes of Friedrich Gottlob Klopstock in the eighteenth century. The general reader will be quick to recognize the powerful hymns of Martin Luther and Paul Gerhardt in the collection, as well as popular folksongs, but he or she may be unfamiliar with many of the beautiful voices represented here: the minnesingers such as Der von Kürenberg, Friedrich von Hausen, Heinrich von Morungen, Walther von der Vogelweide; the baroque stylists Opitz, Weckherlin, Fleming, Gryphius, Lohenstein, and so on. But even flowers whose names we do not know smell just as sweet as the ubiquitous and more famous rose, and so the reader is invited to sample the unknown blossoms of this garden, and, in so doing, to begin to understand the lyric tradition that preceded, and was indispensable to, the powerful verse of Goethe, Schiller, Hölderlin, Novalis, and Heine. (Short biographies of each author are included on pages 313–27 and may be of interest.)

The selection offered here is not a scholarly one. Some poets have never been translated and appear not at all, others are underrepresented, not because they have not been translated, but because their work appears extensively in translation elsewhere. In an effort to be representative, I have sometimes had to resort to translations (including my own), which may be less than successful, but such flaws are balanced by the powerful renderings of such gifted translators as George C. Schoolfield, Frederick Goldin, J. W. Thomas, Alexander Gode, and Henry W. Longfellow. My special thanks is due to those who, perhaps against their own better judgment, spent many agonized hours composing new translations for this volume. My hope is that it will reveal to the English reader the breadth and beauty of German poetry before 1750.

I. W.-E.

German Poetry
from the Beginnings to 1750

Anonymous

Erster Merseburger Zauberspruch*

Eiris sazun idisi,†   sazun hera duoder.
suma hapt heptidun,   suma heri lezidun,
suma clubodun   umbi cuoniouuidi:
insprinc haptbandun,   inuar uigandun!—

Zweiter Merseburger Zauberspruch

P*h*ol ende Uuodan‡   uuorun zi holza.
du uuart demo Balderes uolon   sin uuoz birenki*t*.
thu biguol en Sin*th*gunt,   Sunna era suister,
thu biguol en Friia,   Uolla era suister,
thu biguol en Uuodan,   so he uuola conda:
sose benrenki,   sose bluotrenki,
      sose lidirenki,
ben zi bena,   bluot zi bluoda,
lid zi geliden,   sose gelimida sin!—

---

*Two magic spells recorded in a missal in Merseburg in the tenth century. Pre-Christian in origin, the first spell is designed to procure the release of a captive, whereas the second will heal a lame horse.
†*idisi:* probably a kind of Valkyrie.
‡Germanic gods.

Anonymous

First Merseburg Spell

Once upon a time, the goddesses settled down,
Sat down here, and sat down there.
Some fettered the foe, others hindered the hostile forces.
Still others loosed the fetters of the friendly ones:
Spring forth from the fetters, flee the foe!

Carroll Hightower

Second Merseburg Spell

Phol and Wotan rode through the forest;
There Wotan's mount injured his leg.
Then Sindgund spoke over him, and Sunna, her sister;
Then Frija said a spell, and Volla, her sister.
Then Wotan as well, as best he knew how!
As the injury of the bone, so that of the blood,
So that of the whole limb!
Bone to bone, blood to blood, limb to limb,
May they hold fast anew!

Carroll Hightower

Muspilli*

. . . sin tac piqueme, daz er touuan scal.
uuanta sar so sih diu sela   in den sind arheuit
enti si den lihhamun   likkan lazzit,
so quimit ein heri   fona himilzungalon,
daz andar fona pehhe: dar pagant siu umpi.
Sorgen mac diu sela,   unzi diu suona arget,
za uuederemo herie   si gihalot uuerde.
uuanta ipu sia daz Satanazses   kisindi kiuuinnit,
daz leitit sia sar   dar iru leid uuirdit,
in fuir enti in finstri: daz ist rehto uirinlih ding.
Upi sia auar kihalont die,   die dar fona himile quemant,
enti si dero engilo   eigan uuirdit,
die pringent sia sar uf in himilo rihi:
dar ist lip ano tod   lioht ano finstri,
selida ano sorgun, dar nist neoman siuh.
denne der man in pardisu   pu kiuuinnit,
hus in himile,   dar quimit imo hilfa kinuok.
Pidiu ist durft mihhil
allero manno uuelihemo,   daz in es sin muot kispane,
daz er kotes uuillun   kerno tuo
enti hella fuir   harto uuise,
pehhes pina.   dar piutit der Satanaz altist
heizzan lauc.   so mac huckan za diu,
sorgen drato,   der sih suntigen uueiz.
uue demo in uinstri scal   sino uirina stuen,
prinnan in pehhe: daz ist rehto paluuic dink,
daz der man haret ze gote   enti imo hilfa ni quimit.
uuanit sih kinada   diu uuenaga sela.
ni ist in kihuctin   himiliskin gote,
uuanta hiar in uuerolti   aftar ni uuerkota.
So denne der mahtigo khuninc   daz mahal kipannit,
dara scal queman   chunno kilihaz.
denne ni kitar parno nohhein   den pan furisizzan,
ni allero manno uuelih   ze demo mahale sculi.
Dar scal er uora demo rihhe   az rahhu stantan,
pi daz er in uuerolti   kiuuerkot hapeta.

*The meaning of the title, conferred on the work in 1832, is unclear, but refers to
the destruction of the world by fire. This fragment of the ninth century Bavarian work
deals with the Day of Judgment and the end of the world.

Muspilli

. . . comes the day, when he must die.
When the soul goes on its way
And leaves its earthly body behind,
A host comes from the stars of the heavens,
Another from the fires of hell; they will fight for the soul.
In sorrow the soul must stand its ground, until the settlement
    comes,
To which of the two hosts it will fall as the spoils of battle.
For, if the people of Satan obtain it, they will lead it downward
    without delay, where only pain awaits it,
In fire and in shadow; that is truly a cruel sentence.
But if they, who come from heaven, take up the soul, and it falls
    to the lot of the angels
Then they conduct it quickly into the kingdom of heaven;
There is life without death, light without darkness,
An abode without cares, there no man suffers from sickness.
When a mortal man receives a place in Paradise,
A home in heaven, he is accorded aid in abundance.
For this reason, every man is required
That his heart prompt him to do God's will with joyful assent,
And to avoid in fear and trembling the flames of Hell,
The torment of hellish fire.
There ancient Satan awaits him with hot flames.
He who knows himself to be sinful,
Should reflect on this, and consider it with care.
Woe to him who must repent of his sins in the shadows, who must
burn in eternal flame, that is truly an evil fate,
When a man cries out to God, and help no longer comes.
The unhappy soul still hopes for grace.
But it is no longer sustained by the loving thoughts of heavenly
God, because here in this life
It did not prove himself worthy of him in deed.

When the mighty king ordains the day of judgment, every race
    must appear there.
Then no son of man dare miss the appointed day, believing not

Daz hortih rahhon   dia uueroltrehtuuison,
daz sculi der antichristo   mit Eliase pagan.
der uuarch ist kiuuafanit,   denne uu*i*rdit *u*ntar in uu*ic* arhapan.
khenfun sin*t* so kreftic,   diu kosa ist so mihhil.
*E*lias stritit   pi den *eu*uigon lip,
uuili den rehtkernon   da*z* rihhi kistarkan.
pidiu scal imo helfan   der himiles kiuualtit.
der antichristo   stet pi demo altfiante,
stet pi demo Satanase,   der inan uarsenkan *s*cal.
pidiu scal er in deru uu*ic*steti   u*u*unt piuallan
enti in demo sinde   sigalos uuerdan.—
Doh uuanit des *u*ilo gotmanno,
daz *E*lias in demo uuige   aruuartit *uuerde.*
so daz Eliases pluot   in erda kitriufit,
*s*o inprinnan*t* die perga,   poum ni kistentit
enihc in erdu,   aha artrukn*e*nt,
muor uarsuuilhit sih,   suilizot lougiu der himil,
mano uallit,   prinnit mittilagart.
denni kisten ti teikin *in* erdu,   uerit denne tuatago in lant,
uerit mit diu uuiru   u*iri*ho uuison.
Dar ni mac denne mak andremo   helfan uora demo muspille.
denne daz preita uuasal   allaz uarprinnit
enti uu*i*r enti luft   iz allaz arfurpit,
uuar ist denne diu marha,   dar man dar *e*o mit sinen magon
Diu marha ist farprunnan,   *diu* sela stet pidungan,   [piehc?
ni uu*e*iz mit uuiu puaze,   so uerit si za uu*i*ze.—
Pidiu ist d*e*mo manne so guot,   denner ze demo mahale quimit,
daz er rahono *u*ueliha   reh*t*o arteile.

Denne ni darf*f* er sorgen,   denn*e* er ze deru suonu qu*i*mit.
ni uu*e*iz der uuenago man,   uuielihan uu*a*rtil er habet,
denner mit den miaton   marrit daz reh*t*a,
*d*az der tiuual dar pi   kitar*n*it st*e*ntit.
*d*er hapet in ruouu   rahono *u*ueliha.
daz der man *er* ent*i* si*d   u*piles kifrumita,
daz er iz allaz kisaget,   denne er *ze deru* suonu quimit.
Ni scolta sid man*n*o nohhein   miatun *intfahan.*
So daz *h*imilis*ca* horn kilutit uuirdit,
enti sih der *s*uanar*i   ana den* sind arheuit,

every man is duty bound to the day of judgment.
There he must answer to the Ruler for all he did in this life.
I have heard how men learned in worldly law said
The Antichrist would contend with Elijah:
The foe is armed, the struggle between them begins.
The warriors are so mighty, the matter so momentous:
Elijah is fighting for eternal life, he wants to insure the rule
    of the just.
Therefore, He who rules Heaven will hold him up.
But the Antichrist stands on the side of the old adversary,
Stands for Satan, who must let him cease to live.
The Antichrist must sink to the ground, wounded on the field of
    slaughter,
Must be conquered in this conflict of weapons.
But many servants of God say that Elias will be wounded in
    warfare,
When his blood moistens the earth, the mountains will begin to
    blaze,
Not a single tree on earth will stay standing.
The waters will dry up, the moors devour themselves
The skies ignite, the moon plunge down to the earth,
The middle earth will seethe in flames.
When these signs appear on the earth, then the day of judgment
    will move into the land,
It will come with fire, in order to afflict men.
No one can aid his kinsman in the face of the *muspilli*.
When the whole world is consumed by flame, fire and air sweep
    everything away.
Where, then, is the land, which one always defended with the help
    of his kinsmen?
The land will be swallowed by flame, the soul stands there full
    of sorrow; thus it travels to hell.

Thus, it is useful for man, when he comes before the court,
To have already judged aright over all himself.
Then he need not have a care.
A frail man does not know who is following him, when he wounds
    justice through bribery,
Does not know that the devil is always there in various guises;

der dar *suan*nan scal   toten enti lepen*ten,*
denne heuit sih mit imo   herio meista.
daz ist allaz so pa*l*d,   daz imo nioman kip*a*gan ni mak.
Denne uerit er *ze deru* mahalsteti,   deru dar kimarchot ist.
dar uuirdit d*iu su*ona,   die man dar *i*o sageta.
Denne u*a*rant engila   uper d*i*o marha,
u*u*echant deota,   uuissant ze dinge.
denne *scal* mann*o* gilih   *f*ona deru moltu arsten.
lossan sih ar der*o* le*uu*o uazz*o*n,   scal imo *a*uar sin lip piqueman,
daz er sin reht allaz   kirahhon muozzi
enti imo after sinen tatin   art*eili*t u*u*erde.
Denne der gisizzit,   der dar suonnan scal
enti arteillan scal   toten enti quekkhen,
*de*nne stet dar umpi   engilo menigi,
guotero gomono: gart ist so mih*h*il,
dara qu*i*mit ze deru rihtungu so uilo,   dia da*r ar resti a*rstent.
so dar manno nohhein   u*ui*ht pimidan ni mak,
*dar sca*l denne hant sprehhan,   houpit sagen,
*a*ller*o l*i*d*o u*u*elihc   unzi in den luzigun ui*n*ger,
uuaz er untar *desen* mannun   *m*ordes kifrumita.
Dar ni ist *eo* so listi*c man,*   der dar *i*ouuiht arliugan megi,
daz er kita*rn*an megi   tato dehheina,
*u*zzan er iz mit alamusanu furi*m*egi
enti mit fastun   d*i*o u*i*rina kipuazt*i.*
Denne *der paldet,*   der gipuazzit *h*apet,
denner ze deru *suonu quimit.*
*uui*rdit denne furi kitragan   daz frono ch*ruci,*
dar *der h*eligo Christ   ana arhangan uua*r*d.
denne augit er dio masun,   dio er in deru m*enniski anfenc,*
dio er duruh desse mancunnes   minna f(*ardoleta*) . . .

He holds it all firmly in his hand, deeds which a man has done,
To be presented when he appears at the last judgment.
Therefore, no man should let himself be bribed.
When the divine horn sounds, and the judge who holds court over
    the quick and the dead commences,
The greatest of heavenly armies rises up with him.
It is so full of courage and boldness that no man can contend
with it.
He moves on to the place of judgment, which is arranged exactly.
Then the angels will advance over the land, bestir the peoples,
beckon them before the court.
Each man will arise from the dust, unbind himself from the burden
    of the grave,
He will receive his body back, so that he may answer without
    hindrance, be judged according to his acts.
Then he, who will judge there, judge the quick and the dead,
    takes his seat,
Around him the mass of the angels stands, a host of holy men;
The place of judgment is vast
So many come here for disposition, who arise from the sleep of
    death,
Here no man can hide anything, otherwise
The hand will speak, the head confess it,
Each of the limbs of the body to the small finger
Will confess what murderous deeds the man has done to others.
Before this court, the best of ruses is of no use to deny
    anything, or to conceal any deed;
It will become known to the king, unless he has made amends for
    his guilt
With previous munificence, and with fasting.
He who has already confessed can be comforted, when he comes
    before this court.
There, too, the noble Cross will be carried on before, on which
    holy
Christ was killed,
Then he will see the stigmata, which he received while incarnate,
    which he received for his love of mankind . . .

Carroll Hightower

Weingartner Reisesegen*

Ic dir nâch sihe,   ic dir nâch sendi
mit mînen funf fingirin   funvi undi funfzic engili.
Got mit gisundi   heim dich gisendi.
offin sî dir diz sigidor,   sami sî dir diz segildor:
Bislozin sî dir diz wâgidor,   sami sî dir diz wâfindor.

From Carmina Burana†

Chume, chume, geselle min,
ih enbite harte din!
ih enbite harte din,
chum, chum, geselle min!

Sûzer roservarwer munt,
chum vnde mache mich gesunt!
chum vnde mache mich gesunt,
sûzer roservarwer munt!

Swaz hie gat umbe,
daz sint alle megede;
die wellent an man
allen disen sumer gan!

---

*Dating from the twelfth century, this alliterative blessing was doubtless held to have protective magical power.

†A collection of medieval Latin songs, including songs both in German and a mixture of Latin and German, this thirteenth-century manuscript was discovered in, and named for, the abbey of Benediktbeuren in Bavaria.

The Weingarten Travel Blessing

I look after you as you go,
With my five fingers I send fifty-five angels after you.
May God send you home in health,
The Gate of victory stands open before you
And the gate of happiness, too.
May the gate of water be closed to you,
And the gate of death by sword.

Carroll Hightower

From Carmina Burana

Come, come, my companion,
I eagerly await you!
I eagerly await you,
come, come, my companion!

Sweet rosered mouth,
come and make me healthy!
Come and make me healthy,
sweet rosered mouth!

Those who circle around here,
those are all maidens;
they wish to be without a man
this whole summer long.

Ich wil truren varen lan;
vf die heide sul wir gan,
vil liebe gespilen min!
da seh wir der blumen schin.
Refl. Ich sage dir, ih sage dir,
min geselle, chum mit mir!

Sůziv Minne, raine Min,
mache mir ein chrenzelin!
daz sol tragen ein stolzer man,
der wol wìben dienen chan!
Refl. Ich sage dir . . .

Anonymous (Twelfth Century)

Dû bist mîn, ich bin dîn:*
des solt dû gewis sîn.
dû bist beslozzen
in mînem herzen:
verlorn ist daz slüzzelîn:
dû muost immer drinne sîn.

*From the second half of the twelfth century, this beautiful poem is the conclusion of a nun's Latin love letter, found with other such letters in a Tegernsee manuscript.

I want to rid myself of sadness;
we shall go to the heath,
my very dear playmates!
There we will see the flowers' brightness.
Refrain I say to you, I say to you
my companion, come with me!

Sweet Minne, pure Minne,
make a garland for me!
A splendid man will wear it,
who can serve women well!
Refrain I say to you, I say to you,
my companion, come with me!

Sylvia Stevens

Anonymous (Twelfth Century)

I have thee, thou hast me.
Of this thou shalt assured be.
Thou art enlocked
In my heart.
Lost is the key:
Thou must forever in it be.

Alexander Gode

Anonymous

»Mich dunket niht sô guotes   noch sô lobesam
sô diu liehte rôse   und diu minne mînes man.
diu kleinen vogellîne
diu singent in dem walde: dêst menegem herzen liep.
mirn kome mîn holder geselle,   in hân der sumerwünne niet.«

Der von Kürenberg*

»Ich stuont mir nehtint spâte   an einer zinnen:
dô hôrte ich einen ritter   vil wol singen
in Kürenberges wîse   al ûz der menigîn:
er muoz mir rûmen diu lant,   ald ich geniete mich sîn.«

Nu brinc mir her vil balde   mîn ros, mîn îsengwant,
wan ich muoz einer frouwen   rûmen diu lant.
diu wil mich des betwingen   daz ich ir holt† sî.
si muoz der mîner minne   iemer darbende sin.

---

*A "Wechsel," a form of indirect dialogue occurring in minnesong. The first verse
is sung by the lady, courting her love, the second, by the knight.
†*holt* denotes the relationship between lord and vassal.

Anonymous

"To me nothing seems as splendid   nor as praiseworthy,
as the shining rose   and the love of my friend.
The tiny birds
they sing in the forest: many a heart is joyful.
Yet if my sweet companion does not come to me, I'll not
                          know summer's bliss."

Sylvia Stevens

Der von Kürenberg

"Late at night I stood on a battlement:
then I heard a knight singing well
a melody of Kürenberg amidst the crowd.
Let him clear out of my land, or let him be mine."

Now bring me my horse and armor, fast,
for I must clear out of a lady's land:
she wants to make me bow and serve.
She will have to live without my love.

Frederick Goldin

»Ich zôch mir einen valken   mêre danne ein jâr.
dô ich in gezamete   als ich in wolte hân
und ich im sîn gevidere   mit golde wol bewant,
er huop sich ûf vil hôhe   und floug in anderiu lant.

Sît sach ich den valken   schône fliegen:
er fuorte an sînem fuoze   sîdîne riemen,
und was im sîn gevidere   alrôt guldîn.
got sende si zesamene   die gerne geliep wellen sîn!«

Der tunkele sterne   sam der birget sich,
als tuo du, frouwe schœne,   sô du sehest mich,
sô lâ du dîniu ougen gên   an einen andern man.
son weiz doch lützel iemen   wiez undr uns zwein ist getân.

Wîp unde vederspil   diu werdent lîhte zam:
swer si ze rehte lucket,   sô suochent si den man.
als warb ein schœne ritter   umb eine frouwen guot.
als ich dar an gedenke,   sô stêt wol hôhe mîn muot.

"I trained me a falcon, for more than a year.
When I had him tamed the way I wanted him
and set gold among his feathers,
he rose up high and flew away to wildness.

Since then I have seen the falcon in lordly flight:
he bore silken jesses on his legs,
and gold and red in his feathers.
God bring together all people who want to be lovers."

Frederick Goldin

The morning star goes under cover.
Beautiful and high born, do the same when you see me
and let your eyes turn to another.
No one will guess what we have together.

Frederick Goldin

Woman and falcons—they are easily tamed.
If a man knows how to lure them right, they come flying.
Just so, to try to win a splendid lady, a handsome knight set out.
My spirit rises when I think of that.

Frederick Goldin

Pseudo-Dietmar von Eist

Ez stuont ein frouwe alleine
und warte über heide
und warte ire liebe,
so gesach si valken fliegen.
»sô wol dir, valke, daz du bist!
du fliugest swar dir liep ist:
du erkiusest dir in dem walde
einen bóum der dir gevalle.
alsô hân ouch ich getân:
ich erkôs mir selbe einen man,
den erwélten mîniu ougen.
daz nîdent schoene frouwen.
owê wan lânt si mir mîn liep?
jô 'ngerte ich ir dekeiner trûtes niet.«

»Sô wol dir, sumerwunne!
daz vogelsanc ist geswunden:
als ist der linden ir loup.
jârlanc truobent mir ouch
mîniu wól stênden ougen.
mîn trût, du solt dih gelouben
anderre wîbe:
wan, helt, die solt du mîden.
dô du mich êrst sâhe,
dô dûhte ich dich zewâre
sô rehte minneclîch getân:
des mane ich dich, lieber man.«

Pseudo-Dietmar von Eist

A Lady Stood Alone

A lady stood alone
and looked out on the plain
and waited for her love;
she saw a falcon high above.
"Lucky falcon there on high!
Whither you wish you fly;
you choose from the forest trees
whichever one you please.
So I too have done:
I chose myself a man,
my two eyes did agree.
But charming women envy me.
Oh, why do they set their snares?
I never wanted a lover of theirs."

J. W. Thomas

Gay Summer's Bliss, Good-bye

"Gay summer's bliss, good-bye!
The bird's sweet song has died,
the linden's leaves are gone,
the fading year beyond
will make these fair eyes weary.
My love, hear this entreaty:
all other charms
avoid, and other arms.
The moment that you met me
your manly form impressed me,
I thought you wondrous fair—
so, lover dear, beware!"

J. W. Thomas

Meinloh von Sevelingen

»Mir erwélten mîniu ougen   einen kindeschen man.
daz nîdent ander frouwen: ich hân in anders niht getân,
wan obe ich hân gedienet   daz ich diu liebeste bin.
dar an wil ich kêren   mîn herze und allen den sin.
swelhiu sînen willen   hie bevor hât getân,
verlôs si in von schulden,
    der wil ich nu niht wîzen,   sihe ichs unfrœlîchen stân.«

»Sô wê den merkæren!*   die habent mîn übele gedâht:
si habent mich âne schulde   in eine grôze rede brâht.
si wænent mir in leiden,   sô si sô rûnent under in.
nu wizzen algelîche   daz ich sîn friundinne bin;
âne nâhe bî gelegen: des hân ich weizgot niht getân.
stæchens ûz ir ougen,
    mir râtent mîne sinne   an deheinen andern man.«

---

*Frequently used in minnesong, the term refers to those who sought to frustrate the union of the lovers, or to uncover and betray them.

Meinloh von Sevelingen

My Eyes Have Seen and Chosen

"My eyes have seen and chosen   for me a handsome youth
and other women envy   my fortune but, in truth,
I only seek to show him   that I am sweet and kind
and to this end give over   my heart and all my mind.
Whoever held his favor   before he was my own
has lost him with good reason,
    yet I'll feel only sorrow   to see her stand alone."

J. W. Thomas

Woe Then to the Gossips

"Woe then to the gossips!   They show their evil will
by spreading wicked rumors,   although I've done no ill.
They think they'll spoil our friendship   by whispering about.
That I am still his sweetheart   they'll have no cause for doubt;
but God shall be my witness,   with him I've never lain.
Although my sense be blinded,
    no other man could ever   cause love for him to wane."

J. W. Thomas

Dietmar von Eist

Ûf der linden óbené   dâ sanc ein kleinez vogellîn.
vor dem walde wart ez lût: dô huop sich aber daz herze mîn
an eine stat da'z ê dâ was.   ich sach die rôsebluomen stân:
die manent mich der gedanke vil   die ich hin zeiner frouwen hân.

»Ez dunket mich wol tûsent jâr   daz ich an liebes arme lac.
sunder âne mîne schulde   fremdet er mich mangen tac.
sît ich bluomen niht ensach   noch hôrte kleiner vogele sanc,
sît was mir mîn fröide kurz   und ouch der jâmer alzelanc.«

Wie möhte mir mîn herze werden   iemer rehte fruot,
daz mir ein edeliu frouwe   sô vil ze leide tuot!
der ich vil gedienet hân,
als ir wille was getân.
nu wil si niht gedenken   der mangen sorgen mîn.
sô hôh ôwî,
    sol ich ir lange frömde sîn.

»Jâ hœre ich vil der tugende sagen   von eime ritter guot:
der ist mir âne mâze komen   in mînen stæten muot,
daz ich sîn ze keiner zît
mac vergezzen,« redte ein wip,
»nu muoz ich al der werlte haben   dur sînen willen rât.
sô hôh ôwî!
    wie schône er daz gedienet hât!«

Dietmar von Eist

Yonder on the linden tree   there sang a merry little bird.
Its voice rang out at the forest's edge   and then my heart, by
   memory stirred,
returned to a place that it once knew.   I saw the roses gently blow;
they bring a host of thoughts about   a certain lady that I know.
   "It seems at least a thousand years   since in my lover's arms I
   lay,
and I am not to blame that he   has left me now for many a day.
Since then I've seen no flowers bloom   and heard no bird's
   enchanting song,
since then my joy has been short-lived,   my pain and sorrow all
   too long."

J. W. Thomas

How can I hope a wise heart to attain
While a highborn lady gives me so much pain?
I've served her much, to the full measure
As was her each and every pleasure.
My many sorrows she refuses to see:
Woe, woe is me,
   Shall she long remain indifferent to me?

"Of a good knight and his virtues I have heard much tell,
On him my mind does constantly dwell.
I can never forget him, not a moment," said she.
"Woe, woe is me!
   How wonderfully he has earned this from me!"

Nu ist ez an ein ende komen, dar nâch mîn herze ie ranc,
daz mich ein edeliu frouwe hât genómen in ir getwanc.
der bin ich worden undertân,
als daz schif dem stiurman,
swanne der wâc sîn ünde sô gar gelâzen hât.
sô hôh ôwî!
  si benímt mir mange wilde tât.

Friedrich von Hausen

Deich von der guoten schiet
und ich zir niht ensprach
alsô mir wære liep,
des lîde ich ungemach.
daz liez ich durch die diet
von der mir nît geschach.
ich wünsche ir anders niet,
wan der die helle brach,
der füege ir wê unt ach.

»Si wænent hüeten mîn
die sîn doch niht bestât,
und tuont ir nîden schîn;
daz wênic si vervât.
si möhten ê den Rîn
gekêren in den Pfât,
ê ich mich iemer sîn
getrôste, swiez ergât,
der mir gedienet hât.«

My heart's eternal striving has reached its end
A noble lady my will does bend.
To her I owe all devotion
Like a ship on the ocean
To the sailor o'er the becalmed sea
Woe, woe is me!
   From wild deeds she discourages me.

Carroll Hightower

Friedrich von Hausen

When I parted from my Good*
and did not tell her
how she was dear to me,
I suffer for it now.
I left it out because of all those hypocrites
whose envy ruined my pleasure.
I wish them nothing else
but that the One who harried Hell
make them hurt and yell.

"They think they can spy on me,
though this is none of their business,
and show their envy,
but it does them little good.
They could sooner make
the Rhine flow into the Po
before I'd give him up
who served me,
no matter how things go."

Frederick Goldin

*A literal translation of the Middle High German, referring to the good and
virtuous lady. The first verse is spoken by the man and the second by the lady.

Wâfenâ, wie hât mich Minne gelâzen!
diu mich betwanc daz ich lie mîn gemüete
an solhen wân der mich wol mac verwâzen,
ez ensî daz ich genieze ir güete,*
von der ich bin   alsô dicke âne sin.
mich dûhte ein gewin,   und wolte diu guote
wizzen die nôt diu wont in mînem muote.

Wâfen, waz habe ich getân sô zunêren
daz mir diu guote niht gruozes engunde?
sus kan si mir wol daz herze verkêren.*
daz ich in der werlte bezzer wîp iender funde,*
seht dêst mîn wân,   dâ für sô wil ichz hân,
und dienen nochdan   mit triuwen der guoten,
diu mich dâ bliuwet vil sêre âne ruoten.

Waz mac daz sîn daz diu werlt heizet minne,
unde ez mir tuot alsô wê zaller stunde
unde ez mir nimt alsô vil mîner sinne?
in wânde nicht daz ez ieman erfunde.
getorste ich es jên   daz ichz hête gesên
dâ von mir ist geschêhen   alsô vil herzesêre,*
sô wolte ich gelouben dar an iemer mêre.

Minne, got müeze mich an dir rechen!*
wie vil du mîm herzen der fröiden wendest!*
und möhte ich dir din krumbez ouge ûz gestechen,†
des het ich reht, wan du vil lützel endest
an mir solhe nôt   sô mir dîn lîp gebôt.
und wærest du tôt,   sô dûhte ich mich rîche.
sus muoz ich von dir leben betwungenlîche.

---

*These lines are from the third edition of *Des Minnesangs Frühling,* ed. Friedrich
Vogt (Leipzig: S. Hirzel, 1920).
†She has looked askance at him, has withheld her favor.

Help! How Minne has deserted me—
she made me give my soul up
to a dream that will destroy me
if I am not relieved by kindness from that one woman,
the cause why I so often have no sense.
I would think I'd gotten something if she were willing
to know the distress that has settled in my mind.

Help! What dishonor have I done
that the Good does not let me have her greeting?
This way she can lead my heart into a trap.
Behold my mad faith: that I could never find a better
    woman
in this world. As my faith I shall uphold it
and serve her loyally,
this good woman who scourges me hard without whips.

What may that be which the world calls Minne,
which makes me feel continual pain
and deprives me of so much sense?
I don't think anyone can really find it out.
If I could claim that I had seen it,
the cause of so much sorrow come my way,
then I would believe in it ever more.

Minne, God let me get revenge on you.
How many joys have you detoured away from my heart!
And if I could stick out that squinting eye of yours,
I would be right to do it, because you make no end
to the distress you commanded against me,
and if you were dead, I would think I was rich,
yes, only now I have to live beneath your power.

Frederick Goldin

Ich denke under wîlen,
ob ich ir nâher wære,
waz ich ir wolte sagen.
daz kürzet mir die mîlen,
swenn ich ir mîne swære
sô mit gedanken klage.
mich sehent mange tage
die liute in der gebære
als ich niht sorgen habe,
wan ichs alsô vertrage.

Het ich sô hôher minne
nie mich underwunden,
mîn möhte werden rât.
ich tete ez âne sinne:
des lîde ich zallen stunden
nôt diu nâhe gât.
mîn stæte mir nu hât
daz herze alsô gebunden,
daz siz niht scheiden lât
von ir als ez nu stât.

Ez ist ein grôzez wunder:
diech aller sêrest minne,
diu was mir ie gevê.
nu müeze solhen kumber
niemer man bevinden,
der alsô nâhe gê.
erkennen wânde i'n ê,
nu kan i'n baz bevinden:
mir was dâ heime wê,
und hie wol drîstunt mê.

Swie kleine ez mich vervâhe,
sô vröuwe ich mich doch sêre
daz mir sîn niemen kan
erwern, ichn denke ir nâhe
swar ich landes kêre.
den trôst sol si mir lân.

I think sometimes about
what I would tell her
if I were near enough.
It makes the miles shorter
to call my sorrow out
to her, with thoughts.
Often the people here
see in me the figure
of a carefree man,
for so I let it seem.

Had I not taken on
such lofty love,
I might be saved.
I did it without thinking.
And every moment now I suffer
pain that presses deep.
Now my own constancy
has tied down my heart
and will not let it part
from her, as things are now.

It is a great wonder:
she whom I love with greatest torment
has always acted like my enemy.
Now may no man ever get to know
what such a burden is,
it weighs down hard.
I thought I knew what it was before,
now I know it better.
Over there, where home is, I was sad,
and here three times more.

However little good it does me,
still I have this pleasure:
no one can stop me
from thinking close to her,
wherever on earth I turn.
This comfort she must let me have.

wil siz für guot enpfân,
daz fröut mich iemer mêre,
wan ich für alle man
ir ie was undertân.

Si darf mich des zîhen niet,
ichn hête si von herzen liep.
des mohte si die wârheit an mir sên,
und wil sis jên.
ich quam sîn dicke in solhe nôt,
daz ich den liuten guoten morgen bôt
engegen der naht.
ich was sô verre an si verdâht
daz ich mich underwîlent niht versan,
und swer mich gruozte daz ichs niht vernam.

Mîn herze unsanfte sînen strît
lât, den ez nu mange zît
haldet wider daz aller beste wîp,
der ie mîn lîp
muoz dienen swar ich iemer var.
ich bin ir holt: swenn ich vor gote getar,
so gedenke ich ir.
daz ruoche ouch er vergeben mir:
ob ich des grôze sünde solde hân,
zwiu schuof er si sô rehte wol getân?

Mit grôzen sorgen hât mîn lîp
gerungen alle sîne zît.
ich hâte liep daz mir vil nâhe gie:
dazn liez mich nie
an wîsheit kêren mînen muot.
daz was diu minne, diu noch mangen tuot
daz selbe klagen.

If she takes it well,
that gives me joy forever,
for I, more than any other man,
was always hers.

Frederick Goldin

She may not accuse me
of not loving her with all my heart.
In me she may well perceive the truth of this,
if she is willing to concede it.
I was often in such distress,
that I wished people "Good morning"
towards evening.
I was so absorbed in my thoughts of her,
that at times I didn't remember a single thing,
and if someone greeted me, I didn't hear them.

My heart unwillingly abandons
its struggle, which it has carried on at length
against the very best woman,
whom I must serve forever
wherever I shall go.
I am devoted to her: if I am worthy to go before God,
I will remember her.
For that He may well forgive me;
if I have committed a great sin for that,
why did He form her so beautifully?

With many cares I
constantly struggled.
I loved what affected me so deeply:
it never allowed me to direct
my senses towards prudence.
That was Minne, which still similarly afflicts
many another person.

nu wil ich mich an got gehaben:
der kan den liuten helfen ûzer nôt.
nieman weiz wie nâhe im ist der tôt.

Einer fróuwen was ich undertân,
diu âne lôn mîn dienest nam.
von der enspriche ich niht wan allez guot,
wan daz ir muot
zunmilte wider mich ist gewesen.
vor aller nôt sô wânde ich sîn genesen,
dô sich verlie
mîn herze ûf genâde an sie,
der ich dâ leider funden niene hân.
nu wil ich dienen dem der lônen kan.

Ich quam von minne in kumber grôz,
des ich doch selten ie genôz.
swaz schaden ich dâ von gewunnen hân,
sô friesch nie man
daz ich ir spræche iht wan guot,
noch mîn munt von frouwen niemer tuot.
doch klage ich daz
daz ich sô lange gotes vergaz:
den wil ich iemer vor in allen haben,
und in dâ nâch ein holdez herze tragen.

Mîn herze und mîn lîp diu wellent scheiden,
diu mit ein ander varnt nu mange zît.
der lîp wil gerne vehten an die heiden:
sô hât iedoch daz herze erwelt ein wîp
vor al der welt. daz müet mich iemer sît,
daz si ein ander niene volgent beide.
mir habent diu ougen vil getân ze leide.
got eine müeze scheiden noch den strît.

Now I want to entrust myself to God:
He can help people out of their distress.
No one knows how near death is to him.

I served a lady
who received my service without reward.
About her I will say nothing but what is good,
except that her disposition
towards me was too unmerciful.
I thought I had recovered from all distress,
when my heart
depended on her mercy,
though unfortunately, I never found it there.
Now I want to serve the one, who knows how to reward.

Because of Minne I suffered great anguish,
never enjoying a single thing from it.
Whatever harm I have known from that,
no one has ever heard
me speak anything but well of her,
or heard my lips utter otherwise about women.
But I complain of this:
that I have forgotten God for so long:
Him I want to place forever before all of them,
and only then serve them with a devoted heart.

Sylvia Stevens

My heart and my body want to separate,
that have ridden together all my life.
The body wants to strike against the heathen,
but the heart has chosen out a woman
before all the world. It has weighed on me ever since,
that one will not go in the steps of the other.
My eyes have brought me to grief.
May God alone break up that strife.

Ich wânde ledic sîn von solher swaere,
dô ich daz kriuze in gotes êre nam.
ez waere ouch reht deiz herze als ê dâ waere,
wan daz sîn staetekeit im sîn verban.
ich solte sîn ze rehte ein lebendic man,
ob ez den tumben willen sîn verbaere.
nu sihe ich wol daz im ist gar unmaere
wie ez mir an dem ende süle ergân.

Sît ich dich, herze, niht vol mac erwenden,
dun wellest mich vil trûreclîchen lân,
sô bite ich got daz er dich ruoche senden
an eine stat dâ man dich wol enpfâ.
owê wie sol ez armen dir ergân!
wie torstest eine an solhe nôt ernenden?
wer sol dir dîne sorge helfen enden
mit solhen triuwen als ich hân getân?

Heinrich von Veldeke

Wê mich scadę anę mîner vrouwen,
demę wunschę ich des dorres rîses
dâ dî dîvę anę nemen ende.
wê mîn scônę anę herę bit trouwen,
demę wunschę ich des paradîses
ende valdę hemę mîne hende.
vrâgę îman wê sî sî,
dê kenne sî dâ bî:
het is dî wale gedâne.
genâde, vrouwe, mich.
der sunnen an ich dich,
sô schîne mich der mâne.

I had hoped to be free of this great weight
when I took the cross for the glory of God.
It would be right if the heart were in it too,
but its own faith held it back.
I would truly be a living man again
if it would stop its ignorant desiring.
I see now, to the heart it's all one
how I shall fare at last.

Heart, since I cannot turn you back
from deserting me so sadly,
I pray God reach down to send you
where they will welcome you in.
Alas, poor Heart, how will it go with you?
How could you dare to go boldly into this danger all
    alone?
Who will help you end your cares
with such loyalty as I have shown?

Frederick Goldin

Heinrich von Veldeke

Whoever hurts my favor with my lady,
I wish him the dead branch
on which thieves snatch death.
Whoever helps me with her faithfully,
I wish him paradise
and fold my hands to him.
If anyone asks who she is,
let him know her this way:
it is The Beautiful One.
Lady, pity me.
To you I yield the sun:
then let the moon have light for me.

Wî min nôt gevûger wâre,
sô gewunnę ich lîf nâ leide
ende blîtscap manechfalde,
want ich weit velę lîve mâre:
blûmen springen anę der heiden,
vogelę singen in den walde.
dâ wîlen lach der snê,
dâ steit nû grûne clê,
bedouwet anę den morgen.
wê welę dê vrouwe sich.
nîman ne nôde's mich.
ich bin unledech sorgen.

Tristrant mûstę ânę sînen danc
stâde sîn der koninginnen,
want poisûn hemę dâr tû dwanc
mêre dan dî cracht der minnen.
des sal mich dî gûde danc
weten dat ich nînę gedranc
sulįc pîment endę ich sî minne
bat dan hê, endę mach dat sîn.
walę gedâne,   valsches âne,
lât mich wesen dîn
ende wis dû mîn.

In den aprillen   sô dî blûmen springen,
sô louven dî linden   endę grûnen dî bûken,
sô heven bit willen   dî vogelę hęrę singen,
sint sî minne vinden   al dâ sî sûken
anę hęręn genôt,   want hęrę blîtscap is grôt
der mich nîne verdrôt,   want sî swegen.al den winter stille.

Were my misery more bearable,
I could reach to pleasure after pain,
to joys and joys,
for I hear lovely news:
the flowers are springing on the heath, tra la,
the birds are singing in the woods;
where snow once lay
green clover grows,
covered with dew in the morning.
So, whoever wants to, let him rejoice—
but let him not press me.
I am unfree of sorrows.

Frederick Goldin

Tristan had no choice
but to be faithful to the Queen,
for poison drove him to it
more than the power of love.
Therefore, let The Good One be grateful
to me, for I never drank
such spiced wine and I love her
more than he loved, if that might be.
O beautiful and faultless,
let me be yours,
and you be mine.

Frederick Goldin

In April when the flowers spring,
the lindens leaf out, the beeches turn green,
with a will the birds begin to sing,
for they all find love where they seek it,
in their mates, so their joy is great—
which I never minded, for all winter long they keep still.

Dû sị anẹ den rîsen   dî blûmen gesâgen
bî den bladen springen,   dû wâren sî rîke
herẹ manẹchfalder wîsen,   der sî wîlen plâgen.
sî hûven herẹ sîngen   lûdẹ ende vrôlîke,
nederẹ endẹ hô.   mîn mût stéit ouch alsô
dat ich wíllẹ wesen vrô.   recht is dat ich mîn gelucke prîse.

Mochtẹ ich erwerven   mînér vrouwen hulde!
kundẹ ích dî gesûken   alsẹ hérẹ walẹ getâme
ich sal noch verderven   al dorẹ mîne sculde,
sî nẹ wolde gerûken   dat sî van mich nâme
bûtẹ âne dôt   up genâdẹ endẹ dorẹ nôt,
want et gôt nînẹ gebôt   dat negein man gerne solde sterven.

Albrecht von Johannsdorf

»Wie sich minne hebt daz weiz ich wol;
wie si ende nimt des weiz ich niht.
ist daz ich es inne werden sol
wie dem herzen herzeliep geschiht,
sô bewar mich vor dem scheiden got,
daz wæn bitter ist.
    disen kumber fürhte ich âne spot.

Swâ zwei herzeliep gefriundent sich
unde ir beider minne ein triuwe wirt,
die sol niemen scheiden, dunket mich,
al die wîle unz si der tôt verbirt.
wær diu rede mîn, ich tæte alsô:
verlüre ich mînen friunt,
    seht, sô wurde ich niemer mêre frô.

When they saw on the branches the blossoms
springing among the leaves, then they were rich
in the varied songs they always sang.
They started to sing, joyfully and loud,
low and high. My mind, too, is such
that I want to know joy. I ought to praise my luck.

If I could win my lady's grace,
could seek it as becomes her!
I shall die, and it will be my fault
unless she consents to accept
a penance other than death for her grace; and so it must
    be,
for God never commanded any man be glad to die.

Frederick Goldin

Albrecht von Johannsdorf

"This I know, how love begins to be.
How love ends, I do not, dare not, know.
If within the heart and soul of me,
I shall feel love's kindling joy a-glow,
Spare me, Lord, the parting, which I deem
Bitterest thing of all.
This I dread beyond the heaviest dream.

"Where two loving hearts in friendship grow,
And their loves unite in one strong tie,
None shall ever part them, living so,
Till the day when one of them must die.
So with me, suppose the case my own.
If I lost my friend,
See, I should be utterly alone.

Dâ gehœret manic stunde zuo
ê daz sich gesamne ir zweier muot.
dâ daz ende denne unsanfte tuo,
ich wæne des wol, daz ensî niht guot.
lange sî ez mir vil unbekant.
und werde ich iemen liep,
    der sî sîner triuwe an mir gemant.«

Der ich diene und iemer dienen wil,
diu sol mîne rede vil wol verstân.
spræche ich mêre, des wurd alze vil.
ich wil ez allez an ir güete lân.
ir genâden der bedarf ich wol.
und wil si, ich bin vrô;
    und wil si, so ist mîn herze leides vol.

Ich vant âne huote
die vil minneclîchen eine stân.
sâ dô sprach diu guote
»waz welt ir sô eine her gegân?«
»frouwe, ez ist alsô geschehen.«
»saget, war umbe sît ir her? des sult ir mir verjehen.«

»Mînen senden kumber
klage ich iu, vil liebe frouwe mîn.«
»wê, waz saget ir tumber?
ir mugt iuwer klage wol lâzen sîn.«
»frouwe, ichn mac ir niht enbern.«
»sô wil ich in tûsent jâren niemer iuch gewern.«

»Neinâ, küniginne!
daz mîn dienest sô iht sî verlorn!«
»ir sît âne sinne,
daz ir bringet mich in solhen zorn.«
»frouwe, iur haz tuot mir den tôt.«
»wer hât iuch, vil lieber man, betwungen ûf die nôt?«

"Many an hour is needed, ere the two
Gently weld their wills and minds as one.
Should the end thereof be bitter rue,
Such I ween, were welcome news to none.
That be far from me as my own death!
And if someone there be
Who loves me, let this warn him to keep faith!"

She whom serving now, I serve for ever,
Cannot fail these words to understand.
More I must not say: this brief endeavour
Made, I yield me to her kind command.
Of her grace and goodness I have need,
And if she will, give joy
She can, and if not, I am poor indeed.

M. L. Richey

I discovered the sweet lovely lady
standing alone without a guardian.
Straightaway the good lady said,
"Why do you walk here so alone?"
"Lady, it has happened so."
"Tell me, why are you here? You must tell me that."

"Of my yearning plight
I will complain to you, dearest lady."
"Alas, what are you saying, imprudent man?
You may well cease your lamenting."
"Lady, I cannot be without it."
"Then in a thousand years. I will never grant you a thing."

"Oh no, queen!
That my service is lost in such a way!"
"You are out of your mind,
to make me so angry."
"Lady, your hatred is my death."
"Who, dearest man, has forced such distress upon you?"

»Daz hât iuwer schœne
die ir hât, vil minneclîchez wîp.«
»iuwer süezen dœne
wolten krenken mînen stæten lîp.«
»frouwe, niene welle got.«
»werte ich iuch, des hetet ir êre; sô wær mîn der spot.«

»Lât mich noch geniezen
daz ich iu von herzen ie was holt.«
»iuch mac wol verdriezen
daz ir iuwer wortel gegen mir bolt.«
»dunket iuch mîn rede niht guot?«
»jâ hât si beswæret dicke mînen stæten muot.«

»Ich bin ouch vil stæte,
ob ir ruochet mir der wârheit jehen.«
»volget mîner ræte,
lât die bete diu niemer mac geschehen.«
»sol ich alsô sîn gewert?«
»got der wer iuch anderswâ des ir an mich dâ gert.«

»Sol mich dan mîn singen
und mîn dienest gegen iu niht vervân?«
»iu sol wol gelingen:
âne lôn sô sult ir niht bestân.«
»wie meinet ir daz, frouwe guot?«
»daz ir deste werder sît und dâ bî hôchgemuot.«

Guote liute, holt
die gâbe die got unser herre selbe gît,
der al der welte hât gewalt.
dienet sînen solt,
der den vil sældehaften dort behalten lît

"The beauty, which you possess,
has done this to me, most lovely lady."
"Your sweet song
wishes to weaken my constancy."
"Lady, not at all, God forbid."
"If I yielded to you, you would have honor and I, mockery."

"Let me then still enjoy the benefits
for having been forever faithful to you in my heart."
"You may well weary
of flinging your words against me."
"Don't my words seem favorable to you?"
"Indeed they have often troubled my constancy."

"I am also most constant
if you care to tell me the truth.
"Follow my advice,
abandon the request which may never happen."
"Will I be rewarded in this manner?"
"May God grant you somewhere else what you desire there from
     me."

"Shall my singing then
and my service towards you be in vain?"
"You will certainly succeed:
you will not remain without reward."
"What do you mean, good lady?"
"That you are all the more worthy and, furthermore, noble."

Sylvia Stevens

God's Gifts

Good folk, go gain
The gifts, which by the Lord our God Himself are given,
Who in His might this world doth hold.
His hire obtain,
Which for the blessed lies stored up in Heaven

mit vröiden iemer manecvalt.
lîdet eine wîle willeclîchen nôt
vür den iemermêre wernden tôt.
got hât iu beide sêle un lîp gegeben:
gebt im des lîbes tôt; daz wirt der sêle ein iemerleben

Lâ mich, Minne, vrî.
du solt mich eine wîle sunder liebe lân.
du hâst mir gar den sin benomen.
komest du wider bî
als ich die reinen gotes vart volendet hân,
sô wis mir aber willekomen.
wilt ab du ûz mînem herzen scheiden niht
(daz vil lîhte unwendic doch geschiht),
vüer ich dich dan mit mir in gotes lant,
sô sî der guoten hie   er umbe halben lôn gemant.

»Owê« sprach ein wîp,
»wie vil mir doch von liebe leides ist beschert!
waz mir diu liebe leides tuot!
vröidelôser lîp,
wie wil du dich gebâren, swenne er hinnen vert,
dur den du wære ie hôchgemuot?
wie sol ich der werlde und mîner klage geleben?
dâ bedorfte ich râtes zuo gegeben.
kund ich mich beidenthalben nu bewarn,
des wart mir nie sô nôt.   ez nâhet, er wil hinnen varn.«

Wol si sælic wîp
diu mit ir wîbes güete daz gemachen kan
daz man si vüeret über sê.
ir vil guoten lîp
den sol er loben, swer ie herzeliep gewan,
wand ir hie heime tuot sô wê,
swenne si gedenket stille an sîne nôt.
»lebt mîn herzeliep, od ist er tôt«
sprichet si, »sô müeze sîn der pflegen
durch den er süezer lîp sich dirre werlde hât bewegen.«

With lasting pleasures manifold.
Gladly for a little bear with suffering sore,
To 'scape from death that lasteth evermore.
God did to you both soul and body give:
Give Him the body's death! So shall the soul forever live.

Love, release me now!
Free me for a little from thy vassalage!
My reason thou hast robbed from me.
Later on if thou
Come, when I have finished God's high pilgrimage,
Once more welcome shalt thou be.
Yet, if from my heart thou wilt not be removed,
(Like enough, in sooth, it may be proved)
If to the land of God with me thou fare,
I pray He grant my lady half of all I win me there.

"Alas!" a lady cried,
"What sorrow have I won from what was sweet and dear!
Sweet bliss hath brought me bitter smart.
How shall I abide
Bereft of all my joy, when he hath sailed from here,
Who made me ever high of heart?
Can I face the world and bear my sorrow too?
Sore I need good counsel what to do.
Would I could do what's right in either case!
Ne'er was my need so sore. The hour of parting comes apace."

Blessèd be her name,
Who by her grace and sweetness brings a man to this,
That he bears her o'er the sea!
He must sing the fame
Of his lady, if he e'er hath won such bliss.
For here she bides in misery,
In silence thinking how he's sore bestead.
"Does my lover live, or is he dead?"
So she speaks, "Then may my dear love find
With *Him* fair comfort, for whose sake this world he
    hath resigned!

F. C. Nicholson

Heinrich von Morungen

Hete ich tugende niht sô vil von ir vernomen
unde ir schône niht sô vil gesên,
wie wêre si mir danne alsô ze herzen komen?
ich muoz iemer dem gelîche spên,
als der mâne, der sînen schîn
   von des sunnen schîn enpfêt:
alsô kument mir dicke
ir wol liehten ougen blicke
in mîn herze, dâ si vor mir gêt.

Birgets ab ir liehten ougen schîn,
sô kumt mir diu nôt daz ich muoz klagen.
solde ab ieman an im selben schuldic sîn,
sô het ich mich selben selbe erslagen,
dô ichs in mîn herze nam
   unde ich si vil gerne sach,
noch gerner danne ich solde,
unde ich des niht mîden wolde,
in hôhte ir lop, swâ manz vor mir gesprach.

Mîme kinde wil ich erben dise nôt
und diu klagenden leit diuch hân von ir.
wênet sî dan ledic sîn, ob ich bin tôt,
ich lâz einen trôst doch hinder mir,
daz noch schône wirt mîn sun,
   daz si wunder an im spê
alsô daz er mich reche
und ir herze gar zerbreche,
sô sin alsô schônen selten sê.

Heinrich von Morungen

The Legacy

Had I not perceived so much of worth in her,
Of her beauty had not seen so much,
How could she have ever touched my heart so near?
Now my lot must evermore be such
As befalls the moon, that gets
   From the shining sun its light;
So it ever chances,
In my heart her eyes' bright glances
Enter, when she steps before my sight.

When her bright eyes reach my heart and enter in,
I must needs lament for bitter pain.
Might one 'gainst oneself commit so great a sin,
Mine own self I surely should have slain,
When I took her in my heart
   And was fain on her to gaze
(All too fain, I fear me!)
And, if any praised her near me,
Could not choose but add unto the praise.

I shall make my child heir to this sorrow sore
She hath brought me, and my grief of mind.
Tho' she fancy she'll be free, when I'm no more,
Yet one comfort I shall leave behind,—
   That so fair my son shall wax
He'll do marvels past compare,
Vengeance for me taking,
And her hard heart wholly breaking,
When she sees him grown so wondrous fair.

F. C. Nicholson

Von den elben wirt entsên vil manic man:
sô bin ich von grôzer minne entsên
von der besten die ie man ze friunt gewan.
wil si aber mich dar umbe vên,
mir zunstaten stên,   mac si dan rechen sich,
tuo des ich si bite: si fröit sô sêre mich,
daz mîn lîp vor liebe muoz zergên.

Sie gebiutet unde ist in dem herzen mîn
frouwe und hêrer danne ich selbe sî:
hei wan müeste ich ir alsô gewaltic sîn
daz si mir mit triuwen wêre bî
ganzer tage drî   und eteslîche naht!
so verlüre ich niht den lîp und al die maht.
nust si leider vor mir alze frî.

Mich enzündet ir vil liehter ougen schîn
same daz fiur den dürren zunder tuot,
und ir fremden krenket mir daz herze mîn
same daz wazzer die vil heize gluot:
und ir hôher muot,   ir schône, ir werdecheit,
und daz wunder daz man von ir tugenden seit,
deist mir übel und wirt noch lîhte guot.

Swenne ir liehten ougen sô verkêren sich
daz si mir aldurch mîn herze sên,
swer da 'nzwischen danne stêt und irret mich,
dem müez al sîn wunne gar zergên,
wan ich danne stên   und warte der frouwen mîn
rehte alsô des tages diu kleinen vogellîn:
wenne sol mir iemer liep geschên?

Many a man gets bewitched by the elves.
I have been bewitched with love
by the best a man ever won as friend.
If she wants to be my enemy for that
and destroy me, let her get her vengeance
by doing what I ask: then she delights me so sorely
I pass away with pleasure.

She commands and in my heart
is Lady, her rule is mightier than mine.
O if I could get the power over her somehow
and she stayed with me obediently
three full days, and some nights.
My body's strength would not be ebbing away.
But now she is all too free of me.

The light of her eyes burns me up
like fire on dry tinder.
Her distance damps my heart
like water on a rising flame.
And her rejoicing spirit, her beauty, and her worth,
and the miraculous virtues that have won her fame—
it's my sickness now, but maybe it will be my health.

When her glowing eyes turn
and she looks through my heart,
the fool that steps between us then and gets in my way,
may all his pleasures evaporate,
because I am standing there looking out for her,
like the little bird that waits for day.
I wait for joy—how long must I wait?

Frederick Goldin

Ich wêne nieman lebe der mînen kumber weine,
den ich eine trage,
ez entuo diu guote, diech mit triuwen meine,
vernimt si mîne klage.
wê wie tuon ich sô, daz ich sô herzeclîche
bin an si verdâht, daz ich ein künicrîche
für ir minne niht ennemen wolde,
obe ich teilen unde welen solde?

Dô si mir alrêrst ein hôhgemüete sande
in daz herze mîn,
des was bote ir güete, die ich wol erkande,
und ir liehter schîn.
si sach mich güetlîch ane mit ir spilnden ougen;
lachen si began ûz rôtem munde tougen.
sâ zehant enzunte sich mîn wunne,
daz mîn muot stuont hô alsam diu sunne.

Swer mir des erban, ob ich si minne tougen,
sêt der sündet sich.
swenne ich eine bin, si schînt mir vor den ougen.
sô bedunket mich
wie si gê dort her ze mir aldur die mûren.
ir red und ir trôst enlâzent mich niet trûren.
swenn si wil, sô füeret si mich hinnen
mit ir wîzen hant hô über die zinnen.

Ich wêne, si ist ein Vênus hêre, diech dâ minne:
wan si kan sô vil.
si benimt mir leide, fröide und al die sinne.
swenne sô si wil,
sô gêt si dort her zuo einem vensterlîne,
und siht mich an reht als der sunnen schîne:
swanne ich si dan gerne wolde schouwen,
ach sô gêt si dort zuo andern frouwen.

Wê waz rede ich? jâ ist mîn geloube bœse
und ist wider got.
wan bit ich in des daz er mich hinnen lœse?
ich was ie ir spot.

I believe there is no one alive who weeps for my sorrow,
which I bear alone,
unless the Good, whom I love loyally, should weep
    for me,
if she hears my cry.
O lord, what do I do, that I so lose
myself in thought of her, I would not take
a kingdom for her love,
were I to set them apart and choose?

The first time she sent a jubilation
into my heart,
it was her gentleness that brought the message, as I
    could recognize,
and her brilliant light.
She looked on me with kindness in her playing eyes,
and on her red mouth a secret smile.
Right then my joy lit up
and my mind stood as high as the sun.

Whoever grumbles at my loving her in secret,
behold: that man does wrong:
when I am alone, she gleams before my eyes.
Then I think I see:
There, she comes this way, to me, through the castle walls.
Her greeting and her comfort do not let me grieve.
If she wills, she leads me out away from here,
with her white hand, high up, over the battlements.

I think it is there the noble Venus that I love,
for she has great power.
She takes away my sadness, and my joy, and all my
    senses.
If she wills,
she comes this way to a little window there
and looks down on me like the light of the sun.
Then when I would like to look at her,
ach, she goes to the other women, she goes back in.

ich tuon sam der swan, der singet swenne er stirbet.
waz ob mir mîn sanc daz lîhte noch erwirbet,
swâ man mînen kumber sagt ze mêre,
daz man mir erbunne mîner swêre?

Ich hôrt ûf der heide
lûte stimme und süezen klanc.
dâ von wart ich beide
fröiden rîch und trûrens kranc.
nâch der mîn gedanc   sêre ranc   unde swanc,
díe vant ich ze tanze dâ si sanc.
âne leide   ich dô spranc.

Ích vant si verborgen
eine und ir wengel naz,
dô si an dem morgen
mînes tôdes sich vermaz
dér vil lieben haz   tuot mir baz   danne daz
dô ich vor ir kniete dâ si saz
und ir sorgen   gar vergaz.

Ích vants an der zinnen,
éine, und ich was zir besant.
dâ moht ichs ir minnen
wol mit fuoge hân gepfant.
dô wând ich diu lant   hân verbrant   sâ zehant,
wán daz mich ir süezen minne bant
an den sinnen   hât erblant.

Woe, what have I said? What I believe is evil
and strikes against God.
Why do I not pray Him set me free from here?
To her I was always a thing to ridicule.
I am like the swan, that sings when it is dying.
What if my song should yet gain me this one thing,
wherever they tell about my sorrow:
that they envy me my suffering?

Frederick Goldin

I heard on the meadow
bright voices and sweet tones
and was at once
rich in joys, in sorrows poor.
The one toward whom my thoughts have struggled and
    soared—
I found her in the dance, singing.
Free of sorrow, I danced too.

I found her withdrawn,
by herself, and her cheeks wet,
in the morning where
she fathomed my death.
I would rather the hate of my beloved than how it felt
kneeling before her where she sat
and let go of all her pain.

I found her on the battlement, alone,
and I had been sent for—
and could have taken, quite without uncourtliness,
the proof of her love from her hand.
I thought I had burnt up the land,
it was only that love with its gentle bind
had darkened my mind.*

Frederick Goldin

---

*Literally, "I thought I burnt up the land straightaway (that is, with the fire of my love), but the bond of her sweet love blinded my senses." In other words, the tryst and the promise of her love were only a fantasy.

Owê, sol aber mir iemer mê
geliuhten dur die naht
noch wîzer danne ein snê
ir lîp vil wol geslaht?
der trouc diu ougen mîn:
ich wânde, ez solde sîn
des liehten mânen schîn,
dô taget ez.

"Owê, sol aber er immer mê
den morgen hie betagen?
als uns diu naht engê,
daz wir niht durfen klagen:
'owê, nu ist ez tac,'
als er mit klage pflac
do'r jungest bî mir lac.
dô taget ez."

Owê, si kuste âne zal
in deme slâfe mich.
dô vielen hin ze tal
ir trêne nidersich,
iedoch getrôste ich sî,
daz si ir weinen lî
und mich alummevî.
dô taget ez.

"Owê, daz er sô dicke sich
bî mir ersêen hât!
als er endahte mich,
sô wolte er sunder wât
mich armen schouwen blôz.
ez was ein wunder grôz.
daz in des nie verdrôz.
dô taget ez."

Alas, shall I not see again,
glimmering in the dark
of night, whiter, than snow,
her beautiful body?
It fooled my eyes,
I thought it must be
the bright light of the moon.
Then it dawned.

"Alas, will he not again
stay here till the light?
May the night so pass between us
we've no reason to lament
'Alas, now it is day,'
as he lamented then
when he last lay by me.
Then it dawned."

Alas, she did not stop,
as I was sleeping, kissing me.
Then her tears came
falling.
But I gave her comfort,
and she left her weeping
and held me all around again.
Then it dawned.

"Alas, how many times he lost
himself looking at me,
as he took the cover off,
he wanted to see
poor me naked without clothes.
It was wonderful,
he never got tired of that.
Then it dawned."

Frederick Goldin

Mirst geschênals eime kindelîne,
daz sîn schônez bilde in eime glase ersach
unde greif dar nâch sîn selbes schîne
sô vil biz daz ez den spiegel gar zerbrach.
dô wart al sîn wünne ein leitlich ungemach.
alsô dâhte ich iemer frô ze sîne,
dô'ch gesach die lieben frouwen mîne,
von der mir bî liebe leides vil geschach.

Minne, diu der werlde ir fröide mêret,
sêt, diu brâhte in troumes wîs die frouwen mîn
dâ mîn lîp an slâfen was gekêret
und ersach sich an der besten wünne sîn.
dô sach ich ir werden tugende, ir liehten schîn,
schône und für alle wîp gehêret;
niwan daz ein lützel was versêret
ir vil fröiden rîchez rôtez mündelîn.

Grôze angest hân ich des gewunnen,
daz verblîchen süle ir mündelîn sô rôt.
des hân ich nu niuwer klage begunnen,
sît mîn herze sich ze solcher swêre bôt,
daz ich durch mîn ouge schouwe solche nôt,
sam ein kint daz wîsheit unversunnen
sînen schaten ersach in einem brunnen
und den minnen muose unze an sînen tôt.

Hôer wîp von tugenden und von sinne,
die enkan der himel niender ummevân,
sô die guoten diech vor ungewinne
fremden muoz und immer doch an ir bestân.
ôwê leider, jô wând ichs ein ende hân,
ir vil wünneclîchen werden minne:
nu bin ich vil kûme an dem beginne.
des ist hin mîn wünne und ouch mîn gerender wân.

It has gone with me as with a child
that saw its beautiful image in a mirror
and reached for its own reflection so
often till it broke the mirror to pieces;
then its contentment turned into a great unrest.
So I, once, thought I would live in continual joy
when I set my eyes on my beloved lady,
through whom, beside some pleasure, I have felt much
    pain.

Minne, who increases men's joy—look,
there, she brought me my lady by way of a dream,
where my body was turned toward sleep,
lost in the vision of its great contentment.
Then I gazed on all her nobleness, her shining image,
beautiful, exalted among women. Only,
it was just that there was some damage
to her small red mouth, that always laughed.

It frightened me
to see her small mouth pale, that was so red.
Now for this I have raised up new laments:
my heart stood ready for the grief it knew,
and I found this terror with my eyes—
like that child without experience
who found his own reflection in a spring
and had to love it till he died.

Heaven itself cannot contain
women higher in virtue and mind
than this good lady. I have been brought down,
I must stay far away and cleave to her forever.
O sorrow, how for a moment it could seem
I had reached and won her joyful, noble love.
Now here I stand, just starting out,
my contentment is gone, and my soaring dream.

Frederick Goldin

Vil süeziu senftiu tôterinne,
war umbe welt ir tôten mir den lîp,
und i'uch sô herzeclîchen minne,
zewâre, frouwe, gar für elliu wîp?
wênet ir . . . . ob ir mich tôtet,
daz ich iuch danne niemer mê beschouwe?
nein, iuwer minne hât mich des ernôtet
daz iuwer sêle ist mîner sêle frouwe.
sol mir hie niht guot geschên
von iuwerm werden lîbe,
sô muoz mîn sêle iu des verjên
dazs iuwerr sêle dienet dort   als einem reinen wîbe.

Hartmann von Aue

Ich sprach, ich wolte ir iemer leben:
daz liez ich wîte mære komen.
mîn herze hete ich ir gegeben:
daz hân ich nu von ir genomen.
swer tumben antheiz trage,
der lâze in ê der tage
ê in der strît
beroube sîner jâre gar.
alsô hân ich getân.
der kriec sî ir verlân;
für dise zît
sô wil ich dienen anderswar.

Ich was untriuwen ie gehaz:
und wolte ich ungetriuwe sîn,
mir tæte untriuwe verre baz
dan daz daz mich diu triuwe mîn
von ir niht scheiden liez

You sweet soft murderess,
why do you want to kill me,
when I have loved you with an honest heart,
in truth, above all women?
Do you really think if you kill me
I shall never look on you again?
No! Love of you has driven me
to make your soul the lady of my soul.
If nothing good shall come my way down here
from your noble self,
my soul must swear this oath to you:
it will serve your soul as its perfect lady there.*

Frederick Goldin

Hartmann von Aue

I said I would always live for her
and had the word spread far and wide:
I had given her my heart.
And now I have taken it back.
Whoever carries a foolish oath,
let him set it down
before the struggle
robs him of his days and years.
That is what I have done.
Let the battlefield be hers,
from this time forth
I shall serve elsewhere.

I always hated disloyalty—
and if I ever wanted to be disloyal,
disloyalty would do me much more good
than the way my loyalty stops
me from ever leaving her

*In the next world.

diu mich ir dienen hiez.
nu tuot mir wê,
sî wil mir ungelônet lân.
ich spriche ir niuwan guot:
ê ich beswære ir muot,
sô wil ich ê
die schulde zuo dem schaden hân.

Waz solte ich arges von ir sagen
der ich ie wol gesprochen hân?
ich mac wol mînen kumber klagen
und sî drumb ungevelschet lân.
sî nimt von mir für wâr
mîn dienest manic jâr.
ich hân gegert
ir minne unde vinde ir haz.
daz mir dâ nie gelanc,
des habe ich selbe undanc:
dûht ich sis wert,
sî hete mir gelônet baz.

Sît ich ir lônes muoz enbern,
der ich manc jâr gedienet hân,
so geruoche mich got eines wern,
daz ez der schœnen müeze ergân
nâch êren unde wol.
sît ich mich rechen sol,
dêswâr daz sî,
und doch niht anders wan alsô
daz ich ir heiles gan
baz danne ein ander man,
und bin dâ bî
ir leides gram, ir liebes frô.

Mir sint diu jâr vil unverlorn
diu ich an sî gewendet hân:
hât mich ir minne lôn verborn,
doch trœstet mich ein lieber wân.
ichn gerte nihtes mê,
wan müese ich ir als ê

who called me to her service.
Now it makes me grieve
that she will let me go unrequited.
I shall say nothing but good of her:
before I weigh her spirit down
I would rather
take on myself the guilt for all the harm.

What ill thing should I say about this lady
whom I have always spoken well of?
I would rather just cry out in pain
and leave her unaccused.
It is true, she took
my long years' service.
I longed
for her love and came upon her hate.
Well, if I've never found anything better,
it is my fault:
if she had thought me worthy,
she'd have given me something better.

Since I have to get along without her gift
after I have served these many years,
then God let me have this one wish,
that all things good and honorable
fall to this beautiful lady.
And since I am bound to seek revenge,
then let it be
nothing but this,
that I wish her well
with a better wish than any other man,
and may I be
sad for her pain, joyful for her pleasure.

To me the years are never lost
that I bestowed on her:
if courting her has brought no gift,
one beloved dream still comforts me.
I would desire nothing more
but to be able, as before,

ze vrowen jehen.
manc man der nimt sîn ende alsô
daz im niemer liep geschiht,
wan daz er sich versiht
deiz sül geschehen,
und tuot in der gedinge frô.

Der ich dâ her gedienet hân,
dur die wil ich mit fröiden sîn,
doch ez mich wênic hât vervân.
ich weiz wol daz diu frowe mîn
niwan nâch êren lebt.
swer von der sîner strebt,
der habe im daz.
in betrâget sîner jâre vil.
swer alsô minnen kan,
der ist ein valscher man.
mîn muot stât baz:
von ir ich niemer komen wil.

Manger grüezet mich alsô
(der gruoz tuot mich ze mâze frô),
»Hartman, gên wir schouwen
ritterlîche frouwen.«
mac er mich mit gemache lân
und île er zuo den frowen gân!
bî frowen triuwe ich niht vervân,
wan daz ich müede vor in stân.

Ze frowen habe ich einen sin:
als sî mir sint als bin ich in;
wand ich mac baz vertrîben
die zît mit armen wîben.
swar ich kum dâ ist ir vil,

to proclaim her my lady.
Many men reach the end
and have never known pleasure,
but they had faith
that it would come,
and the hope made them rejoice.

She whom I have served to this day—
through her I shall be with joy,
though I come away with little to hold.
I know that my lady
lives in honor.
Whoever seeks to leave his lady:
my curse.
His years will lie on him like a weight.
Whoever can love like that
is a counterfeit man.
My mind is set on something better:
I shall never come away from her.

Frederick Goldin

Often a friend will greet me thus
(his greeting doesn't make me very glad):
"Hartmann, let us visit
courtly ladies."
Let him leave me in peace
and rush himself to his ladies.
From these ladies I expect no pleasure
but waiting till I'm weary.

I have one mind with ladies:
as they treat me, I treat them;
because I get more for my time
with just plain women.
Wherever I come, there they are in droves,

dâ vinde ich die diu mich dâ wil;
diu ist ouch mînes herzen spil:
waz touc mir ein ze hôhez zil?

In mîner tôrheit mir geschach
daz ich zuo zeiner frowen sprach
»frow, ich hân mîne sinne
gewant an iuwer minne.«
dô wart ich twerhes an gesehen.
des wil ich,des sî iu bejehen,
mir wîp in solher mâze spehen
diu mir des niht enlânt geschehen.

Ich var mit iuwern hulden, herren unde mâge:
liut unde lant diu müezen sælic sîn.
es ist unnôt daz iemen mîner verte vrâge:
ich sage wol für wâr die reise mîn.
mich vienc diu Minne und lie mich vrî ûf mîne sicherheit.
nu hât sî mir enboten bî ir liebe daz ich var.
ez ist unwendic: ich muoz endelîchen dar:
wie kûme ich bræche mîne triuwe und mînen eit!

Sich rüemet manger waz er dur die Minne tæte:
wâ sint diu werc? die rede hœre ich wol.
doch sæhe ich gerne dazs ir eteslîchen bæte
daz er ir diente als ich ir dienen sol.
ez ist geminnet, der sich dur die Minne ellenden muoz.
nû seht wies mich û mîner zungen ziuhet über mer.
und lebt mîn herre, Salatîn und al sîn her
dienbræhten mich von Vranken niemer einen fuoz.

and there I find one that wants me,
and she is my heart's delight.
A lofty goal beyond my reach—frankly, who needs it?

In my inexperience it happened once,
I said to one of these ladies:
"Lady, I have set my mind
to loving you."
She looked at me down her nose.*
So I tell you I want
to find the kind of women
who will save me from such woes.

Frederick Goldin

I go, with your good grace, lords and kinsmen:
bless this people and this land.
No man need ask about my voyage:
I shall tell you all truly why I go.
Love took me captive and on my sworn word set me free.
Now by the love I owe her she has commanded me to go.
It is unalterable: I must surely go:
how unwillingly I would forswear my loyalty and vow.

Many men boast about what they would do for Love:
where are their works? I hear their speeches well enough,
but I would like to see her ask a single one of them
to serve her as I am setting out to serve.
A man who must go into exile for love—there is a man
    who loves.
Now behold how she draws me across the sea away from
    my native tongue.
And if my lord were living, Saladin and all his army
could not move me one foot away from home.

---

*Literally, "Then I was looked at askance."

Ir minnesinger, iu muoz ofte misselingen:
daz iu den schaden tuot daz ist der wân.
ich wil mich rüemen, ich mac wol von minne singen,
sît mich diu minne hât und ich sî hân.
daz ich dâ wil, seht daz wil alse gerne haben mich:
sô müezt ab ir verliesen under wîlen wânes vil:
ir ringent umbe liep daz iuwer niht enwil:
wan mügt ir armen minnen solhe minne als ich?

Reinmar der Alte

Waz ich nu niuwer mære sage
desn darf mich nieman frâgen: ich enbin niht vrô.
die friunt verdriuzet mîner klage.
des man ze vil gehœret, dem ist allem sô.
nu hân ich es beidiu schaden unde spot.
waz mir doch leides unverdienet, daz erkenne got,
und âne schult geschiht!
ichn gelige herzeliebe bî,
    son hât an mîner vröide nieman niht.

Die hôhgemuoten zîhent mich,
ich minne niht sô sêre als ich gebâre ein wîp.
si liegent unde unêrent sich:
si was mir ie gelîcher mâze sô der lîp.
nie getrôste si dar under mir den muot.
der ungenâden muoz ich, und des si mir noch getuot,
erbeiten als ich mac.
mir ist eteswenne wol gewesen:
    gewinne ab ich nu niemer guoten tac?

You minnesingers, you have to fail again and again:
it is foolish hope that damages your song.
I boast that I know how to sing of Love,
for Love has me, and I have her,
that which I desire—see!—desires me as much:
but you must often lose your hopeless hope:
you struggle for a love that wants none of you:
when will you poor fellows love such Love as I?

Frederick Goldin

Reinmar der Alte

No one needs to ask
what's the latest news with me: I am not happy.
My friends are sick and tired of my complaints—
which always happens when something is too often heard.
Now I must put up with insults and mockery as well.
And yet, God be my witness, what I have suffered
unjustly, quite without fault.
If I do not lie with my beloved,
   no one will gain from my joy—till then, not one happy
   word.*

Those who *are* happy bring me accusations:
I couldn't love a woman as much as I pretend to, they
   say.
They lie, and dishonor themselves.
She was always as dear to me as my own self,
and never, for all that, gave me any comfort for my love.
This unkindness and whatever else she may yet do to me
I have to abide as well as I can.
I used to have some pleasure, sometimes.
   Will I ever have one good day again?

* "till then, not one happy word": added.

Sô wol dir, wîp, wie reine ein nam!
wie sanfte er doch z'erkennen und ze nennen ist!
ez wart nie niht sô lobesam,
swâ duz an rehte güete kêrest, sô du bist.
dîn lop níemán mit rede volenden kan.
swes du mit triuwen phligest, wol im, derst ein sælic man
und mac vil gerne leben.
du gîst al der werlde hôhen muot:
    wan maht och mir ein lützel fröiden geben?

Zwei dinc hân ich mir für geleit,
diu strîtent mit gedanken in dem herzen mîn:
ob ich ir hôhen werdekeit
mit mînem willen wolte lâzen minre sîn,
ode ob ich daz welle daz si græzer sî
und si vil sælic wîp stê mîn und aller manne vrî.
diu tuont mir beidiu wê:
ich enwirde ir lasters niemer vrô;
    vergât si mich, daz klage ich iemer mê.

Ob ich nu tuon und hân getân
daz ich von rehte in ir hulden solte sîn,
und si vor aller werlde hân,
waz mac ich des, vergizzet si dar under mîn?
swer nu giht daz ich ze spotte künne klagen,
der lâze im mîne rede beide singen unde sagen

  . . . . .

unde merke wa ich ie spræche ein wort,
    ezn læge ê i'z gespræche herzen bî.

Bless you, *woman*—how pure a name,
how pleasant to come upon it and say it!
There never was anything so worthy of praise—
when you have a mind to goodness—as you.
No one can fulfill your praise with words.
The man you care for loyally, he is blessed, a happy man
and can gladly live.
You exalt the whole world's spirit:
   when will you give me a few joys too?

I have set myself two questions
that argue with each other in my thoughts:
would I really want
her towering virtue down somewhat,
or would I want it higher still
and have her—blessed woman—free of me and every
      other man?
For me, either way means pain:
I could never rejoice in her dishonor,
   but if she passes over me, I will forever complain.

If there is in everything I do, or ever did,
no other thought but to make me worthy of her grace,
and I cherish her above the whole world,
what can I do, if she forgets me while I'm impressing her?*
Whoever says I only pretend to complain, as a joke,
let him have my answer in music and verse

. . . . . .

and take note whether I ever spoke one word
   that did not lie in my heart before I spoke.

Frederick Goldin

*Literally, "meanwhile."

»Lieber bote, nu wirp alsô,
sich in schiere und sage im daz:
vert er wol und ist er frô,
ich leb iemer deste baz.
sage im durch den willen mîn
daz er íemer solhes iht getuo
  dâ von wir gescheiden sîn.

Frâge er wie ich mich gehabe,
gich daz ich mit fröiden lebe.
swâ du mügest dâ leite in abe
daz er mich der rede begebe.
ich bin im von herzen holt
und sæhe in gerner denne den tac:
  daz ab du verswîgen solt.

Ê dazd iemer im verjehest
deich im holdez herze trage,
sô sich dazd alrêrst besehest
und vernim waz ich dir sage:
meine er wol mit triuwen mich,
swaz danne im müge ze vröiden komen,
  daz mîn êre sî, daz sprich.

Spreche er daz er welle her,
daz ichs immer lône dir,
sô bit in daz er verber
rede dier jungest sprach ze mir:
sô mac ich in an gesehen.
wes wil er des besweren mich
  daz doch nimmer mac geschehen?

Des er gert daz ist der tôt
und verderbet mangen lîp;
bleich und eteswenne rôt
alsô verwet ez diu wîp.
minne heizent ez die man,
und möhte baz unminne sîn.
  wê im ders alrêst began!

"Messenger, hear what I say,
seek him out and tell him this:
if he's well and feeling gay,
then I, too, find naught amiss.
Warn him also, for my sake
to be careful. What might part us
   he should never undertake.

If he asks, you should admit
that I'm always well and merry;
if you can, get him to quit
plaints which are not necessary.
For I love him from my heart
and would rather see him than
   the day—but do not tell that part.

Ere you let my sweetheart know
that his lady loves him dearly,
first find out how matters go
and hear what I tell you clearly:
if he's faithful to his vow,
tell him what will give him joy
   and my honor will allow.

Should he say he'll soon appear,
I'd be always in your debt;
what he said the last time here
you must tell him to forget
ere he comes again to me.
Why give ear to his request
   when such a thing may never be?

It is death and will not fail
to bring to many grief and dread.
It can make a woman pale
and it often makes them red.
Men may call it love, but they
should call it not-love; woe to him
   who first led woman thus astray.

Daz ich alsô vil dâ von
hân geredet, daz ist mir leit,
wande ich was vil ungewon
sô getâner arebeit
alse ich tougenlîchen trage—
dune sólt im nimmer niht verjehen
alles des ich dir gesage.«

Walther von der Vogelweide

Ich saz ûf eime steine,
und dahte bein mit beine;
dar ûf satzt ich den ellenbogen:
ich hete in mîne hant gesmogen
daz kinne und ein mîn wange.
dô dâhte ich mir vil ange,
wie man zer welte solte leben:
deheinen rât kond ich gegeben,
wie man driu dinc erwurbe,
der keines niht verdurbe.
diu zwei sint êre und varnde guot,
daz dicke ein ander schaden tuot:
daz dritte ist gotes hulde,
der zweier übergulde.
die wolte ich gerne in einen schrîn.
jâ leider desn mac niht gesîn,
daz guot und weltlich êre
und gotes hulde mêre
zesamene in ein herze komen.
stîg unde wege sint in benomen:

That I spoke of this so much
shows how great is my despair.
I have not been used to such
nor to sorrows that I bear
and must suffer all unknown.
You must never tell him this;
    it was said for you alone."

J. W. Thomas

Walther von der Vogelweide

I sat down on a rock,*
crossed one leg over the other leg,
set my elbow on top,
nestled my chin and one
cheek in my hand.
Then I thought very hard
about how a man should live in the world.
I could not find a way
for a man to gain three things at once
and not one of them be ruined.
Two are the honor and the goods of this life,
which often damage one another;
the third is God's grace,
more precious than the other two.
I'd like all three in one chest,
yes, but in these times it cannot be
that wealth and honor in the world
and God's grace ever
come into one heart in one accord.
The paths and ways are blocked before them,

*The earliest and most famous of Walther's political poems. In 1197 the emperor Heinrich VI died, leaving an infant son, Friedrich, who had earlier been elected as successor. Friedrich's uncle, Philip of Swabia, and Otto of Brunswick contended for the throne, and each was crowned by his supporters in 1198. The result was the disorder and violence that the poet here decries. In the opening lines the poet assumes the ancient symbolic posture of the prophet and thinker.

untriuwe ist in der sâze,
gewalt vert ûf der strâze:
fride unde reht sint sêre wunt.
diu driu enhabent geleites niht, diu zwei enwerden ê gesunt.

Ich hôrte ein wazzer diezen
und sach die vische fliezen,
ich sach swaz in der welte was,
velt walt loup rôr unde gras.
swaz kriuchet unde fliuget
und bein zer erde biuget,
daz sach ich, unde sage iu daz:
der keinez lebet âne haz.
daz wilt und daz gewürme
die strîtent starke stürme,
sam tuont die vogel under in;
wan daz si habent einen sin:
si dûhten sich ze nihte,
si enschüefen starc gerihte.
si kiesent künege unde reht,
si setzent hêrren unde kneht.
sô wê dir, tiuschiu zunge,
wie stêt dîn ordenunge!
daz nû diu mugge ir künec hât,
und daz dîn êre alsô zergât.
bekêrâ dich, bekêre.
die cirkel sint ze hêre,
die armen künege dringent dich:
Philippe setze en weisen ûf, und heiz si treten hinder sich.

Ich sach mit mînen ougen
mann unde wîbe tougen,
daz ich gehôrte und gesach
swaz iemen tet, swaz iemen sprach.
ze Rôme hôrte ich liegen
und zwêne künege triegen.
dâ von huop sich der meiste strît

treachery lies in ambush,
violence rides in the streets,
peace and justice are badly hurt.
The three shall not have safe conduct till the two* are
    first restored.

I heard a stream rushing
and saw the fishes swimming;
I saw whatever there was in the world,
field woods leaf reed grass.
Whatever crawls and flies
and bends its legs on the earth,
I saw it, and I tell you this:
not one of them lives without hate.
Wild beasts and creeping things
struggle in violent fights,
and so the birds with each other.
And yet they have one mind:
they would think they are done for
if they did not set up a strong rule.
They decide on kings and law,
they install masters and servants.
Alas for you of the German tongue,
how does your order stand—
flies have their king
and your glory passes away.
Repent, repent!
The coronets are too proud,†
the little kings oppress you.‡
Put the orphan jewel§ on Philip's head and bid them all
    get back.

I saw with my own eyes
the secrets of men and women,
I saw and heard the things
that everyone did, that everyone said.
In Rome I heard how they lied

---

*The two are peace and justice.
†The lesser nobility supporting Otto.
‡The foreign kings who supported Otto.
§A precious stone in the imperial crown.

der ê was oder iemer sît,
dô sich begunden zweien
die pfaffen unde leien.
daz was ein nôt vor aller nôt:
lîp unde sêle lac dâ tôt.
die pfaffen striten sêre:
doch wart der leien mêre.
diu swert diu leiten si dernider,
und griffen zuo der stôle wider:
si bienen die si wolten,
und niht den si solten.
dô stôrte man diu goteshûs.
ich hôrte verre in einer klûs
vil michel ungebære:
dâ weinte ein klôsenære,
er klagete gote sîniu leit,
»owê der bâbest ist ze junc: hilf, hêrre, dîner kristenheit.«

Ir sult sprechen willekomen:
der iu mære bringet, daz bin ich.
allez daz ir habt vernomen,
daz ist gar ein wint: nû frâget mich.
ich wil aber miete:
wirt mîn lôn iht guot,
ich gesage iu lîhte daz iu sanfte tuot.
seht waz man mir êren biete.

and deceived two kings.*
From that the greatest strife rose up
that ever was or ever will be,
for then the priests
and laity took sides.
It was a disaster of disasters,
body and soul lay there dead.
The priests fought hard,
but the laity's number increased.
So the priests lay down their swords
and grabbed up the stole† again
and put the ban on those they wanted out,
not on those they should have.
Then were the houses of God made desolate.
Far off, in a hermit's cell,
I heard great lamentation.
There a hermit wept,
he poured out his sorrows to God:
"Alas, the Pope is too young, help, O Lord, your
    Christendom."‡

Frederick Goldin

You should bid me welcome:§
I'm a man that's bringing news.
Everything you've heard before
is wind. Now just ask me.
But first I want some reward.
If the pay is any good
I may have some news you'll like.
Now let us see the honorarium.

*Philip and his nephew Friedrich.
†Symbol of ecclesiastical office.
‡Innocent III was 37 at this time.
§Probably written for his (re)appearance at the Viennese court in 1203.

Ich wil tiuschen frowen sagen
solhiu mære daz si deste baz
al der werlte suln behagen:
âne grôze miete tuon ich daz.
waz wold ich ze lône?
si sint mir ze hêr:
sô bin ich gefüege, und bite si nihtes mêr
wan daz si mich grüezen schône.

Ich hân lande vil gesehen
unde nam der besten gerne war:
übel müeze mir geschehen,
kunde ich ie mîn herze bringen dar
daz im wol gevallen
wolde fremeder site.
nû waz hulfe mich, ob ich unrehte strite?
tiuschiu zuht gât vor in allen.

Von der Elbe unz an den Rîn
und her wider unz an Ungerlant
mugen wol die besten sîn,
die ich in der werlte hân erkant.
kan ich rehte schouwen
guot gelâz unt lîp.
sem mir got, sô swüere ich wol daz hie diu wîp
bezzer sint danne ander frouwen.

Tiusche man sint wol gezogen,
rehte als engel sint diu wîp getân.
swer si schildet, derst betrogen:
ich enkan sîn anders niht verstân.
tugent und reine minne,
swer die suochen wil,
der sol komen in unser lant: da ist wünne vil:
lange müeze ich lebe dar inne!

Der ich vil gedienet hân
und iemer mêre gerne dienen wil,
diust von mir vil unerlân:

I want to tell German women
such news as should make them all
more pleasing to the world.
I'll do that without asking for much—
what would I want as wages?
They are too high for that.
That's my breeding, and I ask them only
to greet me handsomely.

I have been in many lands
and looked closely at the best they had.
Damn me
if I can bring my heart
to like
foreign ways.
What good does it do me to argue some untruth?
German breeding excels all others.

From the Elbe to the Rhine
and from here again to Hungary
live the greatest people
I have ever seen on earth.
If I know how to judge
handsome figures and handsome acts,
by God I swear plain women here
are nobler than ladies elsewhere.

German men are nobly bred
and the women made like angels.
Whoever reproaches them is deluded—
otherwise I can't understand him.
Valour, and pure love—
anyone looking for these
should come to our land: there's great joy there.
Long may I live in this land!*

The one I have long served
and will gladly serve for ever,

*This line conveys his request to be taken back at court.

iedoch sô tuot si leides mir sô vil.
si kan mir versêren
herze und den muot.
nû vergebez ir got dazs an mir missetuot.
her nâch mac si sichs bekêren.

Lange swîgen des hât ich gedâht:
nû wil ich singen aber als ê.
dar zuo hânt mich guote liute brâht:
die mugen mir wol gebieten mê.
ich sol singen unde sagen,
und swes si gern, daz sol ich tuon: sô suln si mînen kumber
  klagen.

Hœret wunder, wie mir ist geschehen
von mîn selbes arebeit.
mich enwil ein wîp niht an gesehen:
die brâht ich in die werdekeit,
daz ir muot sô hôhe stât.
jon weiz si niht, swenn ich mîn singen lâze, daz ir lop zergât.

Hêrre, waz si flüeche lîden sol,
swenn ich nû lâze mînen sanc!
alle die nû lobent, daz weiz ich wol,
die scheltent danne ân mînen danc.
tûsent herze wurden frô
von ir genâden; dius engeltent, lât si mich verderben sô.

Dô mich dûhte daz si wære guot,
wer was ir bezzer dô dann ich?
dêst ein ende: swaz si mir getuot,
des mac ouch si verwænen sich,
nimet si mich von dirre nôt,
ir leben hât mînes lebennes êre: stirbe ab ich, sô ist si tôt.

she is wholly unrenounced;
yet she causes me much suffering.
She knows how to torment
my heart and mind.
Now God forgive her for the wrongs she's done me.
Later on she may repent.

Frederick Goldin

To be long silent was my thought:
now I shall sing once again as before.
Gentle people brought me back to it:
they have the right to command me.
I shall sing and make up words,
and do what they desire; then they must lament my grief.

Listen to this wonder, how I fared
for all my hard work:
a certain woman will not look at me—
and it was I that brought her up to that esteem
which makes her so high-minded now.
She does not know: when I leave off singing, her praise
    will die away.

Lord what curses she'd endure,
were I now to stop my song!
All those who praise her now, I know
they'll rebuke her then—against my will.
A thousand hearts were made happy
by her kindness to me; they will suffer for it if she lets me
    perish.

When it seemed that she was gentle,
who was more devoted then than I?
But that's all over: whatever she does to me,
she can expect the same—
if she frees me from this distress,
her life receives the glory of my life; if I perish, she is dead.

Sol ich in ir dienste werden alt,
die wîle junget si niht vil.
so ist mîn hâr vil lîhte alsô gestalt,
dazs einen jungen danne wil.
sô helfe iu got, hêr junger man,
sô rechet mich und gêt ir alten hût mit sumerlaten an.

Saget mir ieman, waz ist minne?
weiz ich des ein teil, sô wist ichs gerne mê.
der sich baz denn ich versinne,
der berihte mich durch waz si tuot sô wê.
minne ist minne, tuot si wol:
tuot si wê, so enheizet si niht rehte minne.
    sus enweiz ich wie si danne heizen sol.

Obe ich rehte râten künne
waz diu minne sî, sô sprechet denne jâ.
minne ist zweier herzen wünne:
teilent sie gelîche, sost diu minne dâ:
sol abe ungeteilet sîn,
sô enkans ein herze alleine niht enthalten.
    owê woldest dû mir helfen, frowe mîn!

Frowe, ich trage ein teil ze swære:
wellest dû mir helfen, sô hilf an der zît.
sî abe ich dir gar unmære,
daz sprich endelîche: sô lâz ich den strît,
unde wirde eine ledic man.
dû solt aber einez rehte wizzen, frouwe,
    daz dich lützel ieman baz geloben kan.

Kan mîn frowe süeze siuren?
wænet si daz ich ir liep gebe umbe leit?

If I grow old in her service,
she won't get much younger in that time.
Maybe then my hair'll have such a look
she'll want a young man at her side.
So help you God, avenge me,
you young man, and have a go with switches on her
    ancient hide.

                              Frederick Goldin

Will anyone tell me what Minne is?
Though I know a little, I gladly would know more.
Whoever understands it better,
let him tell me why it causes pain.
Minne is minne if it gives pleasure:
if it causes misery, it isn't right to call it minne—
then I don't know what it should be called.

If I guess right
what Minne is, say "Yes":
Minne is one joy between two hearts.
If they share alike, there is Minne:
but if it isn't shared,
one heart alone cannot contain it.
Alas, my lady, if you would only help me.

Lady, I bear a little too much.
If you want to help me, help in time.
But if I do not mean a thing to you,
say so once and for all: then I'll give up the struggle,
and become a free man.
But, lady, understand one thing:
no other man can sing your praise so well.

Can my lady turn the sweet to sour?
Does she dream I'll give her pleasure in exchange for
    misery?

sol ich si dar umbe tiuren,
daz siz wider kêre an mîne unwerdekeit?
sô kund ich unrehte spehen.
wê waz sprich ich ôrenlôser ougen âne?
    den diu minne blendet, wie mac der gesehen?

»Under der linden
an der heide,
dâ unser zweier bette was,
dâ mugt ir vinden
schône beide
gebrochen bluomen unde gras.
vor dem walde in einem tal,
tandaradei,
    schône sanc diu nahtegal.

Ich kam gegangen
zuo der ouwe:
dô was min friedel komen ê.
dâ wart ich enpfangen,
hêre frouwe,
daz ich bin sælic iemer mê.
kuster mich? wol tûsentstunt:
tandaradei,
    seht wie rôt mir ist der munt.

Dô het er gemachet
alsô rîche
von bluomen eine bettestat.
des wirt noch gelachet
inneclîche,
kumt iemen an daz selbe pfat.
bî den rôsen er wol mac,
tandaradei,
    merken wâ mirz houbet lac.

Should I lend her all that value
just to have her set it against my unworthiness?
That way I must see things wrong.
O lord what am I saying, deaf and blind?
A man dazzled by Minne—how can he see?

Frederick Goldin

"Under the lime tree
on the open field,
where we two had our bed,
you still can see
lovely broken
flowers and grass.
On the edge of the woods in a vale,
tandaradei,
sweetly sang the nightingale.

I came walking
to the meadow,
my love already was there.
And he received me,
Blessed Lady,
the joy of that will last.
Did he kiss me then? A thousand times, at least,
tandaradei,
look now, how my mouth is red.

Then he made
a lordly
place to lie in, all of flowers.

There's a good laugh there
even now
for anyone coming that way:
he could tell, by the roses,
tandaradei,
just where my head lay.

Daz er bî mir læge,
wessez iemen
(nu enwelle got!), sô schamt ich mich.
wes er mit mir pflæge,
niemer niemen
bevinde daz, wan er unt ich,
und ein kleinez vogellîn:
tandaradei,
        daz mac wol getriuwe sin.«

»Nemt, frowe, disen kranz:«
alsô sprach ich zeiner wol getânen maget:
»sô zieret ir den tanz,
mit den schœnen bluomen, als irs ûffe traget.
het ich vil edele gesteine,
daz müest ûf iur houbet,
obe ír mirs geloubet.
sêt mîne triuwe, daz ichz meine.«

»Ir sît sô wol getân,
daz ich iu mîn schapel gerne geben wil,
so ichz aller beste hân.
wîzer unde rôter bluomen weiz ich vil:
die stênt sô verre in jener heide.
dâ si schône entspringent
und die vogele singent,
dâ suln wir si brechen beide.«

Si nam daz ich ir bôt,
einem kinde vil gelîch daz êre hât.
ir wangen wurden rôt,
same diu rôse, dâ si bî der liljen stât.
do erschampten sich ir liehten ougen:
dô neic si mir schône.
daz wart mir ze lône:
wirt mirs iht mêr, daz trage ich tougen.

If anyone found out,
God forbid, he lay by me,
I'd be ashamed.
What he did with me there
may no one ever
know, except for him and me
and one little bird,
tandaradei,
which will not say a word."

Frederick Goldin

"Lady, take this garland."
So I spoke, once, to a pretty girl.
"And when you wear it, with its pretty flowers,
you will adorn the dance.
If I had precious stones,
you would wear them on your head,
now you believe this:
See, by my good faith, I mean what I say.

"You are so beautiful,
I want to give you my chaplet,
the best one I have.
I can show you many flowers—white, and red—
they wait, off there, in that open field.
There, where they bloom so beautifully,
and birds sing,
we will go pick flowers together."

What I offered her she took
like a young girl of great nobility.
Her cheeks grew red,
like a rose among lilies.
It made her glowing eyes bashful,
but she curtsied to me beautifully.
That was my reward.
If I get more, I'll keep still about it.

Mich dûhte daz mir nie
lieber wurde, danne mir ze muote was.
die bluomen vielen ie
von dem boume bî uns nider an daz gras.

seht, dô muost ich von fröiden lachen,
do ich sô wünneclîche
was in troume rîche,
dô taget ez und muos ich wachen.

Mir ist von ir geschehen,
daz ich disen sumer allen meiden muoz
vast under dougen sehen:
lîhte wirt mir einiu: so ist mir sorgen buoz.
waz obe si gêt an disem tanze?
frowe, dur iur güete
rucket ûf die hüete.
owê gesæhe ichs under kranze!

Herzeliebez frowelîn,
got gebe dir hiute und iemer guot.
kund ich baz gedenken dîn,
des hete ich willeclîchen muot.
waz mac ich dir sagen mê,
wan daz dir nieman holder ist? owê, dâ von ist mir vil wê.

Sie verwîzent mir daz ich
sô nidere wende mînen sanc.
daz si niht versinnent sich
waz liebe sî, des haben undanc!
sie getraf diu liebe nie,
die nâch dem guote und nâch der schœne minnent; wê wie
  minnent

[die?

It seemed to me I never
knew it better than it was then.
Flowers fell all the time
from the tree beside us on the grass.
Look now, I had to laugh for joy.
As I was dreaming
in such lordly pleasure,
day broke, and I had to wake up.

The way I am now, because of her
this whole summer I have to look
every girl square in the eyes:
maybe one of them is the one—then I'm rid of my
    sorrows.
What if she's here at this dance?
Ladies, by your good grace,
push back your hats.
O if underneath a garland I saw her face.

Frederick Goldin

Dearly beloved gentle girl,
God bless you today and every day.
If I could put my thoughts of you in better words,
I would have a willing mind to it.
What is there more to say
but no one loves you more? Oh, I suffer much for that.

They censure me, saying
I set my song too low:
they do not know
what love is—bad luck to them,
love never touched them,
their love goes after skin and gold—lord, what kind of
    love is that?

Bî der schœne ist dicke haz:
zer schœne niemen sî ze gâch.
liebe tuot dem herzen baz:
der liebe gêt diu schœne nâch.
liebe machet schœne wîp:
desn mac diu schœne niht getuon, sin machet niemer lieben lîp.

Ich vertrage als ich vertruoc
und als ich iemer wil vertragen.
dû bist schœne und hâst genuoc:
waz mugen si mir dâ von gesagen?
swaz si sagen, ich bin dir holt,
und nim dîn glesîn vingerlîn für einer küneginne golt.

Hâst dû triuwe und stætekeit,
sô bin ich sîn ân angest gar
daz mir iemer herzeleit
mit dînem willen widervar.
hâst ab dû der zweier niht,
son müezest dû mîn niemer werden. owê danne, ob daz geschiht!

Ir reinen wîp, ir werden man,
ez stêt alsô daz man mir muoz
êr unde minneclîchen gruoz
noch volleclîcher bieten an.
des habet ir von schulden grœzer reht dan ê:
welt ir vernemen, ich sage iu wes.
wol vierzec jâr hab ich gesungen oder mê
von minnen und als iemen sol.
dô was ichs mit den andern geil:
nu enwirt mirs niht, ez wirt iu gar.

Beauty often comes with hate:*
let no man rush toward beauty.
Love is kinder to the heart,
love comes first, then beauty,
love makes a woman beautiful—
but beauty does not have such power, beauty cannot
     make a woman worthy of love.

I bear it as I have borne
and will bear it as long as I must.†
You are beautiful, and you own enough—
what can they say to me?
Let them talk—I love you
and would not take the gold ring of a queen for your
     ring of glass.

If you have loyalty and constancy,
then I need not fear the day
will come when you will want
the anguish of the heart to fall on me.
But if you have neither,
then may you never be mine, and then oh god if it works
     out that way.

Frederick Goldin

You excellent women, you valiant men,
it is fitting now to give me
honor and greetings of love
in greater measure yet.
You have more cause to do this now than ever before.
If you will hear, I shall tell you why:
for forty years and more I have sung
of love, and how we must live.
In those days I had joy in it, with the others,
now I get nothing from it, it is all for you.

*That is, hateful qualities.
†That is, their reproaches.

mîn minnesanc der diene iu dar,
und iuwer hulde sî mîn teil.

Lât mich an eime stabe gân
und werben umbe werdekeit
mit unverzageter arebeit,
als ich von kinde habe getân,
sô bin ich doch, swie nider ich sî, der werden ein,
genuoc in mîner mâze hô.
daz müet die nideren. ob mich daz iht swache? nein.
die werden hânt mich deste baz.
diu wernde wirde diust sô guot,
daz man irz hœhste lop sol geben.
ezn wart nie lobelîcher leben,
swer sô dem ende rehte tuot.

Welt, ich hân dînen lôn ersehen:
swaz dû mir gîst, daz nimest dû mir.
wir scheiden alle blôz von dir.
scham dich, sol mir alsô geschehen.
ich hân lîp unde sêle (des was gar ze vil)
gewâget tûsentstunt dur dich:
nû bin ich alt und hâst mit mir dîn gampelspil:
und zürn ich daz, sô lachest dû.
nû lache uns eine wîle noch:
dîn jâmertac wil schiere komen,
und nimet dir swazt uns hâst benomen,
und brennet dich dar umbe iedoch.

Ich hât ein schœnez bilde erkorn:
owê daz ich ez ie gesach
ald ie sô vil zuoz ime gesprach!
ez hât schœn unde rede verlorn.
dâ wonte ein wunder inne: daz fuor ine weiz war:
dâ von gesweic daz bilde iesâ.
sîn liljerôsevarwe wart sô karkelvar,
daz ez verlôs smac unde schîn.
mîn bilde, ob ich bekerkelt bin
in dir, sô lâ mich ûz alsô

May my courtly song go on serving you,
and let your good wishes be my pay.

Say I walked with a staff
and struggled with undaunted
labor for excellence and honor,
as I have from childhood to this day:
I would walk lowly, yes, but I would stand among the
    valiant,
all bent down, yet in my stature high enough.
This galls the truly low.   Does it cast me down?   No.
Courtly men and women hold me all the higher.
Long merit is so precious,
let us give it our highest praise.
There never was a nobler life
if a man remembers the end as he lives out his days.

World, I know what your rewards are like—
whatever you give me you take away.
Naked are we all when we go from you;
it will be your shame when I, too, go that way.
I have risked my body and my soul—it was too much–
a thousand times for you.
Now I am old, and in me you have a thing to play with
and when I am enraged over that, you laugh.
Well, laugh at us a little while more—
your day of horror is coming soon
and will take everything from you that you took from us
and burn you for it even so.

I made out a beautiful image,
alas that I ever saw it
and spoke with it so many times!
Its beauty is gone, its tongue is still.
A miracle had its dwelling there—it went
I know not where; at once the image was dumb,
its color of lilies and roses became so dungeon gray
it lost its fragrance and its light.
My image, if I am imprisoned

daz wir ein ander vinden frô:
wan ich muoz aber wider in.

Mîn sêle müeze wol gevarn!
ich hân zer welte manegen lîp
gemachet frô, man unde wîp:
künd ich dar under mich bewarn!
lobe ich des lîbes minne, deis der sêle leit:
si giht, ez sî ein lüge, ich tobe.
der wâren minne giht si ganzer stætekeit,
wie guot si sî, wies iemer wer.
lîp, lâ die minne diu dich lât,
und habe die stæten minne wert:
mich dunket, der dû hâst gegert,
diu sî niht visch unz an den grât.

Allerêrst lebe ich mir werde,
sît mîn sündic ouge siht
daz reine lant und ouch die erde
der man sô vil êren giht.
mirst geschehen des ich ie bat,
ich bin komen an die stat
dâ got mennischlîchen trat.

Schœniu lant rîch unde hêre,
swaz ich der noch hân gesehen,
sô bist duz ir aller êre.
waz ist wunders hie geschehen!
daz ein magt ein kint gebar
hêre übr aller engel schar,
was daz niht ein wunder gar?

in you, let me go free, so
that we may find each other once more in joy,
for I shall enter in again one day.

May my soul fare well.
I have given joy to many
in this world, to many women, many men.
If only, doing that, I could have saved myself.
If I praise the body's love, it brings sorrow to my soul,
it says I lie, I rant,
and claims true love alone is constant to the end,
and tells how good love is and how it endures.
Body, leave that love that leaves you all alone
and praise the love that stays.
The thing you crave,
it isn't all meat right down to the bone.*

Frederick Goldin

Now My Life Has Gained Some Meaning

Now my life has gained some meaning
since these sinful eyes behold
the sacred land with meadows greening
whose renown is often told.
This was granted me from God:
to see the land, the holy sod,
which in human form He trod.

Splendid lands of wealth and power,
I've seen many, far and near,
yet of all are you the flower.
What a wonder happened here!
That a maid a child should bear,
Lord of all the angels fair,
was not this a wonder rare?

*Literally, "isn't fish to the bone"; proverbial. The important thing is that he speaks to the body in this down-to-earth peasanty way. Line 18: "all bent down" added.

Hie liez er sich reine toufen,
daz der mensche reine sî.
sît liez er sich hie verkoufen,
daz wir eigen wurden frî.
anders wæren wir verlorn.
wol dir, sper kriuz unde dorn!
wê dir, heiden! deist dir zorn.

Hinnen fuor der sun zer helle
von dem grabe, da'r inne lac.
des was ie der vater geselle,
und der geist, den niemen mac
sunder scheiden: êst al ein,
sleht und ebener danne ein zein,
als er Abrahâme erschein.

Do er den tievel dô geschande,
daz nie keiser baz gestreit,
dô fuor er her wider ze lande.
dô huob sich der juden leit,
daz er hêrre ir huote brach,
und man in sît lebendic sach,
den ir hant sluoc unde stach.

In diz lant hât er gesprochen
einen angeslîchen tac,
dâ diu witwe wirt gerochen
und der weise klagen mac
und der arme den gewalt
der dâ wirt an ime gestalt.
wol im dort, der hie vergalt!

Kristen juden und die heiden
jehent daz diz ir erbe sî:
got müez ez ze rehte scheiden
durch die sîne namen drî.
al diu welt diu strîtet her:
wir sîn an der rehten ger:
reht ist daz er uns gewer.

Here was He baptized, the Holy,
that all people might be pure.
Here He died, betrayed and lowly,
that our bonds should not endure.
Else our fate had been severe.
Hail, O cross, thorns and spear!
Heathens, woe!   Your rage is clear.

Then to hell the Son descended
from the grave in which He lay,
by the Father still attended,
and the Spirit whom none may
give a name: in one are three,
an arrow shaft in unity.
Thus did Abraham once see.

When He there defeated Satan,
ne'er has kaiser battled so,
He returned, our ways to straighten.
Then the Jews had fear and woe:
watch and stone were both in vain,
He appeared in life again,
whom their hands had struck and slain.

To this land, so He has spoken,
shall a fearful judgment come.
Widows' bonds shall then be broken
and the orphans' foe be dumb,
and the poor no longer cower
under sad misuse of power.
Woe to sinners in that hour!

Christians, heathen, Jews, contending,
claim it as a legacy.
May God judge with grace unending
through his blessed Trinity.
Strife is heard on every hand:
ours the only just demand,
He will have us rule the land.

J. W. Thomas

Ouwê, war sint verswunden   alliu mîniu jâr!
ist mir mîn leben getroumet,   oder ist ez wâr?
daz ich ie wânde ez wære,   was daz allez iht?
dar nâch hân ich geslâfen,   und enweiz es niht.
nû bin ich erwachet,   und ist mir unbekant
daz mir hie vor was kündic   als mîn ander hant.
liut unde lant, dar innen   von kinde ich bin erzogen,
die sint mir worden frömde,   als ob ez sî gelogen.
die mîne gespilen wâren,   die sint træge und alt.
gebreitet ist daz velt,   verhouwen ist der walt:
wan daz daz wazzer fliuzet   als ez wîlent flôz,
für wâr mîn ungelücke   wânde ich wurde grôz.
mich grüezet maneger trâge,   der mich bekande ê wol.
diu welt ist allenthalben   ungenâden vol.
als ich gedenke an manigen   wünneclîchen tac,
die mir sint enpfallen   sam in daz mer ein slac,
iemer mêre ouwê.

Ouwê wie jæmerlîche   junge liute tuont,
den ê vil unriuweclîche   ir gemüete stuont!
die kunnen niuwan sorgen,   owê wie tuont si sô?
swar ich zer werlte kêre,   dâ ist nieman vrô.
tanzen, lachen, singen   zergât mit sorgen gar:
nie kristenman gesach   sô jæmerlîche schar.
nû merkent wie den frouwen   ir gebende stât:
jâ tragent die stolzen ritter   dörpellîche wât.

uns sint unsenfte brieve   her von Rôme komen,
uns ist erloubet trûren   und fröide gar benomen.
daz müet mich inneclîchen sêre,   wir lebten ie vil wol,
daz ich nû für mîn lachen   weinen kiesen sol.
die vogel in der wilde   betrüebet unser klage:
waz wunders ist, ob ich   dâ von verzage?
waz spriche ich tumber man   durch mînen bœsen zorn?
swer dirre wünne volget,   der hât jene dort verlorn,
iemer mêre owê.

Ouwê wie uns mit süezen   dingen ist vergeben!
ich sihe die bittern gallen   in dem honege sweben.

Alas, all my years, where have they disappeared?
Have I dreamed my life, or is it real?
That which I thought was something, was it something?
Perhaps I have been sleeping and do not know it.
Now I am awake, and all seems strange
that used to be familiar, once, as my own hand.
The people and the place where I grew up
seem alien, like lies, not of my own land.
The children I played with now are old and slow.
The field is harvested, the woods are hewn.
Were it not that the water flows as it used to flow,
I would think my misery truly great.
Many are slow to greet me that knew me well.
The world is everywhere full of the loss of grace.
When I think of many happy days that have fallen
away from me like a blow struck on the water, then
ever more, alas.

Alas, how miserable are the young today,
whose spirits soared in times gone by.
They know only sorrow—how can they live that way?
Wherever I turn on this earth no one is content,
dancing laughing singing have passed on into care,
no Christian man has ever seen a crowd so wretched.
Look at the women, what they wear on their heads,
and proud knights clothed in peasant dress.

Now cruel letters have come to us from Rome,
we are authorized to suffer, exempt from joy.
It offends me deeply—we used to live well in this land—
that I must give up my laughter and choose to weep.
The birds in the wilderness are cast down by our lament,
it is no wonder, then, that I despair—
But fool that I am, what does my ranting anger make me
    say?
Who runs after pleasures here has lost them *there*,
ever more, alas.

Alas, how the sweet things poison us.
I see the bitter gall floating in the honey.

diu welt is ûzen schœne,   wîz grüen unde rôt,
und innân swarzer varwe,   vinster sam der tôt.
swen si nû habe verleitet,   der schouwe sînen trôst:
er wirt mit swacher buoze   grôzer sünde erlôst.
dar an gedenkent, ritter: ez ist iuwer dinc.
ir tragent die liehten helme   und manegen herten rinc,
dar zuo die vesten schilte   und diu gewîhten swert.
wolte got, wær ich   der sigenünfte wert,
sô wolte ich nôtic man   verdienen rîchen solt:
joch meine ich niht die huoben   noch der hêrren golt.
ich wolte selbe krône   êweclîchen tragen:
die möhte ein soldenære   mit sîme sper bejagen.
möht ich die lieben reise   gevaren über sê,
sô wolte ich denne singen wol,   und niemer mêr ouwê,
niemer mêr ouwê.

Owê, daz wîsheit unde jugent,
des mannes schœne noch sîn tugent,
niht erben sol, sô ie der lîp erstirbet!
daz mac wol klagen ein wîser man,
der sich des schaden versinnen kan,
Reimâr, waz guoter kunst an dir verdirbet.
dû solt von schulden iemer des geniezen,
daz dich des tages wolte nie verdriezen
dun spræches ie den frowen wol mit . . .

des süln si iemer danken dîner zungen.
hetst anders niht wan eine rede gesungen,
"sô wol dir, wîp, wie reine ein nam!," dû hetest alsô
    gestriten
an ir lop daz elliu wîp dir genâden solten biten.

The white green red world is beautiful outside,
and inside black, as dark as death.
Whomever it has seduced, let him look where he will
    find comfort:
with a soft penance he is set free from mighty sin.
Knights, think of this, it is for you, these words,
you wear the bright helms, the hard rings,
the strong shields, the consecrated swords.
Would God that I myself were worthy of the victory.
I, a needy man, would win great wages,
yet not acres of land or the gold of kings.
I myself would wear the crown of ages
that any soldier fighting for money can win with his
    spear.
If I could make that beloved voyage across the sea,
I would sing "Joy!" and never more "Alas,"
never more alas.

Frederick Goldin

Alas, that wisdom, and youth,
and the beauty of man, and his craft
cannot be handed down when the body dies away.
A man who has lived can mourn for this,
who is awake to human hurt.
Reinmar, what great art dies with you.
You've the right to rejoice till the end of days
that you never lost the taste, not once,
for singing noble women's praise.

They ought to thank your tongue forever.
If you had sung but the one theme—if that were all—
"Joy to you, Woman, how pure a name," with that alone
    you would have striven
so for their praise's sake, let every woman pray for mercy
    on your soul.

Dêswâr, Reimâr, dû riuwes mich
michels harter danne ich dich,
ob dû lebtes und ich wær erstorben.
ich wilz bî mînen triuwen sagen,
dich selben wolt ich lützel klagen:
ich klage dîn edelen kunst, daz sist verdorben.
dû kundest al der werlte fröide mêren,

sô duz ze guoten dingen woltes kêren.
mich riuwet dîn wol redender munt und dîn vil süezer
    sanc,
daz die verdorben sint bî mînen zîten.
daz dû niht eine wîle mohtest bîten!
sô leiste ich dir gesellschaft: mîn singen ist niht lanc.
dîn sêle müeze wol gevarn, und habe dîn zunge danc.

Wolfram von Eschenbach

»Sine klâwen
durch die wolken sint geslagen:
er stîget ûf mit grôzer kraft!
ich sich in grâwen
tegelîch als er wil tagen:
den tac, der im geselleschaft
erwenden wil, dem werden man,
den ich bî naht în verliez.
ich bringe in hinnen ob ich kan:
sîn vil manigiu tugent mich daz leisten hiez.«

»Wahtær du singest
daz mir manige vröide nimt
unde mêret mîne klage.
mær du bringest
der mich leider niht gezimt
immer morgens gegen dem tage:

The truth is, Reinmar, I mourn for you
much more than you would mourn for me
if you were living and I had died.
I want to say this on my honor:
you yourself I would not shed a tear for.
I mourn the passing of your noble art.
You could make the joy of the whole world greater

when you had a mind to something good.
I mourn your sweet speaking mouth and tender song,
that I have lived to see them perish,
that you could not stay a while longer in our ranks.
Well, I shall be with you again, my singing is soon over.
May your soul fare well, and your tongue have thanks.

Frederick Goldin

Wolfram von Eschenbach

"Its claws have struck through the clouds,
it rises up with great power,
I see it turning gray, like day about to dawn,
I see day, and day will take
companionship away from him, that worthy man
whom I let in at night with danger.
I shall bring him, if I can, away.
His many virtues made me help him."

"Watchman, what you sing takes my many joys away
and makes my sorrows increase.
You bring news I do not welcome
every morning, alas, toward daybreak.
You must be still about it, all of it,
I command you on your loyalty;
I will make it up to you as well as I can,
just so my friend stays here."

diu solt du mir verswîgen gar!
daz gebiut ich den triuwen dîn.
des lôn ich dir als ich getar—
sô belîbet hie der geselle mîn.«

»Er muoz et hinnen
balde und âne sûmen sich.
nu gip im urloup, süezez wîp!
lâz in minnen
her nâch sô verholne dich,
daz er behalte êre und den lîp.
er gap sich mîner triuwen alsô
daz ich in bræhte ouch wider dan.
ez ist nu tac: naht was ez dô
mit drucken an die brüste dîn kus mir in an gewan.«

»Swaz dir gevalle
wahtær sinc und lâ den hie,
der minne brâht und minne enpfienc.
von dînem schalle
ist er und ich erschrocken ie.
sô ninder morgenstern ûf gienc
ûf in der her nâch minne ist komen,
noch ninder lûhte tages lieht:
du hâst in dicke mir benomen
von blanken armen—und ûz herzen niht.«

Von den blicken,
die der tac tet durch diu glas,
und dô wahtære warnen sanc,
si muose erschricken
durch den der dâ bî ir was.
ir brüstlîn an brust si twanc,
der rîter ellens niht vergaz
(des wold in wenden wahtærs dôn).
urloup nâh und nâher baz
mit kusse und anders gap in minne lôn.

"No, he must go, soon, without delay—
sweet woman, give him leave now.
Let him love you afterwards in secrecy,
and keep his life and honor.
He trusted to my loyalty
to bring him out again.
It is day now; it was night then
when you pressed him to your breast, and kissed him, and
    took him from my side."

"Watchman, sing what you like and leave him here,
who brought love, and received love.
He and I are always startled by your cry—
yes, when the morning star hadn't risen at all
above him, who came here for love,
and not one bit of daylight was shining,
you have often taken him from me—
out of my white arms, not out of my heart."

Because the light of day was shining through the glass,
as the watchman sang his warning,
she was scared, for his sake who lay by her.
She pressed her little breast against his breast.
The knight did not forget his prowess,
that the watchman's song wanted to make him forget.
Love's reward was given in a close
and closer good-bye, with many kisses, and the rest.

Frederick Goldin

Der helnden minne ir klage
du sunge ie gên dem tage,
daz sûre nâch dem süezen.
swer minne und wîplîch grüezen
alsô empfienc,
daz sie sich muosen scheiden,—
swaz du dô riete in beiden,
dô ûf gienc
der morgensterne: wahtære swîc,
dâ von niht langer sinc!

Swer pfliget oder ie gepflac,
daz er bî liebe lac
den merkern unverborgen:
der darf niht durch den morgen
dannen streben.
er mac des tages erbeiten.
man darf in niht ûz leiten
ûf sîn leben:
ein offeniu süeziu wirtes wîp
kan solhe minne geben.

Neidhart von Reuenthal

»Fröut iuch, junge und alte!
der meie mit gewalte
den winder hât verdrungen,
die bluomen sint entsprungen.
wie schôn diu nahtegal
ûf dem rîse   ir süeze wîse   singet, wünneclîchen schal!

You always sang at break of day
the sorrow of hidden love—
the bitter after the sweet:
whoever took love and a woman's greeting
in secret
must now separate.
Whatever you advised the two of them
when the morning star rose up
then—Watchman, be still about that now,
do not sing of it again.

Whoever knows, or ever knew, what it is
to lie with a wife he loves,
with no burrowing when slanderers are near,
that man does not have to steal away
when it is dawn,
he can wait upon the day—
no need to lead him out
in peril of his life.
Such love is in the giving
of the master's honored wife.

Frederick Goldin

Neidhart von Reuenthal

"Young and old, rejoice.
May with its might
has pushed winter out,
the flowers have sprung up.
How sweetly the nightingale
sings on the branch
in varied notes
its echoing song.

Walt nu schône loubet.
mîn muoter niht geloubet,
der joch mit einem seile«,
sô sprach ein maget geile,
»mir bunde einen fuoz,
mit den kinden   zuo der linden   üf den anger ich doch muoz.«

Daz gehôrte ir muoter:
»jâ swinge ich dir daz fuoter
mit stecken umbe den rugge,
vil kleine grasemugge.
wâ wilt dû hüpfen hin
ab dem neste?   sitze und beste   mir den ermel wider in!«

»Muoter, mit dem stecken
sol man die runzen recken
den alten als eim sumber.
noch hiuwer sît ir tumber,
dan ir von sprunge vart.
ir sît tôt   vil kleiner nôt,   ist iu der ermel abe gezart.«

Ûf spranc sî vil snelle.
»der tievel ûz dir belle!
ich wil mich dîn verzîhen;
dû wilt vil übel gedîhen.«
»muoter, ich lebe iedoch,
swie iu troume;   bî dem soume   durch den ermel gât daz loch.«

The woods are in beautiful leaf.
"My mother can't believe it,"
said a joyous maid,
"but I swear if they tied
one foot with a cord,
I still have to go
with the kids
to the lime tree on the meadow."

Her mother heard that—
"And I'll strew you your feed
with a stick on your back,
you little peewee,
where are you hopping to
out of the nest?
Sit down and sew me
my sleeve back on."

"Mother, they should use that stick
to beat out the wrinkles
of the old, like a drum.
This year you're an even greater fool
than you were at the start.
It doesn't take much
to kill you
if you die from a torn-off sleeve."

And up she sprang in a flash.
"May the Devil bark in your mouth,
I give up on you,
you'll come to a bad end."
"Yes, Mother, but I am awake,
and you can only dream.
Where there ought to be a sleeve,
there's just a hole along the seam."

Frederick Goldin

Sumer, dîner süezen weter müezen wir uns ânen:
dirre kalte winder trûren unde senen gît.
ich bin ungetrœstet von der lieben wolgetânen.
wie sol ich vertrîben dise langen swæren zît,
diu die heide velwet unde mange bluomen wolgetân?
dâ von sint die vogele in dem walde   des betwungen,
     daz si ir singen müezen lân.

Alsô hât diu vrouwe mîn daz herze mir betwungen,
daz ich âne vröude muoz verswenden mîne tage.
ez vervæhet niht, swaz ich ir lange hân gesungen;
mir ist alsô mære, daz ich mêre stille dage.
ich geloube niht, daz si den mannen immer werde holt:
wir verliesen, swaz wir dar gesingen   unde gerûnen, ich
     und jener Hildebolt.

Der ist nû der tumbist under geilen getelingen,
er und einer, nennet man den jungen Willegêr:
den enkunde ich disen sumer nie von ir gedringen,
sô der tanz gein abent an der strâze gie entwer.
mangen twerhen blic den wurfen si mich mit den ougen an,
daz ich sunder mînes guoten willen   vor in beiden   ie ze
     sweime muose gân.

Wê, daz mich sô manger hât von lieber stat gedrungen
beidiu von der guoten unde ouch wîlent anderswâ.
œdelîchen wart von in ûf mînen tratz gesprungen.
ir gewaltes bin ich vor in mînem schophe grâ.
iedoch sô neic diu guote mir ein lützel über schildes rant,
gern mugt ir hœren, wie die dörper   sint gekleidet:
     üppiclîch ist ir gewant.

Enge röcke tragent si und smale schaperûne,
rôte hüete, rinkelohte schuohe, swarze hosen.
Engelmâr getet mir nie sô leide an Vriderûne,
sam die zwêne tuont.   ich nîde ir phellerîne phosen,
die si tragent: dâ lît inne ein wurze, heizet ingewer.
der gap Hildebolt der guoten eine   bî dem tanze; die
     gezuhte ir Willegêr.

Summer, now we must live without your sweet weather:
this cold winter gives us grief and longing.
I have no comfort from my dear and beautiful.
How shall I pass this long, slow, heavy time
that has made the moorland pale, and many lovely flowers?
Thus the birds in the woods are driven to forsake their
     song.

My lady has my heart so in her power
I must waste my days without joy.
All that I have sung for so long now—it does no good,
I could just as well be silent from now on.
I do not think she ever will be kind to any man:
whatever I sing, whatever he whispers, we lose—I and
     that Hildebolt.

Among the merry peasants he is now the biggest fool there is,
he and one they call young Willeger—
the whole summer long I never could get him away from her
when the dance went round toward evening in the street.
They gave me many a dirty look with those eyes of theirs,
and I always had to take a walk, against my will, when
     they showed up.

What a pity so many have driven me from a place I loved,
both from my good one and also, before that, another place.
It was hateful the way they danced to spite me.
Because of their violence there is gray in my forelock.
Still, my good one bows her head to me a little, passing by.
You will love to hear how these villagers are dressed, how
     high-class are their clothes.

They wear narrow tunics and small cloaks,
red hats, buckled shoes, black hose.
Engelmar never hurt me so with Vriderun
as these two did. I envy them the silken pouches
they wear—they have a spice in it called ginger.
Hildebolt gave my Good a little of it at the dance;
     Willeger grabbed it away.

Sagte ich nû diu mære, wie siz mit ein ander schuofen,
des enweiz ich niht: ich schiet von danne sâ zehant.
manneglîch begunde sînen vriunden vaste ruofen;
einer der schrê lûte: "hilf gevater Weregant!"
er was lîhte in grôzen nœten, dô er sô nach helfe schrê.
Hileboldes swester hôrte ich eines   lûte schrîen: "wê
mir mîns bruoder, wê!"

Wâ bî sol man mîn geplätze hinne vür erkennen?
hie envor dô kande man iz wol bî Riuwental.
dâ von solde man mich noch von allem rehte nennen:
nust mir eigen unde lêhen dâ gemezzen smal.
kint, ir heizet iu den singen, der sîn nû gewaltic sî.
ich bin sîn verstôzen âne schulde: mîne vriunde, lâzet
mich des namen vri!

Mîner vînde wille ist niht ze wol an mir ergangen:
wolde ez got, sîn mähte noch vil lîhte werden rât.
in dem land ze Oesterrîche wart ich wol enphangen
von dem edeln vürsten, der mich nû behûset hât.
hie ze Medelicke bin ich immer âne ir aller danc.
mir ist leit, daz ich von Eppen und von Gumpen   ie ze
Riuwental sô vil gesanc.

Rädelohte sporen treit mir Fridepreht ze leide,
niuwen vezzel hât er baz dann zweier hende breit.
rucket er den afterreif hin wider ûf die scheide,
wizzet, mîne vriunde, daz ist mir ein herzenleit!
zwêne niuwe hantschuoh er unz ûf den ellenbogen zôch.
mugt ir hœren, wie der selbe gemzinc   von der lieben
hiuwer ab dem tanze vlôch?

Now I ought to tell you all about what they created there with one
    another,
except that I don't know: I got out of there fast.
They all cried out for their friends.
One screamed loud, "Help, Godfather Weregant!"
He must have been in bad trouble, crying out for help like that.
Once I heard Hildebolt's sister screaming, "O my poor
    brother, O!"

How shall anyone recognize my foolish verses any more?
They used to know it by the "Reuental" before.
By right that's what they ought to call me still.
What I own and what I get there comes to very little.
Children, ask the man who owns it now to sing to you.
I've been driven out, and through no fault of mine. My
    friends, let me be free of that name.*

My enemies weren't able to do what they wanted to against me.
God willing, there may be a way out for me yet.
I've been well received in Austria
by the noble prince, who has housed me now.†
I am here in Melk, and they don't like that.
I only regret I ever sang so much about Eppe and Gump
    at Reuental.

Fridepreht wore jing-a-linging spurs, much to my annoyance,
and he had a new sword-belt on, more than two hands wide.
He trailed the loop behind him round the scabbard.
Friends, believe me, that pains my heart.
He drew two brand-new gloves on right up to his elbows.
Would you want to hear how this same jumping buck
    ran from my beloved this year at the dance?

Frederick Goldin

---

*Neidhart often mentions his name in the final strophe of his poems. Since he no
longer has any possessions in "Reuental," he would just as soon give up the name
altogether and stop singing.
†Friedrich of Austria.

»Sinc an, guldîn huon! ich gibe dir weize«,
(schiere dô
wart ich vrô)
sprach si, nâch der hulden ich dâ singe:
alsô vreut den tumben guot geheize
durch daz jâr.
würde ez wâr,
sô gestuont nie mannes muot sô ringe,
alsô mir der mîne danne waere.
mac si durch ir geilicheit
mîniu leit
wenden? ja ist mîn kumber klagebaere.

Los ûz! ich hoer in der stuben tanzen.
junge man,
tuot iuch dan!
da ist der dorefwîbe ein michel trünne.
dâ gesach man schône ridewanzen.
zwêne gigen;
dô si swigen
(daz was geiler getelinge wünne),
seht, dô wart von zeche vor gesungen!
durch diu venster gie der galm.
Adelhalm
tanzet niwan zwischen zwein vil jungen.

Rûmet ûz die schämel und die stüele!
heiz die schragen
vuder tragen!
hiute sul wir tanzens werden müeder.
werfet ûf die stuben, sô ist ez küele,
daz der wint
an diu kint
sanfte waeje durch diu übermüeder!
sô die voretanzer danne swîgen,
sô sult ir alle sîn gebeten,
daz wir treten
aber ein hovetänzel nâch der gîgen:

"Sing, my golden cock, I'll give thee grain!"
(at her voice
I rejoice)
spoke the pretty maid for whom I sigh.
Thus a dunce's hopes are raised in vain
seasons through.
Were it true,
no one's spirit then would be as high,
no one else's heart would beat so light.
Will her careless gaiety
ever free
me from all the sorrows of my plight?

Listen! Hear the dancing at the inn!
Every man
go who can,
there the women wait, a merry throng.
Soon we'll see the *ridewanz* begin.
Tarradiddle
goes the fiddle,
lusty peasant youths break forth in song.
Each in turn sings out his verse with pride,
shakes the room with lungs of brass.
Noblegrass
dances with a maid on either side.

Move out all the chairs and clear the floor;
take the tables
to the stables
and we'll dance till feet and ankles hurt.
Open up the windows and the door;
let the breeze
cool their knees,
blowing through each village wench's skirt.
When the leaders stop to rest a little,
then we'll all, great and small,
short and tall,
step a courtly dance once to the fiddle.

Gôzbreht, Willebolt, Gumpreht und Eppe,
Willebreht,
meiers kneht,
Werenbolt und ouch der junge Tuoze,
Megenbolt, des meiers sun, und Reppe,
Irenwart,
Sigehart,
Gîselher und Fridegêr und Uoze:
der ist ein vil tumber Holingaere;
er gêt vrîen durch daz jâr
(des nemt war!)
unde ist doch den meiden gar unmaere.

Sâht ir ie gebûren sô gemeiten,
als er ist?
wizze Krist!
er ist al ze vorderst anme reien.
niuwen vezzel zweier hende breiten
hât sîn swert.
harte wert
dünket er sich sîner niuwen treien:
diust von kleinen vier und zweinzec tuochen,
di ermel gênt im ûf die hant:
sîn gewant
sol man an eim oeden kragen suochen.

Dörperlîch stât allez sîn gerüste,
daz er treit.
mirst geseit,
er sinn Engelboltes tohter Âven:
den gewerp erteile ich im ze vlüste.
si ist ein wîp,
daz ir lîp
zaeme wol ze minne einem grâven;
dâ von lâze er sich des wîsen tougen!
zecke er anderthalben hin!
den gewin
trüege er hin ze Meinze in sînem ougen.

Gozbreht, Willebolt, Gumpreht, and Eppe,
Willebrand
(hired hand),
Werenbolt, and also youngster Tutze,
Megenbolt (the farmer's son), and Reppe,
Irenwart,
Sigehart,
Giselher and Frideger and Utze—
he's the stupid oaf from Holingare.
He goes courting every day,
so they say,
but the girls don't like him anymore.

Never has a bumpkin looked so grand,
nor so flighty;
God Almighty,
how he struts in line before the rest!
More than two hands wide the leather band
of his sword,
like a lord
in his new and gaily colored vest,
scraps of every shape and hue are there,
fancy shirt, embroidered pants,
see him prance
in a garb no other fool would wear.

His attire is rustic as can be,
it's absurd.
So I've heard,
he's been wooing Engel's daughter, Pearl.
All such hopes are futile, I foresee.
She's a prize
of shape and size
to win the admiration of an earl.
Good advice I'll give him: let him try
someone else; for all his pain
what he'll gain
he can take to Mayence in his eye.

Imst sîn treie nie sô wol zerhouwen
noch sîn kel
nie sô hel,
er enmüge sî sîn wol erlâzen.
disen sumer hât er sî gekouwen
gar vür brôt.
schamerôt
wart ich, dô si bî ein ander sâzen.
wirt si mir, der ich dâ gerne diene,
guotes gibe ich ir die wal,
Riuwental
gar vür eigen: deist mîn Hôhiu Siene.

Mirst von herzen leide,
daz der küele winder
verderbet schœner bluomen vil:
sô verderbet mich ein senelîchiu arebeit.
dise sorge beide
dringent mich hin hinder
ze ende an mîner vreuden zil.
owê, daz diu guote mit ir willen daz vertreit,
sît si wol geringen mac
alle mîne swære!
owê, gelebte ich noch den tac,
daz sî genædic wære!

Swenne ich mich vereine
unde an si gedenke,
wær inder wîbes güete dâ
diune hæte sich sô lange bî ir niht verholn.
sît si lônet kleine
mîner niuwen klenke,
wan mag ich dienen anderswâ?
nein, ich wil mit willen disen kumber langer doln.
waz ob noch ein sælic wîp
gar den muot verkêret?

Though his clothes are colorful and gay
and he's dressed
in his best,
he should know, she simply can't abide him.
He has hung around her every day;
I became
red with shame
when I saw her sitting down beside him.
If I win this maid who looks so pretty,
I shall give to her my all,
Reuenthal,
for her own: this is my fabled city.

J. W. Thomas

There is pain in my heart,
the cold winter
is destroying so many beautiful flowers.
And a great travail of longing is destroying me.
These two cares
always thrust me
back from my goal of joy.
What sorrow that the Good lets this happen willingly,
for she can make
my sorrows small.
Oh, if I could live to see the day
she's kind.

When I go off by myself
and think of her, it seems
if the goodness of a woman were in her
it could never have stayed hidden all this time.
Since she gives small wages
for my foolish songs,
why shouldn't I serve somewhere else?
No! I shall endure this sorrow with a patient will.
Why couldn't a generous woman
change her mind some day?

vreu mîn herze und trœste den lîp!
diu zwei diu sint gesêret.

Zuo dem ungemache,
den ich von ir lîde,
sô twinget mich ein ander leit,
daz vor allem leide mich sô sêre nie betwanc,
swiech dar umbe lache
und gebâre blîde:
mir hât ein dörper widerseit
umbe anders niht wan umbe den mînen üppeclîchen
    sanc.
derst geheizen Adeltir,
bürtic her von Ense.
zallen zîten drôt er mir
als einer veizten gense.

Hiwer an einem tanze
gie er umbe und umbe.
den wehsel het er al den tac:
glanziu schapel gap er umb ir niuwen krenzelîn.
Etzel unde Lanze,
zwêne knappen tumbe,
die phlâgen ouch, des jener phlac.
Lanze der beswæret ein vil stolzez magedîn;
eine kleine rîsen guot
zarte er ab ir houbet,
dar zuo einen bluomenhuot:
wer het im daz erloubet?
Owê sîner hende!
daz si sîn verwâzen!
die vinger müezen werden vlorn,
dâ mit er gezerret hât den schedelîchen zar!
hiete er ir gebende
ungezerret lâzen,
daz kränzel hiete ouch si verkorn.
er ist ungevüeger, danne wîlen Engelmâr,
der gewalticlîchen nam
den spiegel Vriderûne.

May you rejoice my heart and comfort my body,
for both are in distress.

Add to the hardship
I suffer from her
another torment oppressing me,
that hounds me more than any other pain,
though I smile through it all
and act gay—
a peasant has declared himself my enemy
for no other reason than my lordly poetry.
His name is Adeltir,
he came here from Enns.
He looks at me menacingly all the time.
He would look like that at a fat goose.

This year at a dance
he went everywhere
making exchanges all day long:
he gave bright-colored chaplets for their little garlands.
Etzel and Lanze,
these two bungling boys,
were trying to do the same.
Lanze annoyed a splendid girl.
He grabbed a dainty little
kerchief off her head,
and a little garland too.
Who could have stood that?
O his hands!
A curse on them,
may he lose the fingers
he grabbed with, doing such damage!
If he hadn't pulled
her headdress apart,
she would have given up the garland, like the others.
He's a bigger ruffian than Engelmar some time ago,

des bin ich dem dörper gram,
dem selben Walberûne.

Dise alten schulde
wecket mir diu niuwe:
ez hât jener getelinc
hiwer an mir erwecket, swaz mir leides ie geschach.
ê ichz langer dulde,
sêt des mîne triuwe,
gespringe ich zuo zim in den rinc,
er bestât sîn buoze, daz er ir ze vrouwen jach,
der ich lange gedienet hân
her mit ganzer stæte.
wolde er si gerouwet lân,
wie rehte er danne tæte!

Wê, waz hât er muochen!
si kumt im niht ze mâze.
zwiu sol sîn pîneclîch gebrech?
im enmac gehelfen niht sîn hovelîch gewant.
er sol im eine suochen,
diu in werben lâze.
diu sînen rôten buosemblech
diu sint ir ungenæme gar, dar zuo sîn hiufelbant.
enge ermel treit er lanc,
die sint vor gebræmet,
innen swarz und ûzen blanc.
mit sîner rede er vlæmet.

who took the mirror
from Vriderun by force.*
For that I am angry at that peasant,
that Galoot.

This new violence
makes me remember the old—
that lummox has awakened
in me this year all the wrongs I ever suffered.
But I shall suffer it no longer—
I swear—
if I spring upon him in the ring,
he'll pay for claiming her his lady—
whom I have served
for so long faithfully.
If he'd leave her alone,
how right he would be acting.

Oh lord, what wild conceits he has.
He does not measure up to her.
What does he expect, with his rough tearing-off?
His courtly raiment cannot do him any good.
Let him find some woman
who'll let him court her.
His red breastplate
and his hip belt must strike my lady as so many blemishes.
He wears long narrow sleeves,
trimmed in front,
black inside and white outside,
and when he talks he flemishes.†

Frederick Goldin

---

*The theft of Vriderun's mirror is a frequent theme in Neidhart's poetry. Its meaning is not fully understood, but it is clearly intended to convey the brutality and degredation of the "peasants."

†That is, apes the speech of the knights of Flanders, who were considered exemplary.

Steinmar

Ein knecht der lac verborgen,
bî einer dirne er slief
unz ûf den liehten morgen:
der hirte lûte rief
»Wol ûf, lâz, ûz, die hert!«
Des erschrac diu dirne und ir geselle wert.

Daz strou das muost er rûmen
und von der lieben varn.
Er torste sich niht sûmen,
er nam si an den arn.
Daz höi daz, ob im lac
daz ersach diu reine ûf fliegen in den tac.

Dâ von si muoste erlachen,
ir sigen diu ougen zuo.
Sô suoze kunde er machen
in deme morgen fruo
mit ir daz bettespil;
wer sach ân geræte ie fröiden mê sô vil!

Sît si mir niht lônen wil
der ich hân gesungen vil,
seht sô wil ich prîsen
den der mir tuot sorgen rât,
herbest der des meien wât
vellet von den rîsen.
ich weiz wol, ez ist ein altez mære
daz ein armez minnerlîn ist rehte ein marteræere.
seht, zuo den was ich geweten:
wâfen!   die wil ich lân und wil inz luoder treten.
Herbest, underwint dich mîn,

Steinmar

A farmhand lay all hidden,
A farm girl by his side.
The morning rays had smitten:
A herdsman then outcried—
"Get up! Let out the herd . . ."
It startled them as they both heard.

He had to push the straw away
And from the farm girl fly.
He dared to brook no great delay,
But clasped her closely by.
The hay that around the maiden lay
Flew away in the sun's bright ray.

Ah! how she had to laugh aloud
As she saw him standing nude.
Tomorrow morning he'll be allowed
To take his place with her anew
And play those games* again with joy.
Who ever saw such bliss with so few ploys?

James J. Wilhelm

Since She Gives So Little Pay

Since she gives so little pay†
whom I've sung in many a lay,
hear, my praises now
go to autumn, who will bring
rewards, and let the clothes of spring
fall from every bough.
It's an ancient tale they often tell;
that a lover is a wretched martyr, I know well.

---

*That is, games of love.
†That is, she will not reward him for his service.

wan ich wil dîn helfer sîn
gegen dem glanzen meien.
durh dich mîde ich sende nôt.
sît dir Gebewîn ist tôt,
nim mich tumben leien
vür in zeime stæten ingesinde.
»Steimâr, sich daz wil ich tuon, swenn ich nu baz bevinde,
ob du mich kanst gebrüeven wol.«
wâfen! ich singe daz wir alle werden vol.

   Herbest, nu hœr an mîn leben.
wirt, du solt uns vische geben
mê dan zehen hande,
gense hüener vogel swîn,
dermel pfâwen sunt dâ sîn,
wîn von welschem lande.
des gib uns vil und heiz uns schüzzel schochen:
köpfe und schüzzel wirt von mir unz an den grunt erlochen.
wirt, du lâ dîn sorgen sîn:
wâfen! joch muoz ein riuwic herze trœsten wîn.

   Swaz du uns gîst, daz würze uns wol
baz dan man ze mâze sol,
daz in uns werde ein hitze
daz gegen dem trunke gange ein dunst,
alse rouch von einer brunst,
und daz der man erswitze,
daz er wæne daz er vaste lecke.
schaffe daz der munt uns als ein apotêke smecke.
erstumme ich von des wînes kraft,
wâfen! sô giuz in mich, wirt, durh geselleschaft.

   Wirt, durh mich ein strâze gât:
dar ûf schaffe uns allen rât,
manger hande spîse.
wînes der wol tribe ein rat
hœret ûf der strâze pfat.
mînen slunt ich prîse:
mich würget niht ein grôziu gans so ichs slinde.
herbest, trûtgeselle mîn, noch nim mich zingesinde.
mîn sêle ûf eime rippe stât,
wâfen! diu von dem wîne drûf gehüppet hât.

Look, I've suffered in this strife;
I'll exchange it for a gayer, lusty life.
    Autumn, I have been betrayed
and would like to give you aid
against the Maytime's splendor.
You protect from love's design.
Now that you've lost Gebewine,
take me, young and tender,
in his place, to be your loyal thane.
"Steinmar, see, that I shall do, if you can make it plain
that your praise will be as sweet."
Fine, I'll sing a song to make all want to eat.
    Autumn, hear how I would live:
landlord, fish! And you must give
us ten different brands,
geese and chickens, birds and swine,
peacocks, sausages, and wine
brought from foreign lands.
Bring so much we'll have to stack the dishes,
and I'll empty every one, from wine to fowl to fishes.
Landlord, let your cares depart;
hasten, for your wine consoles a saddened heart.
    All you bring must be well spiced,
more than merely what sufficed;
build in us a fire.
May fumes arise our drinks to meet
like the smoke from flaming heat;
cause us to perspire
so that we feel wetter than a mop.
Give our mouths the smell of an apothecary shop,
and, if wine should still my tongue,
landlord, pour down more until my song is sung.

J. W. Thomas

Oswald von Wolkenstein

Simm Gredlin, Gret, mein Gredelein,
mein zarter bül, herz lieb gemait,
dein züchtlich er an mir nicht weich!"
„Halt wie es get, mein Öselein,
inn deiner schül treu stetikait,
die wil ich leren ewikleich."
„Die wort sol ich behalten mier
und schreiben in meins herzen grund
von deinem röselochten mund."
„Mein hort, das selb ist wol mein gier,
wann ich wil nicht wencken."
„Gedenck, liebs Öselein, an mich,
dein Gredlin sol erfreuen dich."

„Du kanst mich nicht erfreuen bas,
wann das ich läg an deinem arm,
verslossen als ain kleusener."
„in deiner phlicht wurd ich nicht lass,
an sainlich träg mach ich dir warm
und ist mir das ain klaine swër."
„Hab danck, men trauter aidgesell,
das sol ich dir vergessen klain,
wann du bist wol, die ich da main."
„An wanck von mir kain ungevell,
herzlieb, nicht enwarte!"
„danck so hab die zarte."
„zart liebster man, mir ist so wol,
wenn ich dein brust umbsliessen sol."

„Vor aller freud tröst mich dein herz,
dorzu dein wunniklicher leib,
wenn er sich freuntlich zu mir smucket."
„Gesell, so geud ich wol den scherz,
und gailt sich fro dein ainig weib,
wenn mir dein hand ain brüstlin drucket."

Oswald von Wolkenstein

O Margie, Marge, Dear Margaret

"O Margie, Marge,   dear Margaret,
for whom I yearn   and would caress,
may thy good name   thou ever keep."
"Whate'er the charge,   Os, my pet,
from thee I'll learn   true faithfulness
and ever aim   thy praise to reap."
"I greet   these words and shall engrave
them in the bottom of my heart
as from thy rosy lips they part."
"My sweet,   this too is what I crave,
and I'll never waiver."
"I'll think of thy favor."
"Think, dearest Ossie, just of me,
thy Marge will bring delight to thee."

"Thou canst not give,   nor I desire
more joy than when   thou hast my form
held fast, as one locked in a cell."
"For thee I'll live   and shall not tire
of holding then;   I'll keep thee warm
with pleasure, and shall do it well."
"My dear,   I owe thee gratitude
and I shall ne'er forget thy love;
thou'rt always she I'm dreaming of."
"No fear   that I'll be mean or rude
needst thou have, my treasure."
"My thanks can have no measure."
"O, dearest man, I feel so good
when I embrace thee as I would."

"I cannot know   more joy than this:
thy love and wondrous body, too,
which lustfully to mine is pressed."

„Ach frau, das ist mein zucker nar
und süsst mir alle mein gelid,
seid du mir haltst günstlichen frid."
„Getraw mir sicherlichen zwar,
Öslin, gar an ende!"
„Gredlin, das nicht wende!
kain wenden zwischen mein und dir
sei uns mit hail beschaffen schier."

Martin Luther

Ein feste Burg ist unser Gott,
Ein gute Wehr und Waffen.
Er hilft uns frei aus aller Not,
Die uns jetzt hat betroffen.
Der alt böse Feind,
Mit Ernst er's jetzt meint.
Groß Macht und viel List
Sein grausam Rüstung ist.
Auf Erd ist nicht seinsgleichen.

Mit unsrer Macht ist nichts getan,
Wir sind gar bald verloren.
Es streit't für uns der rechte Mann,
Den Gott hat selbst erkoren.
Fragst du, wer der ist?
Er heißt Jesus Christ,
Der Herr Zebaoth,
Und ist kein ander Gott.
Das Feld muß er behalten.

"I overflow   with keenest bliss
and thrill with passion through and through
whene'er thy hands caress my breast."
"My bride,   the best of sugarbread,
whose sweeetness flows through all thy limbs,
is that thy lovelight never dims."
"Abide,   and trust what I have said,
Os, with faith unbending."
"Be thy love unending!"
"Let fortune never separate
us two, nor harm a love so great!"

J. W. Thomas

Martin Luther

A Mighty Fortress is Our God

A mighty fortress is our God,
A sword and shield victorious;
He breaks the cruel oppressor's rod
And wins salvation glorious.
The old satanic foe
Has sworn to work us woe.
With craft and dreadful might
He arms himself to fight.
On earth he has no equal.

No strength of ours can match his might.
We would be lost, rejected.
But now a champion comes to fight,
Whom God himself elected.
You ask who this may be?
The Lord of hosts is he,
Christ Jesus, mighty Lord,
God's only Son, adored.
He holds the field victorious.

Und wenn die Welt voll Teufel wär
Und wollt uns gar verschlingen,
So fürchten wir uns nicht so sehr,
Es soll uns doch gelingen.
Der Fürst dieser Welt,
Wie saur er sich stellt,
Tut er uns doch nicht.
Das macht, er ist gericht't.
Ein Wörtlein kann ihn fällen.

Das Wort sie sollen lassen stahn
Und kein' Dank dazu haben.
Er ist bei uns wohl auf dem Plan
Mit seinem Geiste und Gaben.
Nehmen sie den Leib,
Gut, Ehr, Kind und Weib,
Laß fahren dahin.
Sie haben's kein Gewinn.
Das Reich muß uns doch bleiben.

Aus tiefer Not schrei ich zu dir,
Herr Gott, erhör mein Rufen.
Dein gnädig Ohren kehr zu mir
Und meiner Bitt sie offen.
Denn so du willt das sehen an,
Was Sünd und Unrecht ist getan,
Wer kann, Herr, vor dir bleiben?

Bei dir gilt nichts denn Gnad und Gonst,
Die Sünden zu vergeben.
Es ist doch unser Tun umsonst
Auch in dem besten Leben.
Vor dir niemand sich rühmen kann.
Des muß dich fürchten jedermann
Und deiner Gnade leben.

Though hordes of devils fill the land
All threatening to devour us,
We tremble not, unmoved we stand;
They cannot overpower us.
Let this world's tyrant rage;
In battle we'll engage.
His might is doomed to fail;
God's judgment must prevail!
One little word subdues him.

God's Word forever shall abide,
No thanks to foes, who fear it;
For God himself fights by our side
With weapons of the Spirit.
Were they to take our house,
Goods, honor, child, or spouse,
Though life be wrenched away,
They cannot win the day.
The Kingdom's ours forever!

Lutheran Book of Worship, 1978

From Depths of Woe I Cry to You

From depths of woe I cry to you.
O Lord, my voice is trying
To reach your heart and, Lord, break through
With these my cries and sighing.
If you keep record of our sin
And hold against us what we've been,
Who then can stand before you?

Your grace and love alone avail
To blot out sin with pardon.
In your gaze our best efforts pale,
Develop pride and harden.
Before your throne no one can boast
That he escaped sin's deadly coast.
Our haven is your mercy.

Darum auf Gott will hoffen ich,
Auf mein Verdienst nicht bauen.
Auf ihn mein Herz soll lassen sich
Und seiner Güte trauen,
Die mir zusagt sein wertes Wort.
Das ist mein Trost und treuer Hort,
Des will ich allzeit harren.

Und ob es währt bis in die Nacht
Und wieder an den Morgen,
Doch soll mein Herz an Gottes Macht
Verzweifeln nicht noch sorgen.
So tu Israel rechter Art,
Der aus dem Geist erzeuget ward
Und seines Gotts erharre.

Ob bei uns ist der Sünden viel,
Bei Gott ist viel mehr Gnaden.
Sein Hand zu helfen hat kein Ziel,
Wie groß auch sei der Schaden.
Er ist allein der gute Hirt,
Der Israel erlösen wird
Aus seinen Sünden allen.

Vom Himmel hoch, da komm ich her.
Ich bring euch gute, neue Mär.
Der guten Mär bring ich so viel,
Davon ich sing'n und sagen will.

Euch ist ein Kindlein heut geborn,
Von einer Jungfrau auserkorn,
Ein Kindelein so zart und fein,
Das soll eur Freud und Wonne sein.

In God I anchor all my trust,
Discarding my own merit.
His love holds firm; I therefore must
His fullest grace inherit.
He tells me, and my heart has heard,
The steadfast promise of his Word,
That he's my help and haven.

Though help delays until the night
Or waits till morning waken,
My heart shall never doubt his might
Nor think itself forsaken.
All you who are God's own indeed,
Born of the Spirit's Gospel seed,
Await his promised rescue.

Though sins arise like dunes of sand,
God's mercy-tides submerge them.
Like oceans pouring from his hand,
Strong flows the grace to purge them.
Our shepherd will his Israel lead
To uplands out of every need
And ransom us from sinning.

F. Samuel Janow

From Heaven Above to Earth I Come

From heaven above to earth I come
To bring good news to everyone!
Glad tidings of great joy I bring
To all the world and gladly sing:

To you this night is born a child
Of Mary, chosen virgin mild;
This newborn child of lowly birth
Shall be the joy of all the earth.

Es ist der Herr Christ, unser Gott.
Der will euch führn aus aller Not.
Er will eur Heiland selber sein,
Von allen Sünden machen rein.

Er bringt euch alle Seligkeit,
Die Gott der Vater hat bereit't,
Daß ihr mit uns im Himmelreich
Sollt leben nun und ewiglich.

So merket nun das Zeichen recht:
Die Krippen, Windelein so schlecht.
Da findet ihr das Kind gelegt,
Das alle Welt erhält und trägt.

Des laßt uns alle fröhlich sein
Und mit den Hirten gehn hinein,
Zu sehn, was Gott uns hat beschert
Mit seinem lieben Sohn verehrt.

Merk auf, mein Herz, und sieh dort hin.
Was liegt doch in dem Krippelein?
Wes ist das schöne Kindelein?
Es ist das liebe Jesulein.

Mitten wyr ym leben sind /
mit dem tod vmbfangen /
Wen suchen wyr der hulffe thu /
das wyr gnad erlangen /
Das bistu Herr alleyne /
vns rewet vnser missethat /
die dich Herr erzurnet hat /
Heyliger herre Gott /
Heyliger starcker Gott /

This is the Christ, God's Son most high,
Who hears your sad and bitter cry;
He will himself your Savior be
And from all sin will set you free.

The blessing which the Father planned
The Son holds in his infant hand
That in his kingdom, bright and fair,
You may with us his glory share.

These are the signs which you will see
To let you know that it is he:
In manger bed, in swaddling clothes
The child who all the earth upholds.

How glad we'll be to find it so!
Then with the shepherds let us go
To see what God for us has done
In sending us his own dear Son.

Look, look, dear friends, look over there!
What lies within that manger bare?
Who is that lovely little one?
The baby Jesus, God's dear Son.

Lutheran Book of Worship, 1978

In the Very Midst of Life

In the very midst of life
Death has us surrounded.
When shall we a helper find,
Hear his coming sounded?
For you, our Lord, we're waiting.
We sorrow that we left your path,
Doing what deserves your wrath.
Holy, most mighty God!
Holy and most merciful Savior!

Heyliger barmhertziger Heyland /
du ewiger Gott /
las vns nicht versincken /
ynn des bittern todes not /
   Kyrieleyson.

Mitten ynn dem tod anficht /
vns der Hellen rachen /
Wer will vns aus solcher not /
frey vnd ledig machen /
Das thustu Herr alleyne /
Es iamert deyn barmhertzikeyt /
vnser klag vnd grosses leyd /
Heyliger Herre Gott /
Heyliger starcker Gott /
Heyliger barmhertziger Heyland
du ewiger Gott /
las vns nicht verzagen /
fur der tieffen hellen glut /
   Kyrieleyson.

Mitten ynn der Hellen angst /
vnser sund vns treyben /
Wo soln wyr denn flihen hyn /
da wyr mugen bleyben.
Zu dyr herr Christ alleyne /
Vergossen ist deyn thewres blut /
das gnug fur die sunde thut /
Heyliger Herre Gott /
Heyliger starcker Gott /
Heyliger barmhertziger Heyland /
du ewiger Gott /
las vns nicht entfallen /
von des rechten glaubens trost /
   Kyri.

Forever our Lord!
Keep us from despairing
In the bitter pain of death.
Have mercy, O Lord!

In the midst of bitter death,
Sharp the hell-drawn harrow.
Who will break its teeth and save
Faith's most inner marrow?
Lord, you alone, our Savior.
Though you were grieved by our misdeed,
Pity drew you to our need.
Holy, most righteous God!
Holy, most mighty God!
Holy and most merciful Savior!
Forever our Lord!
Let despair not bind us
With its threats of deepest hell.
Have mercy, O Lord!

Through the midst of hells of fear
Our transgressions drive us.
Who will help us to escape,
Shield us, and revive us?
Lord, you alone, our Savior.
Your shed blood our salvation won;
Sin, death, hell now undone.
Holy, most mighty God!
Holy and most merciful Savior!
Forever our Lord!
Give us grace abounding;
Keep us, keep us in the faith.
Have mercy, O Lord!

F. Samuel Janow

Ulrich von Hutten

Ein neu Lied Herr Ulrichs von Hutten

Ich hab's gewagt mit Sinnen
Und trag des noch kein Reu,
Mag ich nit dran gewinnen,
Noch muß man spüren Treu;
Dar mit ich mein   nit eim allein,
Wenn man es wolt erkennen:
Dem Land zu gut,   wie wol man tut
Ein Pfaffenfeind mich nennen.

Da laß ich jeden lügen
Und reden was er will;
Hätt Wahrheit ich geschwiegen,
Mir wären hulder vil:
Nun hab ich's gsagt,   bin drum verjagt,
Das klag ich allen Frummen,
Wie wol noch ich   nit weiter fliech,
Vielleicht werd wider kummen.

Um Gnad will ich nit bitten,
Dieweil ich bin ohn Schuld;
Ich hett das Recht gelitten,
So hindert Ungeduld,
Daß man mich nit   nach altem Sitt
Zu Ghör hat kummen lassen;
Vielleicht wills Gott   und zwingt sie Not
Zu handlen dieser Maßen.

Nun ist oft dieser gleichen
Geschehen auch hie vor,
Daß einer von den Reichen
Ein gutes Spiel verlor,

Ulrich von Hutten

Ulrich von Hutten's Song

I've ventured* it of purpose free,
   Nor yet my deed I rue;
I may not win, but men will see
   My heart and life were true.
'Tis not my own I seek alone,
   This they must know at least;
'Tis good of all, though me they call
   A foe to Church and priest.

But I will let them spread their lies
   And chatter as they will;
If I would but the truth disguise,
   And tongue and pen keep still,
Flatterers enow were mine, I trow,
   Now I'm a banished man;
Yet think not I afar to fly,
   Time yet may change the ban.

But nought of pardon will I pray,
   For nought of guilt I own;
I would have bowed to Justice' sway,
   Here Passion reigns alone,
Nor grants my cause by ancient laws
   A hearing fair and free;—
But God ordains and need constrains
   That thus they deal with me.

Yet oft ere now it hath been seen
   When rich men felt secure,
They yet have lost the game, I ween,
   They deemed their own full sure.

*"Ich habs gewagt," "I have ventured it," was Hutten's motto.

Oft großer Flamm   von Fünklin kam;
Wer weiß ob ich's werd rechen!
Stat schon im Lauf,   so setz ich drauf:
Muß gehen oder brechen!

Dar neben mich zu trösten
Mit gutem Gwissen hab,
Daß keiner von den Bösten
Mir Ehr mag brechen ab,
Doch sagen, daß   uf einig Maß
Ich anders sei gegangen,
Denn Ehren nach,   hab diese Sach
In Gutem angefangen.

Will nun ihr selbs nit raten
Die frumme Nation,
Ihrs Schaden sich ergatten
Als ich vermahnet han,
So ist mir leid;   hie mit ich scheid,
Will mengen baß die Karten!
Bin unverzagt,   ich habs gewagt
Und will des Ends erwarten!

Ob dann mir nach tut denken
Der Curtisanen List:
Ein Herz läßt sich nit kränken,
Das rechter Meinung ist;
Ich weiß, noch viel   wölln auch ins Spiel
Und solltens drüber sterben:
Auf, Landsknecht gut   und Reuters Mut,
Laßt Hutten nit verderben!

A mighty flame from sparks oft came;
   Who knows, my turn may come?
I've played my stake, the risk I'll take,
   And here abide my doom.

And 'midst it all my solace is
   A conscience void of spot;
My direst foes must grant me this,
   My honor hath no blot.
For there is nought I've said or sought,
   But it doth well appear,
That all was done before the sun
   In honor bright and clear.

Now if my nation's gallant youth
   Will not my warning take,
And bravely stand for Right and Truth,
   It grieves me for her sake,
I must depart, with heavy heart;
   Yet deem not all is o'er,
Come foul or fair I'll not despair,
   But mix the cards once more.

No courtiers' crafts shall me affright,
   Though deep the game they've played;
An honest heart that loves the Right
   Can never be dismayed.
Full many a name will join the game,
   Nor life nor wealth will cherish;
Up! burghers grave, and horsemen brave,
   And let not Hutten perish!

Catherine Winkworth

Hans Sachs

Ein schöne Tagweis: von dem Wort Gottes

Wach auf, meins Herzen Schöne,
Du christenliche Schar,
Und hör das süß Getöne,
Das rein Wort Gottes klar,
Das jetzt so lieplich klinget,
Es leucht recht als der helle Tag
Durch Gottes Güt her dringet!

Der Propheten Weissage
Hört man jetzt wiederumb,
Die lang verborgen lage;
Das Evangelium
Man jetzt auch süßlich höret:
Da wird manich Gewissen frei,
Das vor ward hart beschwöret.

Mit viel Menschengesetzen,
Mit Bannen und Gebott,
Mit Geldstrick und Seelnetzen:
Die werden jetzt zu Spott,
Vor jedermann zu Schande,
Für eitel Lüg und Finsternüs
Durch alle Teutsche Lande.

Christus viel Boten sendet,
Die verkünden sein Wort;
Ihr viel werden geschändet,
Gefangen und ermordt,
Die Wahrheit zu verstecken:
O Christenheit, du Gottes Braut,
Laß dich nit mit abschrecken!

Hans Sachs

A Fair Melody: To Be Sung by Good Christians

Awake, my heart's delight, awake
   Thou Christian host, and hear
These tones that lovely music make,
   God's Word most pure and clear,
That now is sweetly sounding,
While dawn is piercing through the night
   Through God's dear love abounding.

The prophets' message now at last
   Our ears may hear again,
Locked up therewith in silence fast
   Long had the Gospel lain;
But now we hear their voices,
And many an anxious burdened soul
   In freedom now rejoices.

For conscience lay oppressed and bound
   By bans and men's commands,
Soul-traps and nets were all around;
   But now our German lands,
Behold the sun is risen,
And those foul shapes were ghosts and lies,
   And dare to burst their prison.

Christ sends us many messengers
   His gospel to proclaim,
And all the realm of darkness stirs
   To work them death or shame,
And quench the Truth in error;—
O Christendom, thou Bride of God,
   Fear not for all their terror!

Keim Gleißner tu mehr trauen,
Wie viel ihr immer seind,
Vor Menschen Lehr hab Grauen,
Wie gut sie immer scheint;
Glaub dem Wort Gotts alleine,
Darin uns Gott verkündet hat
Den guten Willen seine!

Dem Wort gib dich gefangen!
Was es verbieten tut,
Nach dem hab kein Verlangen,
Was es dich heißt ist gut,
Was es erlaubt ist freie:
Wer anders lehrt, wie Paulus spricht,
Vermaledeiet seie!

Das Wort dir wendet Schmerzen
Für Sünd und Helle Pein;
Gelaubstu ihm von Herzen,
Du wirst von Sünden rein
Und von der Helle erloste:
Es lehret dich, allein Christus
Sei dein einiger Troste.

Selig sei der Tag und Stunde,
Darin das göttliche Wort,
Dir wiederumb ist kunde,
Der Seelen höchster Hort!
Nichts Liebers soll dir werden,
Kein Engel noch kein Kreatur
Im Himmel noch auf Erden!

O Christenheit, merk eben
Auf das wahr Gottes Wort!
In ihm so ist da Leben
Der Seelen hie und dort;
Wer darin tut abscheiden,
Der lebet darin ewiglich
Bei Christo in den Freuden!

Trust thou in flattering tongues no more,
    Though many they may be;
All human teachings dread thou sore,
    Though good they seem to thee;
But put thy whole affiance
In God's goodwill and holy Word,
    There is our one reliance.

There yield thy heart and soul entire,
    What if commands is good;
Where it forbids let no desire
    E'er stir within thy blood;
Where it allows, maintain thou
Thy Christian freedom as Paul saith,
    Yet from offense refrain thou.

The Word will save thee from the smart
    Of sin and pains of hell,
If thou believe it with thy heart
    No evil there can dwell;
'Twill make thee pure and holy,
And teach thee that in Jesus lies
    Our hope and comfort solely.

Blest be the day and blest the hour
    When thou didst see revealed
The Word of God in all its power,
    The soul's true strength and shield;
Let nought to thee be dearer
In heaven or earth, no creature-love
    E'er to thy heart be nearer.

O Christendom, here give thou heed,
    By no false lore perplexed,
Here seek and find true life indeed
    For this world and the next;
For he who dies believing
In Christ alone, shall live with Him,
    His heavenly joys receiving.

Catherine Winkworth

Anonymous (Lyrics of the fifteenth to seventeenth centuries)

Es waren zwei Königskinder,
Die hatten einander so lieb;
Sie konnten beisammen nicht kommen,
Das Wasser war viel zu tief.

»Ach Schätzchen, ach könntest du schwimmen,
So schwimm doch herüber zu mir!
Drei Kerzchen will ich anzünden,
Und die solln leuchten zu dir.«

Das hört ein falsches Nönnchen,
Die tat, als wenn sie schlief;
Sie tät die Kerzlein auslöschen,
Der Jüngling ertrank so tief.—

»Ach Fischer, lieber Fischer,
Willst dir verdienen Lohn,
So senk deine Netze ins Wasser,
Fisch' mir den Königssohn!«

Sie faßt ihn in ihre Arme
Und küßt seinen roten Mund:
»Ach Mündlein, könntest du sprechen,
So wär mein jung Herze gesund.«

Sie schwang sich um ihren Mantel
Und sprang wohl in die See:
»Gut Nacht, mein Vater und Mutter,
Ihr seht mich nimmermeh!«

Da hört man Glockenläuten,
Da hört man Jammer und Not:
Hier liegen zwei Königskinder,
Die sind alle beide tot.

Anonymous (Lyrics of the fifteenth to seventeenth centuries)

There were two royal children,
They loved one another so true,
Yet they could not come to each other,
Cross waters so deep and so blue.

"Oh darling, if only you'd swim to me,
Just swim right across to my arms,
Three candles will I light for you.
And their light will keep you from harm."

A wicked nun heard their scheming,
She pretended to be asleep,
And so she extinguished the candles,
And the royal youth drowned in the deep.

"Oh Fisherman, dear Fisherman,
There's fair reward to be won,
Just cast your nets in the water
And fetch me the king's royal son."

Into her arms she gathered him,
And she kissed his mouth so red,
"Oh mouth, could you but speak to me,
My young heart would not be dead."

She wrapped her cloak tight about her,
And jumped straight into the sea:
"Good night, my mother and father,
Never more I'll dwell with thee.

And the bells rang out their sorrow,
There was mourning and bitter dread,
Here lie those two royal children,
And both of them are dead.

Ingrid Walsøe-Engel

Wenn ich ein Vöglein wär
und auch zwei Flüglein hätt,
flög ich zu dir.
Weils aber nicht kann sein,
bleib ich allhier.

Bin ich gleich weit von dir,
bin doch im Schlaf bei dir
und red mit dir.
Wenn ich erwachen tu,
bin ich allein.

Es vergeht kein Stund in der Nacht,
daß mein Herz nicht erwacht
und an dich denkt,
daß du mir vieltausendmal
dein Herz geschenkt.

Innsbruck, ich muß dich lassen,
ich fahr dahin mein Straßen,
in fremde Land dahin.
Mein Freud ist mir genommen,
die ich nit weiß bekommen,
wo ich im Elend bin.

Groß Leid muß ich jetzt tragen,
das ich allein tu klagen
dem liebsten Buhlen mein.
Ach Lieb, nun laß mich Armen
im Herzen dein erbarmen,
daß ich muß dannen sein.

Mein Trost ob allen Weiben,
dein tu ich ewig bleiben,
stät, treu, der Ehren frumm.
Nun müß dich Gott bewahren,

If I were but a bird,
And two small wings had I,
To thee I'd fly.
But as that cannot be,
Here must I lie.

Though I am far from thee,
In sleep I cleave to thee,
and speak with thee.
But when my dreams depart,
I am alone.

With every hour of night,
My heart awakes, my light,
And thinks of thee,
That thousandfold, thy love,
Thou gavest me.

Ingrid Walsøe-Engel

Innsbruck, now I must depart,
My journey's road I'm forced to start,
To foreign lands I'll roam.
Sweet happiness has vanished,
Joy stolen, ever banished,
In climes so far from home.

Great sorrow now weighs on me,
Yet I'll ask pity only
From my heart's true delight.
All wretched, I entreat thee,
My love, show thy heart's mercy,
For I must leave tonight.

No other girl will cheer me,
And ever will I love thee,
Your true and steadfast swain.
Now God alone shall guard thee,

in aller Tugend sparen,
biß daß ich wiederkumm.

Es ist ein Ros entsprungen
aus einer Wurzel zart,
als uns die Alten sungen,
aus Jesse kam die Art,
und hat ein Blümlein bracht,
mitten in kaltem Winter,
wohl zu der halben Nacht.

Das Röslein, das ich meine,
darvon Esaias sagt,
hat uns gebracht alleine
Marie die reine Magd;
aus Gottes ewgem Rat
hat sie ein Kind geboren
wohl zu der halben Nacht.

Georg Rudolph Weckherlin

Von dem König von Schweden

O König, dessen Haupt den Weltkreis zu regieren
Und dessen Faust die Welt zu siegen allein gut,
O Herrscher, dessen Herz, Herr, dessen grossen Mut
Gottsforcht, Gerechtigkeit, Stärk, Mass und Weisheit zieren;

In virtue he'll preserve thee,
Till I come back again.

Ingrid Walsøe-Engel

Lo, how a rose is growing,
A bloom of finest grace;
The prophets had foretold it:
A branch of Jesse's race
Would bear one perfect flow'r
Here in the cold of winter
And darkest midnight hour.

The rose of which I'm singing
Isaiah had foretold.
He came to us through Mary,
Who sheltered him from cold.
Through God's eternal will
This child to us was given
At midnight calm and still.

Gracia Grindal

Georg Rudolph Weckherlin

Concerning the King of Sweden

Oh king, whose head alone can rule Earth's company,
Whose hand alone the world in victory can embrace,
Oh chief, whose heart, oh lord, whose courage knows the grace
Of fear of God, restraint, strength, wisdom, equity!

O Held, für dessen Schwert die Verfolger die Wut,
Ihr Klagen, Forcht, Gefahr die Verfolgte verlieren,
Mars, göttlichen Geschlechts, von der Erretter Blut,
Wert, über Tyrannei und Stolz zu triumphieren!

Des Feinds Zorn, Hochmut, Hass, durch Macht, Betrug, Untreu,
Hat schier in Dienstbarkeit, Unrecht, Abgötterei
Des Teutschlands Freiheit, Recht und Gottesdienst verkehret,

Als Euer Haupt, Herz, Hand ganz weis, gerecht, bewehret,
Die Feind bald ihren Wohn und Pracht in Hohn und Reu,
Die Freind ihr Leid in Freud zu verkehren gelehret.

Sie ist die gröste Reichthumb

Das prächtigste Kriegsschiff, dem ie das Meer war kund,
    Hat keinen mast so hoch, als hoch ist mein begehren;
    Kein äncker halb so starck und beissend in den grund,
    Als meine lieb und trew, die unaufhörlich wehren.
So knüpfet auch kein sayl noch leyn ein solchen bund,
    Als die zart krause haar, die meinen gaist beschweren;
    Kein wind bliess jemahl auff die seegel stoltz und rund
    Als mich die süsse lufft des rothen munds bethören.
Kein Schiffman hat iemahls in einer schwartzen nacht
    Ein halb so klares liecht oder gestirn erblicket
    Als hell seind die augstern, mein trost und Amors pracht:
So hat auch noch kein schiff, nach langer fahrt beglicket,
    Ein Kleinoth so viel werth zu uns von Ost gebracht,
    Als dises Kleinoth ist das alle welt erquicket.

Oh hero, at whose sword the hunter halts the chase,
The hunted halt their wails, their fears, their misery,
Oh Mars of blood divine and of the saviors' race,
A worthy conqueror o'er pride and tyranny!

By falseness, force, deceit had hate, pride, rage of foe
Almost to slavishness, injustice, idol's show
The freedom, rights, and faith of German nations brought,

When your hand, heart, and head, tried, just, and wise in thought,
Your foe's vain dream and pomp a change to scorn and woe,
The suffering of your friends a change to gladness taught.

George C. Schoolfield

She Is the Greatest Wealth

The grandest ship-of-war which e'er to sea was known
    Has not a mast that climbs as high as my desire,
    No anchor does such strength or biting fluke-arms own,
    As do my faith and love which never will expire.
Nor is from rope or cord so strong a rigging sewn,
    As from those tender locks which hold my soul in hire,
    And ne'er a wind that sails so proud and round has blown,
    As I'm to madness puffed by her red mouth's sweet choir.
No seaman who his way through murky night has sought
    Has half so clear a light or constellation spied
    As those eye-stars, Love's pride, my comfort, bright are
        wrought.
No vessel has, at last upon the homeward tide,
    So dear a jewel to us from Eastern reaches brought,
    As is this gem wherein the world's delight resides.

George C. Schoolfield

An das Teutschland

Zerbrich das schwere Joch/ darunder du gebunden/
O Teutschland/ wach doch auff/ fass wider einen muht/
Gebrauch dein altes hertz/ und widersteh der wuht/
Die dich/ und die freyheit durch dich selbs uberwunden.

Straf nu die Tyranney/ die dich schier gar geschunden/
Und lösch doch endlich auss die (dich verzöhrend) glut/
Nicht mit dein eignem schwaiss/ sondern dem bösen blut
Fliessend auss deiner feind und falschen brüdern wunden.

Verlassend dich auf Got/ folg denen Fürsten nach/
Die sein gerechte hand will (so du wilt) bewahren/
Zu der Getrewen trost/ zu der trewlosen raach:

So lass nu alle forcht/ und nicht die zeit hinfahren/
Und Got wirt aller welt/ dass nichts dan schand und schmach
Des feinds meynayd und stoltz gezeuget/ offenbahren.

Die Lieb ist Leben und Tod

Das Leben, so ich führ, ist wie der wahre Tod,
Ja über den Tod selbs ist mein trostloses Leben.
Es endet ja der Tod des Menschen Pein und Leben,
Mein Leben aber kann nicht enden dieser Tod.

Bald kann ein Anblick mich verletzen auf den Tod,
Ein andrer Anblick bald kann mich wiedrum beleben,
Dass ich von Blicken muss dann sterben und dann leben,
Und bin in einer Stund bald lebendig bald tot.

Ach, Lieb! Verleih mir doch nunmehr ein anders Leben,
Wenn ich ja leben soll, oder den andern Tod:
Denn weder diesen Tod lieb ich, noch dieses Leben.

To Germany

Destroy the heavy yoke beneath which you are bound!
Oh Germany, awake! Again your courage claim!
Employ your time-tried heart and seek the rage to tame
Which by your aid yourself and freedom would confound!

Let now on tyranny its hangman's arts redound!
At last the fire put out which eats you with its flame!
And let it in the blood from wounds of evil fame,
Of foe and fickle friend (not in your sweat) be drowned!

Entrusting you to God, go at those princes' side
Whose course (just as you will) His righteous hand will chart,
The faithful to console, the faithless to deride.

So let now every fear but not the hour depart,
And God will show the world that, out of hostile pride
And foeman's false-sworn oaths, but shame and pain may start.

George C. Schoolfield

Love Is Life and Death

The life which now I lead is as a perfect death,
Yea, even worse than death is my unhappy life,
For death indeed can end a creature's pain and life,
But yet my life is not concluded by this death.

A glance can deal me wounds unto the point of death,
Another glance can bring me back again to life,
That I from glances first must die and then have life,
And be within the hour now living, now with death.

Oh love, grant me instead another way of life,
If I shall live at all, or then that other death:
For I love not this death, nor this my present life.

Verzeih mir, Lieb, ich bin dein lebendig und tot.
Und ist der Tod mit dir ein köstlich süsses Leben,
Und Leben, von dir fern, ist ein ganz bittrer Tod.

An Brissach von Höchstermeltem Helden Bernhard Hertzogen zu Sachsen eingenommen

Ja, Brissach, dein verlust ist dein gewin und preyss;
    Du hast, in dem du dich verloren, dich gefunden;
    Du hast, von disem schwert erobert überwunden;
    Und uneinnehmlich nu wirst du auff dise weiss.
Dan diser Fürst, Held, Mars (dein Siger) ist so weiss,
    So gütig, mächtig, gross, dass dein verdruss verschwunden,
    Alsbald dich seine faust zu seinem dienst verbunden,
    Darumb mit frewd und danck gehorsam dich erweiss.
Sih doch, bedenck und merck, wie herrlich Er dich zieret,
    Und du mit nichten Ihn; wie durch ihn Got in dir,
    Als durch Got über dich Er (sigreich) triumfieret!
So lern nu seine lehr (und gib ihm danck darfür)
Weil Got den Fürsten selbs, wie der Fürst dich, regieret.
Dass ihm allzeit der Sig, und Got die ehr, gebihr.

Forgive me, love, that I am yours in life and death.
For death becomes with you a sweet and precious life,
And life, far from your side, a more than bitter death.

George C. Schoolfield

To Breisach, Taken by That Supremely Celebrated Hero, Bernhard, Duke of Saxony*

Yes, Breisach, your decrease is profit yet and prize,
    You are, in loss of self, unto that self restored,
    And win the victory, defeated by the sword:
    Impregnable you are become upon this wise.
For this prince-hero-Mars, your victor, is so wise,
    So kind, great, mighty, that your rage became accord,
    The moment his strong hand you to his service warred;
    Therefore with joyful thanks him of your faith apprise.
Behold, consider, mark your splendid ornament
    (Though you are none to him); how God through him in you
    And he through God o'er you his winning passage went.
So learn this lesson now and give him thanks anew,
    (Since God the prince's will, as he your own, has bent)
    That victory may be his and praise God's constant due.

George C. Schoolfield

---

*In 1683, the town of Breisach (in Baden) was besieged and captured by Bernhard, Duke of Sachsen-Weimar (1604–1639), after Gustav of Sweden perhaps the most brilliant Protestant general of the Thirty Years' War.

Martin Rinckart

Nun danket alle Gott
Mit Herzen, Mund und Händen,
Der große Dinge tut
An uns und allen Enden,
Der uns von Mutterleib
Und Kindesbeinen an
Unzählig viel zu gut
Und noch jetzund getan.

Der ewig reiche Gott
Woll uns bei unserm Leben
Ein immer fröhlich Herz
Und edlen Frieden geben
Und uns in seiner Gnad
Erhalten fort und fort
Und uns aus aller Not
Erlösen hier und dort.

Lob, Ehr und Preis sei Gott,
Dem Vater und dem Sohne
Und dem, der beiden gleich
Im höchsten Himmels Throne,
Dem ewig-höchsten Gott,
Als er anfänglich war
Und ist und bleiben wird
Jetzund und immerdar.

Martin Rinckart

Now Thank We All Our God

Now thank we all our God
With hearts and hands and voices,
Who wondrous things has done,
In whom his world rejoices;
Who from our mothers' arms
Has blest us on our way
With countless gifts of love
And still is ours today.

Oh, may this bounteous God
Through all our life be near us,
With ever joyful hearts
And blessed peace to cheer us
And keep us in his grace
And guide us when perplexed
And free us from all harm
In this world and the next!

All praise and thanks to God
The Father now be given,
The Son, and him who reigns
With them in highest heaven.
The one eternal God,
Whom earth and heaven adore;
For thus it was, is now,
And shall be evermore.

Lutheran Book of Worship, 1978

Martin Opitz

An Diss Buch

So wiltu dennoch jetzt auss meinen Händen scheiden
Du kleines Buch und auch mit andern seyn veracht?
Gewiss du weissest nicht wie hönisch man jetzt lacht/
Wie schwerlich sey der Welt Spitzfindigkeit zu meiden.
　Es muss ein jeglich Ding der Menschen Urtheil leiden/
Und/ ob es tauglich sey/ steht nicht in seiner Macht;
Der meiste Theil ist doch auff schmähen nur bedacht/
Und denckt was er nicht kan/ dasselbe muss' er neiden.
　Noch dennoch/ dass du nicht so offt' und viel von mir
Auffs neue dulden dürffst dass ich dich nehme für/
Muss ich dir loss zu seyn und auss zu gehn erleuben.
　So ziehe nun nur hin/ weils ja dir so gefellt/
Und nimb dein Urtheil an/ zieh' hin/ zieh' in die Welt;
Du hettest aber wol zu Hause können bleiben.

Ich wil diss halbe mich/ was wir den Cörper nennen/
Diss mein geringstes Theil/ verzehren durch die Glut/
Wil wie Alcmenen Sohn mit unverwandtem Muth'
Hier diese meine Last/ den schöden Leib/ verbrennen/
　Den Himmel auff zu gehn: mein Geist beginnt zu rennen
Auff etwas bessers zu. diss Fleisch/ die Hand voll Blut/
Muss aussgetauschet seyn vor ein viel besser Gut/
Dass sterbliche Vernunfft und Fleisch und Blut nicht kennen/
　Mein Liecht entzünde mich mit deiner Augen Brunst/
Auff dass ich dieser Haut/ des finstern Leibes Dunst/
Des Kerckers voller Wust und Grauens/ werd entnommen/
　Und ledig/ frey und loss/ der Schwachheit abgethan/

Martin Opitz

To This Book

So you will presently my loving hands abjure,
You little book, and thus with others be despised?
Indeed, men's mockery you have not realized,
And how against the world's sharp cavils to be sure.
  Each thing and everything must men's decree endure:
And nothing's sure that it will properly be prized.
The major part of men in scorn has specialized,
And thinks its feebleness with envy best to cure,
  But since you'll not allow that ever and anew
I take you from the shelf and look your pages through,
Then I must set you free and let you wanton roam.
  Depart now from this place, since you will have it so,
Attempt, attempt the world, and to your judgment go;
And yet you could have stayed as well within your home.

George C. Schoolfield

I'll lay this halfway me, which we the body name,
My least momentous part, beneath the fire's hot blade,
And, like Alcmene's son, with courage undismayed,
This burden and base form I'll cast into the flame,*
  That I to Heaven may climb: toward a better aim
My soul begins to haste, and I this flesh must trade,
This clutch of blood against a ware far better made,
Whose knowledge mortal thought and flesh and blood disclaim.
  My light, let fire to me from your eyes' passion swell,
So that I from this skin, this gloomy body's smell,
This madhouse-dungeon full of terror may be freed;
  And that, loosed from my bonds, my frailty at end,

*Hercules, tormented by the wounds he had received from the shirt of Nessus, immolated himself on Mount Oeta, from whence he was carried up into Olympus and there made immortal.

Weit uber alle Lufft und Himmel fliegen kan
Die Schönheit au zu sehn von der die deine kommen.

Ich gleiche nicht mit dir des weissen Mondens Liecht:
Der Monde fellt und steigt; du bleibt in einem Scheine:
Ja nicht die Sonne selbst: die Sonn' ist gantz gemeine/
Gemein' auch ist ihr Glantz; du bist gemeine nicht.
    Du zwingst durch Zucht den Neid/ wie sehr er auff dich sticht.
Ich mag kein Heuchler seyn/ der bey mir selbst verneine
Dass was ich jetzt gesagt: es gleichet sich dir keine/
Du bist dir ähnlich selbst; ein ander Bild gebricht
    Dass dir dich zeigen kan; du bist dein eigen Glücke/
Dein eigenes Gestirn/ der Schönheit Meisterstücke.
Du hettest sollen seyn wie noch die Tugend war
    Geehret alss ein Gott/ in der Welt ersten Jugend/
So were wol gewiss gewesen deine Tugend
Die Kirch' und Opfferung/ der Weyrauch und Altar.

    Du güldne Freyheit du/ mein wündschen und begehren/
Wie wol doch were mir/ im fall ich jederzeit
Mein selber möchte seyn/ und were gantz befreyt
Der Liebe die noch nie sich wollen von mir kehren/
    Wiewol ich offte mich bedacht bin zu erwehren.
Doch/ lieb' ich gleichwol nicht/ so bin ich wie ein Scheit/
Ein Stock/ und rawes Bley. die freye Dienstbarkeit/
Die sichere Gefahr/ das tröstliche Beschweren/
    Ermuntert meinen Geist/ dass er sich höher schwingt
Alss wo der Pöfel kreucht/ und durch die Wolcken dringt/
Geflügelt mit Vernunfft und mutigen Gedancken.
    Drumb geh' es wie es wil/ und muss ich gleich darvon/
So uberschreit' ich doch des Lebens enge Schrancken:
Der Nahme der mir folgt ist meiner Sorgen Lohn.

I can above the air and every sky ascend,
That beauty to admire from which yours must proceed.

George C. Schoolfield

With snowy light of moon I cannot you compare:
The moon must grow and shrink: you in your strength stay one;
Nor with the sun itself; for everywhere's the sun,
And everywhere its shine: you are not everywhere.
    With courtesy you dull the point of envy's stare.
I am no hypocrite, who've instantly undone
What I have barely said: for like to you is none.
You are most like yourself; no image that might share
    You with yourself exists; your own bliss you will be,
Your beauty's masterpiece, your starry company.
You should have lived that time when virtue was revered
    Even as a deity, in Earth's initial youth;
Then would your virtue have as temple (in all truth),
As altar, frankincense, and sacrifice appeared.

George C. Schoolfield

You golden freedom, both my wish and my desire,
What happiness were mine, if now I might conclude
Always to be myself, and if I might elude
The love that never yet has wanted to retire,
    Though oft I hoped to find some shield against her fire.
Yet, out of loving I am like a log rough-hewed,
A stick, unpolished lead. This chainless servitude,
This certain peril, and this consolation dire
    Arouse my spirit so that it may higher soar
Above the creeping mob, and through the cloudy floor
Ascend on reason's wings and with courageous thought.
    Then let things take their course: if soon I must away,
I'll overstep no less life's bounds too narrow wrought:
The name which follows me my cares' reward will pay.

George C. Schoolfield

Vom Wolffsbrunnen bey Heidelberg

Du edele Fonteyn mit Ruh und Lust umbgeben,
Mit Bergen hier und dar, als einer Burg, umbringt,
Printz aller schönen Quell, auss welchem Wasser dringt
Anmütiger dann Milch, und köstlicher dann Reben,
   Da unsers Landes Kron und Haupt mit seinem Leben,
   Der werden Nymf, offt selbst die Zeit in frewd zubringt,
Da jhr manch Vögelein zu ehren lieblich singt,
Da nur ergetzlichkeit und keusche Wollust schweben,
   Vergeblich bistu nicht in diesem grünen Thal,
Von Klippen und Gebirg beschlossen uberal,
Die künstliche Natur nat darumb dich umbfangen
   Mit Felsen und Gebüsch, auff dass man wissen soll
Dass alle Fröligkeit sey Müh und arbeit voll,
Und dass auch nichts so schön, es sey schwer zu erlangen.

Ach Liebste, laß uns eilen,
   Wir haben Zeit:
Es schadet das Verweilen
   Uns beiderseit.
Der edlen Schönheit Gaben
   Fliehn Fuß für Fuß,
Daß alles, was wir haben,
   Verschwinden muß.
Der Wangen Zier verbleichet,
   Das Haar wird greis,
Der Äuglein Feuer wiechet,
   Die Flamm wird Eis.
Das Mündlein von Korallen
   Wird ungestalt,

Concerning the Wolffsbrunnen near Heidelberg

You noble fountain set in peace and joy's design,
Which mountains here and there do like a keep enring,
Prince of all lovely founts from which these waters spring,
More pleasing still than milk, more precious than the vine,
    Where with his worthy nymph our country's liege benign*
And chieftain often spends the hours' long dallying,
And where the birds' brigade does in her honor sing,
Where only happiness and chaste desire recline:
    You in this greening vale have not been placed in vain;
Enclosed from every side by cliff's and peak's domain,
An artful nature thus has given you a guard
    Of copses and of cliffs, so that we men may know
That all our merriments from pain and labor grow,
That nothing's truly fair lest it to gain be hard.

George C. Schoolfield

    Ah Dearest, let us haste us,
        While we have time;
    Delaying doth but waste us
        And lose our prime.
    The gifts that beauty nourish
        Fly with the year,
    And everything we cherish
        Must disappear.
    The cheeks so fair turn pallid,
        And grey the hair,
    The flashing eyes turn gelid,
        And ice, desire.
    From coral lips must flee then
        The outline bold;

*Opitz was a student at Heidelberg when, on September 25, 1619, Friedrich V of the Palatinate left his land to become the unhappy "winter king" of Bohemia. The young Silesian poet there had the chance to see the last of those happy days that Friedrich spent in Heidelberg with his high-spirited wife, Elizabeth, the "worthy nymph" of this poem.

Die Händ als Schnee verfallen,
    Und du wirst alt.
Drum laß uns jetzt genießen
    Der Jugend Frucht,
Eh dann wir folgen müssen
    Der Jahre Flucht.
Wo du dich selber liebest,
    So liebe mich,
Gib mir, daß, wann du gibest,
    Verlier auch ich.

Friedrich Spee

Die gesponss Jesu klaget ihren Hertzenbrand

Gleich früh wan sich entzündet
    Der silber weisse tag;
Und uns die Sonn verkündet/
    Wass nachts verborgen lag:
Die lieb in meinem hertzen
    Ein flämlein stecket an;
Dass brint gleich einer kertzen
    So niemand leschen kan.

Wan schon Ichs schlag in Winde/
    Gen Ost- und Norden brauss;
Doch ruh/ noch rast ich finde/
    Last nie sich blasen auss.
O wee der qual/ der peine!
    Wo soll mich wenden hin?
Den gantzen tag ich weine/
    Weil stäts in schmertzen bin.

The snowy hands decay then,
    And thou art old.
So therefore let us swallow
    Youth's precious fruit,
E'er we are forc'd to follow
    The years in flight.
As thou thyself then lovest,
    Love also me;
Give me, that when thou givest
    I lose to thee.

        F. Warnke

Friedrich Spee

The Spouse of Jesus Laments Her Heart's Flame

All early, when the day
    In silver-white's revealed,
And us the sun can say
    What nighttime had concealed:
Love has within my heart
    A little flamelet lit;
It takes a candle's part
    And none can smother it.

Though I the flame bore 'round
    'Gainst East- and Northwind's shout,
Nor rest nor respite found,
    No wind has blown it out.
Let woe these worries cry!
    Now whither shall I turn?
I always weep since I
    Fore'er in torments burn.

Wann wider dann entflogen
  Der Tag zur Nacht hinein/
Und sich gar tieff gebogen
  Die Sonn/ und Sonnenschein;
Dass Flämlein so mich queelet
  Noch bleibt in voller glut;
All stundt/ so viel man zehlet/
  Michs je noch brennen thut.

Dass Flämlein dass ich meine/
  Ist JESU süsser nam;
Ess zehret Marck und Beine/
  Frisst ein gar wundersam.
O süssigkeit in schmertzen!
  O schmertz in süssigkeit!
Ach bleibe doch im Hertzen/
  Bleib doch in Ewigkeit.

Ob schon in pein/ und qualen
  Mein Leben schwindet hinn/
Wann JESU Pfeil und Stralen
  Durchstreichet Muth und Sinn;
Doch nie so gar mich zehret
  Die Liebe JESU mein/
Alss gleich sie wider nehret/
  Und schenckt auch frewden ein.

O Flämlein süss ohn massen!
  O bitter auch ohn ziel!
Du machest mich verlassen
  All ander Frewd/ und Spiel;
Du zündest mein gemüthe/
  Bringst mir gross Hertzen leidt/
Du kühlest mein Geblüthe/
  Bringst auch ergetzligkeit.

Ade zu tausent Jahren/
  O Welt zu guter nacht:
Ade lass mich nun fahren/

When once again has fled
　　The day down night's decline,
And sleepwards bend their head
　　Both sun and sunlight's shine:
The gnawing flamelet stays
　　In me at fullest force,
Ignores the hour's swift ways,
　　And burns me in its course.

The flame of which I think
　　Is Jesus Christ's sweet name
And bone and marrow sink
　　All strangely in its flame.
Oh loving born of pain!
　　Oh pain born lovingly!
Oh in my heart remain
　　For all eternity!

Although in wrack and rue
　　My life does swiftly go,
When Jesus wanders through
　　My heart with bolt and bow:
Yet love does never eat
　　My soul to such degree,
Unless she gives me meat,
　　And pours out joy for me.

Sweet fire from endless founts!
　　Oh boundless bitter flame!
You cause me to renounce
　　Each other joy and game!
You set my soul afire
　　And bring me heart-born woes,
You cool my blood's desire
　　And bring me glad repose.

A thousand years' good-night,
　　Oh world, is my farewell:
Now free me from your sight,

Ich längst hab dich veracht.
In JESU lieb Ich lebe/
Sag dir von Hertzen grund:
In lauter Frewd Ich schwebe/
Wie sehr ich bin verwund.

Heinrich Albert

Musicalische Kürbs-Hütte
(Ein Kürbis spricht)

Mit der Zeit ich kommen bin/
Fall' auch mit der Zeit dahin!

Mensch/ hierinnen sind wir gleich/
Du magst Schön seyn/ Jung und Reich:
Unser Pracht kan nicht bestehn/
Beyde müssen wir vergehn.

Nun ich jung noch bin und grüne/
o/ so hält man mich im Wehrt!
Bin ich welck und nicht mehr diene/
Wer ist dann der mein begehrt?

Mensch/ ich kan es leichtlich gläuben
Dass du wünscht/ ich möchte bleiben;
Nicht dein Will'/ auch meiner nicht/
Gottes Wille nur geschicht.

I long have scorned your spell.
In Jesus' love I lie,
From heart's vault tell the news:
In sheerest joy I fly
Despite my cruel abuse.

George C. Schoolfield

Heinrich Albert

Musical Pumpkin-Hut*
(A Pumpkin Speaks)

I with time to life ascend,
And with time do come to end.

Man, in this we are the same:
You wealth, beauty, youth can claim,
Yet our splendor must grow sere,
We must twinlike disappear.

Now that I'm still young and green,
Men do high my worth admire!
When I spent and withered seem,
Who will know for me desire?

Man, I easy can believe
That you'd wish I would not leave;
Not your will, nor mine, has won.
Heaven's will alone is done.

*In his garden, Albert had a so-called pumpkin-hut, where, from 1631 until 1640 the members of the Königsberg circle—among them Simon Dach, Johann Peter Titz, and Robert Roberthin—were accumstomed to hold their summer assemblies. Eventually, the artistic friends came to call their group after its meeting place. In 1645, Albert published a series of verses, set to music by himself (he was the cathedral organist in Königsberg), in which he celebrated the various members of the circle. This collection too was called the "Musikalische Kürbis Hütte."

Wenn der rauhe Herbst nun kömpt/
Fall' ich ab/und muss verderben.
Wenn dein Ziel dir ist bestimmt/
Armer Mensch/ so mustu sterben.

Sieh mich an/
Und dencke dran:
Ich muss fort
Von diesem Ort!
Mit dir helt auch
Gott solchen Brauch.

Dem Herbst verlangt nach mir/
Mich zu verderben;
Dem Tod'/O Mensch/ nach dir/
Auch Du must sterben!
Wer wird nach kurtzen Tagen
    Mich beklagen/
  Wenn ich verwelckt nun bin?
Auch Dir wirds widerfahren
    Nach wenig Jahren/
  Wenn Dich der Tod nimpt hin.

Die Zeit und wir vergehn!
Was wir hie sehen stehn
In diesem grünen Garten/
Verwelckt in kurtzer Zeit/
Weil schon des Herbstes Neid
Scheint drauff zu warten.

Ich/ und meine Blätter/ wissen
Dass wir dann erst fallen müssen
Wenn der rauhe Herbst nun kömpt:
Aber Du/ Mensch/ weist ja nicht
Ob's nicht heute noch geschicht
Dass dir Gott das Leben nimpt?

Ob ich gleich muss bald von hier/
Kriegstu dennoch Frucht von mir;

When the cruel fall holds sway,
I must sick and ruined lie.
When an ending stops your way,
Wretched man, then you must die.

See me aright,
And weigh the sight:
That I am bound
To leave this ground.
God has with you
Such usage too.

That he my end might gain
Does autumn sigh;
Man, death would you obtain,
You too must die!
Who, when brief days are spent,
    Will lament
  How blighted I have grown?
Though death will make you die
    Ere few years fly,
My fate will be your own.

Time goes, we disappear!
What we see standing here
Behind this garden-gate
In little time does fade,
Since autumn's envious shade
Already seems to wait.

I and all my leaves do know
That we then to earth must go
When the cruel fall holds sway.
Man, you ne'er a pledge have won
That God, ere the day be done,
Will not take your life away.

Though but brief I can remain,
You will fruits from me obtain.

Wenn man dich/ Mensch/ wird begraben/
Was wirst Du für Früchte haben

O ich habe schon vernommen
Dass mein Feind/ der Herbst/ wird kommen/
Dessen Raub ich werden sol!
Lieber Mensch/ gehab dich wol!

Simon Dach

Über den Eingang der Schlossbrücke

Du Seule Brandenburgs, du Preussens Sicherheit,
O Fridrich Wilhelm, Trost und Hoffnung vieler Lande,
Sey willkomm deinem Volck hie an des Pregels Rande!
Des Höchsten Ehrendienst ist wegen dein erfreut,

Verspricht Uns undter Dir die alte güldne Zeit;
Gerechtigkeit und Fried in jedem Ort und Stande
Verknüppffen dir sich fest mit einem güldnen Bande
Du machst, dass alles wil genesen weit und breit.

In dem dein Eintzug Uns die Hoffnung aber gidebet,
So wirstu billich nie von uns auch gnug geliebet;
O leb Uns werthes Haupt, sey Uns ein Sonnen-schein,

Der nimmer untergeht! schon jetzt mit deiner Jugend
Dringt Fama durch die Welt, du wirst bey solcher Tugend
Nicht hie nur, sondern auch im Himmel Hertzog seyn.

When you, man, are borne to earth,
To what fruits will you give birth?

Now the news is brought to me
That fall comes, my enemy,
And will me as quarry fell:
Oh, dear human, fare you well.

George C. Schoolfield

Simon Dach

On the Entrance of the Castle Bridge

You Brandenburg's support and Prussia's guarantee,
Oh Frederick William,* whom we for hope's solace thank,
Your people greet you now upon the Pregel's bank!
God's honored hosts rejoice to see your regency,

And do 'neath you for us an Age of Gold desire.
Both righteousness and peace in every place and rank,
Fast joined with golden bands, must march upon your flank;
You lead us, far and wide, to fresh prosperity.

Since this your entry's brought to us new hoping-stuff,
You cannot have from us just love or love enough.
Live for us, worthy head, and be our ray of sun

Which nevermore shall set! Now with your youth, sweet Fame
Goes through the world, and you, who may such virtue claim,
Will have not only earth's, but heaven's dukedom won.

George C. Schoolfield

---

*Friedrich William I, "the Great Elector" to be (1620–88), held his solemn entrance into Königsberg, at whose university Dach was a professor, on November 30, 1641.

Über der Schloss-Pforte, da Ihr Fürstliche Durchl.
Auff dero Beylager einzogen, zu lesen

Komm glücklich, wehrter Held, O Bräutgam, eingezogen,
Dein Auss- und Eingangk muss von Gott gesegnet seyn,
Schau, unser ChurFürst selbst begleitet dich herein,
Thu, was der Himmel längst dich hat zu thun bewogen,

Vollbring dein Liebes-Werck. Mercur kömpft angeflogen,
Und bringt Bericht, der Schluss der Götter in gemein
Sey dissfalls Glück und Heil, nach dem sie wegen dein
Bissher in Gegenwart der Parcen Raht gepflogen.

O Reichthum, den du kömpst zu hohlen in dein Land,
Dergleichen Hoheit hat die Erde kaum erkant,
Mit der vollkommen sich Loys' Charlotte zieret.

Wer wird, O Churland, nun wol fassen deinen Pracht,
So bald dein Hertzog Sie wird haben heim gebracht?
Uns aber wird hiedurch ein Tugend-Bild entführet.

Perstet amicitiae
Semper venerabile foedus!

Der Mensch hat nichts so eigen,
So wohl steht ihm nichts an,
Als daß er Treu erzeigen
Und Freundschaft halten kann;
Wann er mit seinesgleichen
Soll treten in ein Band,
Verspricht sich, nicht zu weichen
Mit Herzen, Mund und Hand.

**To Be Read above the Castle-Gate, When His
Princely Highness Rode in to His Marriage Bed***

Oh happy hero come, oh enter, worthy groom,
Your goings in and out God's blessing must display;
And see, our glorious prince has come with you this way;
What Heaven long has wished, that task tonight assume.

Fulfill your work of love. Let Mercury presume
To read to us the gods' one-voiced report, and say
It's filled with grace and joy, since they till now did stay
And council learn for you before the Parcae's loom.

Oh riches, which you come within your land to bring!
Like majesty on earth has been a seldom thing,
Yet it Louise Charlotte can perfectly adorn.

Who will, Curland, indeed your splendor apprehend,
Now that your Duke with her his way will homeward wend?
But we are thereby of our virtue's crown forlorn.

George C. Schoolfield

The Bonds of Friendship

Man has nought so much his own,
And nought becomes him better,
Than that true faith to him is known,
And friendship's binding fetter;
And when, with souls fraternal,
He takes oath's solemn band,
He pledges trust eternal,
With heart and mouth and hand.

*On October 10, 1645, Louise Charlotte, the sister of Friedrich William, was married to the duke of Curland.

Die Red ist uns gegeben,
Damit wir nicht allein
Für uns nur sollen leben
Und fern von Leuten sein.
Wir sollen uns befragen
Und sehn auf guten Rat,
Das Leid einander klagen,
So uns betreten hat.

Was kann die Freude machen,
Die Einsamkeit verhehlt?
Das gibt ein doppelt Lachen,
Was Freunden wird erzählt.
Der kann sein Leid vergessen,
Der es von Herzen sagt;
Der muß sich selbst auffressen,
Der in geheim sich nagt.

Gott stehet mir vor allen
Die meine Seele liebt;
Dann soll mir auch gefallen,
Der mir sich herzlich gibt:
Mit diesen Bundsgesellen,
Verlach ich Pein und Not,
Geh auf den Grund der Höllen
Und breche durch den Tod.

Ich hab, ich habe Herzen,
So treue, wie gebührt,
Die Heuchelei und Scherzen
Nie wissentlich berührt.
Ich bin auch ihnen wieder
Von Grund der Seelen hold;
Ich lieb euch mehr, ihr Brüder,
Denn aller Erden Gold!

God gave us words for speaking,
That we'd not bide alone,
Self's silent solace seeking,
Companionship unknown;
We should ask one another,
Good counsel ever seek,
Confiding in our brother,
The pain of sorrows bleak.

How can joy hope to fire the soul,
In solitude concealed?
We surely double laughter's role,
When our delight's revealed;
The pain of sorrow passes,
When heartfelt words resound,
No agony surpasses,
A grief in silence bound.

Above all others, holy Lord,
My soul delights in thee,
But next have earned my love's reward
Those, who in turn, love me;
With these my boon companions,
I'd laugh at misery's pain,
Descend to hell's deep canyons,
And break death's heavy chain.

My comrades now are my reward,
Their hearts pure and sincere,
Untouched by cunning's ugly fraud,
By mockery's cruel spear.
And each of them I treasure,
From the bottom of my heart,
My brothers give more pleasure,
Than great wealth can impart.

Ingrid Walsøe-Eng

Klaggedicht bei seiner schmerzlichen Krankheit

Wie? Ist es denn nicht gnug, gern einmal sterben wollen?
Natur, Verhängnüs, Gott, was haltet ihr mich auf?
Kein Säumnüs ist bei mir, vollendet ist mein Lauf;
Soll ich die Durchfahrt euch denn tausendmal verzollen?
Was kränkt es, fertig sein und sich verweilen sollen!
Ist Sterben ein Gewinn? O mir ein teurer Kauf!
Mich töten so viel Jahr und Krankheiten zuhauf;
Ich lebe noch und bin wohl zehnmal tot erschollen.
Weib, Kinder, macht es ihr? Verlängert ihr mein Licht?
Seht meinen Jammer an! Ist dieses Liebespflicht,
Zu schlechtem Vorteil euch mein Vorteil mir nicht gönnen?
Ach kränket mich nicht mehr durch euer Angesicht!
Die allerletzte Pein ist, gläub ich, ärger nicht,
Als leben müssen, tot sein wollen und nicht können.

Anonymous

Annchen von Tharau ist, die mir gefällt;
Sie ist mein Leben, mein Gut und mein Geld.

Annchen von Tharau hat wieder ihr Herz
Auf mich gerichtet in Lieb' und in Schmerz.

Lamentation during His Most Painful Illness

Why is it not enough, to want death's certain peace?
Why, Nature, God, why, Fate—why halt my last retreat,
When I seek no delay; this life of mine, complete?
Am I to pay a thousand times your gateway's cruel surcease?

What bitter fate, to have no life, yet still find no release!
What profit lies in death? Most costly winding-sheet!
Age and disease compete, each painful breath defeat!
And lingering still I hear ten tales of my decease!

Wife, children is it you? Do you prolong my light?
Is this your duteous love? I beg you heed my plight!
Would you your pleasure small, with my great pain enable?

Oh do not wound me more, but get you from my sight!
Could even death's last throes so much my soul benight?
Condemned to life I want to die, yet am unable.

Ingrid Walsøe-Engel

Anonymous

Annie of Tharaw*

Annie of Tharaw, my true love of old,
She is my life, and my goods, and my gold.

Annie of Tharaw her heart once again
To me has surrendered in joy and in pain.

---

*A well-known seventeenth-century poem, often considered a *Volkslied,* it was
long believed to have been written by Dach. But some consider that it may have been
written by Albert.This nuptial song was composed in dialect and the present version
was rendered by Herder.

Annchen von Tharau, mein Reichtum, mein Gut,
Du meine Seele, mein Fleisch und mein Blut!

Käm' alles Wetter gleich auf uns zu schlahn,
Wir sind gesinnet bei einander zu stahn.

Krankheit, Verfolgung, Betrübniß und Pein
Soll unsrer Liebe Verknotigung seyn.

Recht als ein Palmenbaum über sich steigt,
Je mehr ihn Hagel und Regen anficht;

So wird die Lieb' in uns mächtig und groß
Durch Kreuz, durch Leiden, durch allerlei Noth.

Würdest du gleich einmal von mir getrennt,
Lebtest, da wo man die Sonne kaum kennt;

Ich will dir folgen durch Wälder, durch Meer,
Durch Eis, durch Eisen, durch feindliches Heer.

Annchen von Tharau, mein Licht, meine Sonn,
Mein Leben schließ' ich um deines herum.

Was ich gebiete, wird von dir gethan,
Was ich verbiete, das läßt du mir stahn.

Was hat die Liebe doch für ein Bestand,
Wo nicht Ein Herz ist, Ein Mund, Eine Hand?

Wo man sich peiniget, zanket und schlägt,
Und gleich den Hunden und Katzen beträgt?

Annchen von Tharau, das woll'n wir nicht thun;
Du bist mein Täubchen, mein Schäfchen, mein Huhn.

Was ich begehre, ist lieb dir und gut;
Ich laß den Rock dir, du läßt mir den Hut!

Annie of Tharaw, my riches, my good,
Thou, O my soul, my flesh, and my blood!

Then come the wild weather, come sleet or come snow,
We will stand by each other, however it blow.

Oppression, and sickness, and sorrow, and pain
Shall be to our true love as links to the chain.

As the palm-tree standeth so straight and so tall,
The more the hail beats, and the more the rains fall,—

So love in our hearts shall grow mighty and strong,
Through crosses, through sorrows, through manifold wrong.

Shouldst thou be torn from me to wander alone
In a desolate land where the sun is scarce known,—

Through forests I'll follow, and where the sea flows,
Through ice, and through iron, through armies of foes.

Annie of Tharaw, my light and my sun.
The threads of our two lives are woven in one.

Whate'er I have bidden thee thou hast obeyed,
Whatever forbidden thou hast not gainsaid.

How in the turmoil of life can love stand,
Where there is not one heart, and one mouth, and one hand?

Some seek for dissension, and trouble, and strife;
Like a dog and a cat live such man and wife.

Annie of Tharaw, such is not our love;
Thou art my lambkin, my chick, and my dove.

Whate'er my desire is, in thine may be seen;
I am king of the household, and thou art its queen.

Dies ist uns Annchen die süsseste Ruh.
Ein Leib und Seele wird aus Ich und Du.

Dies macht das Leben zum himmlischen Reich,
Durch Zanken wird es der Hölle gleich.

Friedrich von Logau

Epigramme

1. Die unartige Zeit

Die Alten konten frölich singen
Von tapffern, deutschen Heldens-Dingen,
Die ihre Väter aussgeübet.
Wo Gott noch uns ie Kinder gibet,
Die werden unsrer Zeit Beginnen
Beheulen, nicht besingen können.

2. Trunckenheit

Wer vielleichte soll ertrincken,
Darff ins Wasser nicht versincken,
Alldieweil ein Deutscher Mann
Auch im Glas ersauffen kan.

3. Der Ärtzte Glücke

Ein Artzt ist gar ein glücklich Mann.
Was er berühmtes hat gethan,
Das kan die Zeit selbst sagen an;
Sein Irrthum wird nicht viel gezehlet;
Dann wo er etwa hat gefehlet,
Das wird in Erde tief verhölet.

It is this, O my Annie, my heart's sweetest rest,
That makes of us twain but one soul in one breast.

This turns to a heaven the hut where we dwell;
While wrangling soon changes a home to a hell.

H. W. *Longfellow*

Friedrich von Logau

Epigrams

1. Our Naughty Time
The ancients happily could sing
Of German's brave adventuring,
The deeds that were their fathers' will.
If God will grant us children still,
These, seeing what our time has bred,
Will sing no more but howl instead.

2. Drunkenness
He who thinks perchance to drown
Need not in the depths go down,
Since truehearted Germans may
In their goblets pass away.

3. The Physicians' Fortune
A doctor's fortunate indeed:
Where'er his brilliant skills succeed,
Time does itself his glory plead.
Of his mistakes but little's heard,
For where he may perchance have erred,
His error's in the tomb interred.

4. Die Geburt ist der Tod; der Tod ist die Geburt
Der Tod ist nicht der Tod; der Tod ist die Geburt.
Durch diese kam ich kaum, so must ich wieder fort.
Der Tod ist nicht der Tod; er ist das rechte Leben,
Drauss ich mich mehr nicht darff in Ewigkeit begeben.

5. Frantzösische Kleidung

Diener tragen in gemein ihrer Herren Lieverey;
Solls dann seyn, dass Franckreich Herr, Deutschland aber Diener
  sey?
Freyes Deutschland schäm dich doch dieser schnöden Knechterey!

6. Glauben

Luthrisch, Päbstisch und Calvinisch, diese Glauben alle drey
Sind vorhanden; doch ist Zweiffel, wo das Christenthum dann sey.

7. Beute aussm deutschen Kriege

Was gabe der deutsche Krieg für Beute?
Viel Grafen, Herren, Edelleute.
Das deutsche Blut ist edler worden,
Weil so geschwächt der Bauer-Orden.

8. Weiber-Herrschung

Haus, Dorff, Stadt, Land und Reich wird Wolfahrt bald gelosen,
Wo Männer tragen Röck, und Weiber tragen Hosen.

9. Wasser und Wein

Es kan, wer Wasser trinckt, kein gut Getichte schreiben;
Wer Wein trinckt, kriegt die Gicht und muss erschrecklich
  schreyen;
Es sey nun, wie ihm wil; eh mag das tichten bleiben,
Eh dass ich soll so tief in Gichten hin gedeyen.

10. Ein Frosch

Die Stimm ist gross, der Mann ist klein;
Was nahe nichts, hat ferne Schein.

11. Seele und Leib

Seel ist ein Gefangner; Leib ist ein Gefängnüss;
Wer den Leib verzärtelt, gibt der Seele Drängnüss.

4. Birth is Death, Death is Birth

Death is not death, for death is but the borning day.
Through death I've hardly come, and I must pass away.
Death is not death, for death is but life's verity,
From which I may not go for all eternity.

5. French Dress

As a rule all servants dress in their masters' livery;
Can it be that France is lord, and the servant Germany?
German freedom, go in shame at this base servility.

6. Faith

Lutheran, Popish, Calvinistic, all of these confessions three
Stand before us, yet we wonder where then Christendom may be.

7. Booty from the German War*

What booty gave the German war?
Why, nobles, counts, and lords the more.
Our German blood has changed to blue
Because the peasants are made few.

8. Women's Rule

House, village, city, land, and empire harvest hurt
When women trousers wear, and husbands wear the skirt.

9. Water and Wine

Whoever water drinks, writes wretched poetry;
Who lives on wine gets gout, and screams for very pain;
But nonetheless I'd let my rhyming sooner be,
Than that I would at last the joys of gouting gain.

10. A Frog

The voice is large, the man is small;
What far is much, near's not at all.

11. Soul and Body

Soul is a prisoner, and body is its jail;
Who spoils the flesh, his soul's sweet freedom would curtail.

---

*A pointed remark about an abuse common during the baroque age, the bestowal of nobility through the letter patent.

12. Narren und Kluge
Narren herrschen über Kluge; ihre Händel, ihre Sachen,
Die die Narren arg verwirren, müssen Kluge richtig machen.

13. Alter Adelstand
Weiland war dess Adels Brauch in dem Felde durch das Blut,
Nicht im Acker durch den Schweiss, zu erwerben Ehr und Gut.

14. Die Freyheit
Wo dieses Freyheit ist: frey thun nach aller Lust,
So sind ein freyes Volck die Säu in ihrem Wust.

15. Göttliche Rache
Gottes Mühlen mahlen langsam, mahlen aber trefflich klein;
Ob auss Langmuth er sich seumet, bringt mit Schärff er alles ein.

16. Ein Glaube und kein Glaube
Deutschland soll von dreyen Glauben nunmehr nur behalten einen;
Christus meint, wann er wird kummen, dürfft er alsdann finden
keinen.

17. Mächtige Diener
Den grossen Elephant führt offt ein kleiner Mohr,
Und grossen Herren auch schreibt offt ein Bauer vor.

18. Die deutsche Sprache
Kan die deutsche Sprache schnauben, schnarchen, poltern,
donnern, krachen,
Kan sie doch auch spielen, schertzen, liebeln, gütteln, kürmeln,
lachen.

12. Fools and Wise Men

Fools have power over wise men: each transactions, each affair,
Which the fools so badly muddle, wise men's wit must needs
repair.

13. The Old Nobility

Once noble custom was: by blood on battleground
And not by sweat on soil, its gold and fame to found.

14. Freedom

Where this is freedom: free to follow each desire,
Then men are sows set free, delighting in their mire.

15. Divine Revenge

Heaven's mills are grinding slowly, but they grind exceeding small;
Though from patience they be tardy, still they stern do capture all.

16. One Faith and No Faith

Germany of three confessions now shall keep a single one.
Christ must think that, when returning, he most likely will find
none.

17. Powerful Servants

Oft mighty elephants by little Moors are led,
Oft mighty lords must do what some small peasant's said.

18. The German Language

Can the German language crack and snore and rumble, thunder,
snort?
Then it too can jest and love and cuddle, babble, coo, and sport.

George C. Schoolfield

Johann Rist

From O Ewigkeit, du Donnerwort

O Ewigkeit, du Donnerwort,
O Schwert, das durch die Seele bohrt,
O Anfang sonder Ende!
O Ewigkeit, Zeit ohne Zeit,
Ich weiß vor großer Traurigkeit
Nicht, wo ich mich hinwende.
Mein ganz erschrocken Herz erbebt,
Daß mir die Zung am Gaumen klebt.

Solang ein Gott im Himmel lebt
Und über alle Wolken schwebt,
Wird solche Marter währen:
Es wird sie plagen Kält und Hitz,
Angst, Hunger, Schrecken, Feu'r und Blitz
Und sie doch nicht verzehren.
Denn wird sich enden diese Pein,
Wenn Gott nicht mehr wird ewig sein.

O Ewigkeit, du Donnerwort,
O Schwert, das durch die Seele bohrt,
O Anfang sonder Ende!
O Ewigkeit, Zeit ohne Zeit,
Ich weiß vor großer Traurigkeit
Nicht, wo ich mich hinwende.
Nimm du mich, wenn es dir gefällt,
Herr Jesu, in dein Freudenzelt!

Johann Rist

From Eternity, Thou Thunderous Word*

Eternity, thou thunderous word,
O sword that through the soul doth bore,
Beginning with no ending!
Eternity, time lacking time,
I know now faced with deepest grief
Not where to seek my refuge.
So much my frightened heart doth quake
That to my gums my tongue is stuck.

So long a God in heaven dwells
And over all the clouds doth swell,
Such torments shall not be finished:
They will be plagued by heat and cold,
Fear, hunger, terror, lightning's bolt
And still be not diminished.
For only then shall end this pain
When God no more eternal reign.

Eternity, thou thunderous word,
O sword that through the soul doth bore,
Beginning with no ending!
Eternity, time lacking time,
I know now faced with deepest woe
Not where to seek my refuge.
Take me then when thou dost please,
Lord Jesus, to thy joyful tent!

Z. Philip Ambrose

---

*Only excerpts from this powerful poem have been translated.

Sie rühmet ihre Beständigkeit

Mein Hertz' ist nicht von Wachs/ mein Hertz ist nicht zugleichen
Den Winden/ die bald Ost bald West herümmer schleichen/
  Es ist nicht wie ein Schiff/ das nach der Wellen Lust
  Bald hie/ bald dort hinläufft; Ach! mier ist nichts bewust

Als nur bestendig seyn. Mein lieben sol bezeugen
Dass es zu seinem Schatz' als ein Magnet sich neigen
  und tapffer halten will. Kein ande wird gedrückt
  In meine keusche Seel' als den ich erst erblickt.

Die Sonne zwar steht auff und geht des Abends nieder/
Der bleiche Mond nimt ab und kommt gefüllet wieder/
  Auff Hitze folget Kält'/auff Regen Sonnen-schein/
  Auff Traurigkeit die Freud'/auff schertzen Schmertz und Pein.

Mein Hertz' ist nicht also/ das läst sich nicht erregen/
Das soll kein falscher Sturm in Lieb' und Leid bewegen/
  Ich halte wie ein Felss/ der an den üfern steht
  Bey welchem Wind und Fluth mit Spott fürüber geht.

So lang' ein Thier sich wird mit seines gleichen paaren/
So lang' ein Schiffer wird die Wellen überfahren/
  So lange Sonn' und Mond noch haben ihren Schein
  So lang' O Daphnis solst du mein Hertzliebster seyn.

Paul Gerhardt

Geh aus, mein Herz, und suche Freud
In dieser lieben Sommerzeit
An deines Gottes Gaben:
Schau an der schönen Gärten Zier,
Und siehe, wie sie mir und dir
Sich ausgeschmücket haben.

She Boasts of Her Constancy

My heart is not of wax; nor may it one compare
With winds which east and west go creeping through the air.
  It is not like a ship, which at the wave's desire
  Darts back and forth: Oh, I will to no goal aspire

Save to sheer constancy. My way of love shall prove
That it toward its prize does like a magnet move
  And brave will hold its course. No other may abide
  Within my virtuous soul, save him whom first I spied.

The sun, indeed, ascends, yet seeks its nightly den,
The pale moon loses force, yet, fattened, comes again.
  Cold follows after heat, and sunshine after rain,
  Joy after sadness comes, and after jesting pain.

But thus is not my heart. It adamant shall sit,
Nor shall in weal or woe false storms unsettle it.
  I'll hold fast as a cliff which stands upon the shore:
  Against it wind and tide in foolish rage may roar.

As long as animals but with their like will lie,
As long as seamen will across the billows fly,
  As long as sun and moon may still possess their fire,
  So long, oh Daphnis, shall you be my heart's desire.

George C. Schoolfield

Paul Gerhardt

Go out in this dear summertide
And seek to find the joys that bide
In Heaven's gifts, oh heart:
Behold the gardens' lovely hue,
And see how they for me and you
Are decked by fairest art.

Die Bäume stehen voller Laub,
Das Erdreich decket seinen Staub
Mit einem grünen Kleide:
Narzissus und die Tulipan,
Die ziehen sich viel schöner an
Als Salomonis Seide.

Die Lerche schwingt sich in die Luft,
Das Täublein fleucht aus seiner Kluft
Und macht sich in die Wälder.
Die hochbegabte Nachtigall
Ergetzt und füllt mit ihrem Schall
Berg, Hügel, Tal und Felder.

Die Glucke führt ihr Völklein aus,
Der Storch baut und bewohnt sein Haus.
Das Schwälblein speist die Jungen.
Der schnelle Hirsch, das leichte Reh
Ist froh und kommt aus seiner Höh
Ins tiefe Gras gesprungen.

Die Bächlein rauschen in dem Sand
Und malen sich und ihren Rand
Mit schattenreichen Myrthen.
Die Wiesen liegen hart dabei
Und klingen ganz von Lustgeschrei
Der Schaf und ihrer Hirten.

Die unverdrossne Bienenschar
Zeucht hin und her, sucht hier und daar
Ihr edle Honigspeise.
Des süssen Weinstocks starker Saft
Kriegt täglich neue Stärk und Kraft
In seinem schwachen Reise.

Der Weizen wächset mit Gewalt,
Darüber jauchzet Jung und Alt
Und rühmt die grosse Güte
Des, der so überflüssig labt

The trees in fullest leafage rise,
The earth, to give its dust disguise,
Has put a green dress on.
Narcissus and the tulip-bloom
Far finer vestment do assume
Than silks of Solomon.

The lark soars high into the air,
The little dove departs its lair
And takes the woodland's way.
The sweetly gifted nightingale
Fills hill and mountain, field and dale
With song, and makes them gay.

The hen leads out her little troop,
The stork does build and fill his stoop,
Its young the swallow feeds.
The hasty stag, the agile doe
Are glad, and from their heights do go
A-running through the reeds.

The brooklets rustle in the sand
And o'er them and their banks a band
Of shady myrtles keep.
The meadowlands lie close thereby,
Resounding from the happy cry
Of shepherds and their sheep.

The bee-host back and forth has made
Its trips, thus seeking unafraid
Its noble honey-food.
The goodly vine, with juice grown big,
Gets daily in its weakest sprig
Its strength and force renewed.

The wheat grows large with all its might,
And does both young and old delight:
They sing the bounteousness
Of Him Who soothes so generously

Und mit so manchem Gut begabt
Das menschliche Gemüte.

Ich selbsten kann und mag nicht ruhn,
Des grossen Gottes grosses Tun
Erweckt mir alle Sinnen.
Ich singe mit, wenn alles singt,
Und lasse, was dem Höchsten klingt,
Aus meinem Herze rinnen.

Nun Ruhen Alle Wälder

Nun ruhen alle Wälder,
Vieh, Menschen, Städt und Felder,
Es schläft die ganze Welt;
Ihr aber, meine Sinnen,
Auf auf, ihr sollt beginnen,
Was eurem Schöpfer wohlgefällt.

Wo bist du, Sonne, blieben?
Die Nacht hat dich vertrieben,
Die Nacht, des Tages Feind;
Fahr hin! Ein ander Sonne,
Mein Jesus, meine Wonne,
Gar hell in meinem Herzen scheint.

Der Tag ist nun vergangen,
Die güldnen Sterne prangen
Am blauen Himmelssaal;
Also werd ich auch stehen,
Wenn mich wird heißen gehen
Mein Gott aus diesem Jammertal.

Der Leib eilt nun zur Ruhe,
Legt ab das Kleid und Schuhe,

And does such countless property
Upon man's spirit press.

Now I can neither rest, nor will:
Great God's great manufactures thrill
Awake my every sense.
I sing along, when all does sing,
And let what shall to Heaven ring
From out my heart commence.

George C. Schoolfield

Evensong

The woods sleep bathed in shadow,
Beast, borough, man, and meadow;
The whole world is at rest:
But you, my waking senses,
Up, up, your task commences:
Obedient to God's fond request.

Lo sun, where have you vanished?
By night your light is banished;
The night, dark foe of day:
Yet go! a sweeter sunlight,
My Jesus, souls' delight,
Inside my heart shines bright its ray.

Now day has taken flight,
The golden stars, with light
Ignite the glimmering firmament:
I too will just as they,
My Lord's command obey
and pass beyond earth's sad lament.

The body hastes to rest,
Casts off worn shoes and dress,

Das Bild der Sterblichkeit;
Die zieh ich aus. Dagegen
Wird Christus mir anlegen
Den Rock der Ehr und Herrlichkeit.

Nun geht, ihr matten Glieder,
Geht hin und legt euch nieder,
Der Betten ihr begehrt;
Es kommen Stund und Zeiten,
Da man euch wird bereiten
Zur Ruh ein Bettlein in der Erd.

Das Haupt, die Füß und Hände
Sind froh, daß nun zu Ende
Die Arbeit kommen sei;
Herz, freu dich, du sollst werden
Vom Elend dieser Erden
Und von der Sünden Arbeit frei.

Breit aus die Flügel beide,
O Jesu, meine Freude,
Und nimm dein Küchlein ein!
Will Satan mich verschlingen,
So laß die Englein singen:
Dies Kind soll unverletzet sein.

Auch euch, ihr meine Lieben,
Soll heinte nicht betrüben
Ein Unfall noch Gefahr.
Gott laß euch selig schlafen,
Stell euch die güldnen Waffen
Ums Bett und seiner Engel Schar.

Mortality's token sign:
These gladly I'll lay down,
For Christ my soul will gown
In honor's robe of glorious design.

My head and hands and feet,
Contented, gladly greet
The end of daily toil:
Heart, sing! rejoice to be
From earth's sad trials soon free,
Released from sin's oppressive moil.

Weary limbs worn aching-raw,
Seek now rest; to sleep withdraw!
A bed is all you crave:
Yet comes the hour and day,
When deep in mortal clay,
God lays the cradle of your grave.

Spread forth a sheltering wing,
Lord Jesus, joy's true spring,
This fledgling chick encompass!
When Satan hurls hell's fire
Then sing the angels' choir:
Keep safe this child from Lucifer's distress.

And you, my kindred all,
Let not night's purple pall
Awaken thoughts of hazard's awful menace.
God grant you restful sleep,
And round your bedposts keep
His heavenly host with golden swords of grace.

Ingrid Walsøe-Engel

O Haupt voll Blut und Wunden,
Voll Schmerz und voller Hohn,
O Haupt, zu Spott gebunden
Mit einer Dornenkron!
O Haupt, sonst schön gezieret
Mit höchster Ehr und Zier,
Jetzt aber hoch schimpfieret,
Gegrüßet seist du mir!

Die Farbe deiner Wangen,
Der roten Lippen Pracht
Ist hin und ganz vergangen,
Des blassen Todes Macht
Hat alles hingenommen,
Hat alles hingerafft,
Und daher bist du kommen
Von deines Leibes Kraft.

Nun, was du, Herr, erduldet,
Ist alles meine Last,
Ich hab es selbst verschuldet,
Was du Getragen hast!
Schau her, hier steh ich Armer,
Der Zorn verdienet hat,
Gib mir, O mein Erbarmer,
Den Anblick deiner Gnad.

Ich will hier bei dir stehen,
Verachte mich doch nicht!
Von dir will ich nicht gehen,
Wann dir dein Herze bricht.
Wann dein Haupt wird erblassen
Im letzten Todesstoß,
Alsdann will ich dich fassen
In meinen Arm und Schoß.

Ich danke dir von Herzen,
O Jesu, liebster Freund,
Für deines Todes Schmerzen,

O sacred head, now wounded,
With grief and shame weighed down,
Now scornfully surrounded
With thorns, your only crown.
O sacred head, what glory
And bliss did once combine;
Though now despised and gory,
I joy to call mine!

How pale you are with anguish,
With sore abuse and scorn!
Your face, your eyes, now languish,
Which once were bright as morn.
Now from your cheeks has vanished
Their color once so fair;
From loving lips is banished
The splendor that was there.

All this for my transgression,
My wayward soul to win;
This torment of your Passion,
To set me free from sin.
I cast myself before you,
Your wrath my rightful lot;
Have mercy, I implore you,
O Lord, condemn me not!

Here will I stand beside you,
Your death for me my plea;
Let all the world deride you,
I clasp you close to me.
My awe cannot be spoken,
To see you crucified;
But in your body broken,
Redeemed, I safely hide!

What language can I borrow
To thank you, dearest friend,
For this your dying sorrow,

Da du's so gut gemeint.
Ach gib, daß ich mich halte
Zu dir und deiner Treu
Und, wenn ich nun erkalte,
In dir mein Ende sei.

Erscheine mir zum Schilde,
Zum Trost in meinem Tod
Und laß mich sehn dein Bilde
In deiner Kreuzesnot.
Da will ich nach dir blicken,
Da will ich glaubensvoll
Dich fest an mein Herz drücken.
Wer so stirbt, der stirbt wohl.

Der 121. Psalm Davids

Ich erhebe, Herr, zu dir
    meiner beiden Augen Licht;
mein Gesicht ist für und für
    zu den Bergen aufgericht,
zu den Bergen, da herab
ich mein Heil und Hülfe hab.

Meine Hülfe kömmt allein
    von des Schöpfers Händen her,
der so künstlich, hübsch und fein
    Himmel, Erden, Luft und Meer
und was in den allen ist
uns zum besten ausgerüst.

Er nimmt deiner Füsse Tritt,
    o mein Herz, wohl in acht,
wenn du gehest, geht er mit
    und bewahrt dich Tag und Nacht:

Your mercy without end?
Bind me to you forever,
Give courage from above;
Let not my weakness sever
Your bond of lasting love.

Lord, be my consolation,
My constant source of cheer;
Remind me of your Passion,
My shield when death is near.
I look in faith, believing
That you have died for me;
Your cross and crown receiving,
I live eternally.

Lutheran Worship, 1982

The 121st Psalm of David

Now the twin-light of my eyes,
   Oh my Lord, to You I raise;
Lifted up, my vision flies
   To the mountains all my days,
To the mountains, from whose crown
I fetch strength and succor down.

My salvation's sole design
   From the Maker's hands does fare:
He has, artfully and fine,
   Earth and heaven, sea and air
(And whate'er their bounds admit)
Decked out in our benefit.

He with vigilance does guide,
   Oh my heart, your footsteps' way;
Where you go, He at your side
   Goes and keeps you night and day.

Sei getrost, das Höllenheer
wird dir schaden nimmermehr.

Siehe, wie sein Auge wacht,
wenn du liegest in der Ruh!
Wenn du schläfest, kömmt mit Macht
   auf dein Bett geflogen zu
seiner Engel güldne Schar,
dass sie deiner nehme wahr.

Alles was du bist und hast,
   ist umringt mit seiner Hut.
Deiner Sorgen schwere Last
   nimmt er weg, macht alles gut.
Leib und Seel hält er verdeckt,
wenn dich Sturm und Wetter schreckt.

Wenn der Sonnen Hitze brennt
   und des Leibes Kräfte bricht,
wenn dich Stern und Monde blendt
   mit dem klaren Angesicht,
hat er seine starke Hand
dir zum Schatten vorgewandt.

Nun, er fahre immer fort,
   der getreue, fromme Hirt;
bleibe stets dein Schild und Hort.
   Wenn dein Herz geängstet wird,
wenn die Not wird viel und gross,
schliess er dich in seinen Schoss.

Wenn du sitzest, wenn du stehst,
wenn du redest, wenn du hörst,
wenn du aus dem Hause gehst,
   und zurücke wieder kehrst,
wenn du trittst aus oder ein,
   woll er dein Gefährte sein.

Have good cheer: the hellish swarm
Nevermore will do you harm.

See now, his wakeful eye
   E'en to your repose is led!
When you slumber, there does fly
   All in armor to your bed
Quick his angels' golden host,
Taking round you sentry-post.

All you are and all you own,
   He will with His guard defend,
And but take care's heavy stone
   From your back, and make you mend.
He holds soul and body warm,
Though you tremble in the storm.

When the sun's hot fevers smite
   And the body's powers break,
When the stars', the moon's clear light
   Would from you your vision take,
He His mighty hand has laid
Round about you like a shade.

May He thus for evermore
   Be the Shepherd, good and true;
May He stay your shield and store.
   When cruel fears your heart pursue,
When despair is mightiest,
May He close you to His breast.

When you stand and when you sit,
   When you listen, when you speak,
When your household's door you quit,
   Then once more its shelter seek,
Whether out or in you wend,
He will be your constant friend.

George C. Schoolfield

Paul Fleming

An die grosse Stadt Moskaw, als er schiede
1636 Juni 25

Prinzessin deines Reichs, die Holstein Mume nennt,
du wahre Freundin du, durch welcher Gunst wir wagen,
was Fürsten ward versagt und Kön'gen abgeschlagen,
den Weg nach Aufgang zu, wir haben nun erkennt,
   wie sehr dein freundlichs Herz in unsrer Liebe brennt.
Die Treue wollen wir mit uns nach Osten tragen,
und bei der Wiederkunft in unsern Landen sagen,
das Bündnuss ist gemacht, das keine Zeit zertrennt.
   Des frommen Himmels Gunst, die müsse dich erfreuen,
und alles, was du tust, nach Wundsche dir gedeien,
kein Mars und kein Vulkan dir überlästig sein.
   Nim itzo diss Sonnet. Komm ich mit Glücke wieder,
so will ich deinen Preis erhöhn durch stärkre Lieder,
dass deiner Wolgen Schall auch hören sol mein Rhein.

Von sich selber

Ich feure gantz und brenne liechter Loh.
Die Trähnen hier sind meiner Flammen Ammen/
Die mich nicht lässt diss stete Leid verthammen;
Ich kenn' es wohl/ was mich kan machen froh/
   Dass ich fortan nicht dürffte weinen so.
Wo aber ists? So müssen nun die Flammen
hier über mir nur schlagen frey zusammen.
Mein Schirm ist weg/ mein Schutz ist anders wo.
   Ist gantz nichts da/ daran ich mich mag kühlen/

Paul Fleming

To the Great City of Moscow, as He Was Leaving
June 25, 1636

Oh princess of your land, whom Holstein* cousin names,
True mistress you, through whose good offices we dare
That which to kings was barred, denied to princes' prayer:
The way towards the dawn. Our wisdom now acclaims
    How much your friendly heart in our devotion flames.
This faith we will with us toward the Orient bear
And, when we have returned within our lands, declare:
Alliance has been made to flout all future blames.
    May heaven's pious boon your heart with gladness fill,
And all you undertake show fortune at your will.
May Vulcan not, nor Mars, e'er give you cause to grieve.
    This sonnet then accept. Should I with luck return,
Your praise I'll lift on high and stronger stanzas learn
So that my Rhine may too your Volga-sounds perceive.

George C. Schoolfield

Concerning Himself

I'm all afire and from bright blaze annealed.
These tears are of my love the nursing dame,
Who does not wish that I this grief should tame;
I know full well what can such gladness yield
    That instantly my tears would be congealed.
    But where's it hid? For freely may the flame
Here over me its mastery proclaim.
My guard is gone and elsewhere is my shield.
    And is there naught upon which I may cool

*Friedrich III of Holstein-Gottorp sponsored the expeditions that took Fleming on his journeys to Russia and Persia.

In solcher Gluth/ die meine Geister fühlen?
Der Liebes Durst verzehrt mir Marck und Bein.
Diss Wasser ists/ die Kühlung meiner Hitze.
Das ich zum Trunck' aus beyden Augen schwitze.
Ich zapfe selbst/ und Amor schenckt mir ein.

An den Mon

Du, die du standhaft bist in deinem Unbestande,
Steig, Hekate, herab; ich singe dir ein Lied,
Ein Lied von meiner Zier, die itzt auch nach dir sieht,
Ob ich schon bin sehr weit von ihr und ihrem Lande.

Komm, Berezynthie, zu dieses Stromes Rande,
An dem ich geh herum, da meine Hoffnung blüht,
Du weisst es Delie, was itzt mit ihr geschieht,
Du weisst es, wie es steht um meine Salibande.

Komm, Phöbe, Tag der Nacht, Diane, Borgelicht,
Wahrsägrin, Liederfreund; komm, Lune, säume nicht!
Die ganze Welt, die schläft. Ich wache, dich zu loben.

Stromfürstin, Jägerfrau, Nachtauge, Horngesicht,
Herab! Itzt fang ich an das süsse Lobgedicht.
Und kömmst du nicht herab, so hör es nur dort oben!

The awful fires which now my senses rule?
Love's thirsts my marrow and my bone destroy.
  This water is the cooling of my fire,
Which I as drink from both my eyes perspire.
I tap myself and Love's my serving boy.

George C. Schoolfield

To the Moon

You, who inconstancy so constantly can squander,
Great Hecate, descend; to you a song I'll sing
About my pride, whose eyes now to your brilliance cling,
Although I've journeyed far from land and loved one yonder.

Come, Berecynthia,* and join me where I ponder
Beside this river's banks, because my hope's in spring;
You know, oh Delian,† what now her fate may bring,
You know full well what ways my Salibande may wander.

Come, Phoebe,‡ loan-o'-light, Diana, midnight's day,
Song's friend and prophetess, come, Luna, nor delay.
The whole world is asleep. I wake to sing your praises.

Stream-princess, huntress fair, night-eye, and horn-cut face,
Descend! For I'll begin a song to praise your grace.
And if you'll not descend, then hear in Heav'n my phrases.

George C. Schoolfield

---

*One of the many appelations of Hecate–Cybele: after Mount Berecyntus in Phrygia, which was sacred to the goddess.
†Delos was celebrated as the natal island of Apollo and Artemis (Diana).
‡A special name of Artemis–Diana as moon goddess. Note that Fleming uses all the names applied in classical times to the moon goddess: he does not distinguish between such very different goddess "constellations" as Hecate–Cybele and Artemis–Diana.

An Sich

Sei dennoch unverzagt, gib dennoch unverloren,
Weich keinem Glücke nicht, steh höher als der Neid,
Vergnüge dich an dir und acht es für kein Leid,
Hat sich gleich wider dich Glück, Ort und Zeit verschworen.

Was dich betrübt und labt, halt alles für erkoren,
Nimm dein Verhängnüs an, lass alles unbereut.
Tu was getan muss sein, und eh man dirs gebeut.
Was du noch hoffen kannst, das wird noch stets geboren.

Was klagt, was lobt man doch? Sein Unglück und sein Glücke
Ist ihm ein jeder selbst. Schau alle Sachen an:
Dies alles ist in Dir. Lass deinen eitlen Wahn,
Und eh du förder gehst, so geh in dich zurücke.
Wer sein selbst Meister ist und sich beherrschen kann,
Dem ist die weite Welt und alles untertan.

Wie er wolle geküsset sein

Nirgends hin als auf den Mund,
Da sinkts in des Herzen Grund.
Nicht zu frei, nicht zu gezwungen,
Nicht mit gar zu fauler Zungen.

Nicht zu wenig, nicht zu viel,
Beides wird sonst Kinderspiel.
Nicht zu laut und nicht zu leise,
Bei der Mass ist rechte Weise.

Nicht zu nahe, nicht zu weit;
Dies macht Kummer, jenes Leid,
Nicht zu trucken, nicht zu feuchte,
Wie Adonis Venus reichte.

To Himself

Yet do not be afraid, yet give no post forlorn,
Rise over jealousy, and to each joy assent,
Think it no ill but stay with your own self content,
If fortune, place, and time 'gainst you a league have sworn.

Assume that all has plan, if it do soothe or scorn,
Accept your fate and leave each deed without repent,
What must be done, that do, ere orders speed event.
Whate'er you still can hope, can each day still be born.

Why do men mourn or praise? His fortune, weal or woe,
Is each man to himself. Into each thing inquire—
All this resides in you. Your vain dreams let expire,
And go into yourself, before you farther go:
Who's master of himself and rules his own desire
Has subject unto him the mighty globe entire.

George C. Schoolfield

How He Should Like to Be Kissed

Nowhere else but on the mouth,
So that it heart's depths should touch.
Not too free, not too constrained,
Not with tongues too soiled and stained.

Not too little, not too much,
Children's play would each be such.
Not too loud and not too soft,
Moderation keep aloft.

Not too near and not too far,
One brings grief, the other harm.
Not too dry, and not too wet,
As Adonis Venus met.

Nicht zu harte, nicht zu weich,
Bald zugleich, bald nicht zugleich.
Nicht zu langsam, nicht zu schnelle,
Nicht ohn Unterscheid der Stelle.

Halb gebissen, halb gehaucht,
Halb die Lippen eingetaucht.
Nicht ohn Unterscheid der Zeiten,
Mehr alleine, denn bei Leuten.

Küsse nun ein jedermann,
Wie er weiss, will, soll und kann!
Ich nur und die Liebste wissen,
Wie wir uns recht sollen küssen.

Andacht

Ich lebe. Doch nicht ich. Derselbe lebt in mir,
Der mir durch seinen Todt das Leben bringt herfür.
Mein Leben war sein Todt, sein Todt war mir mein Leben,
Nur geb' ich wieder Ihm, was Er mir hat gegeben.
Er lebt durch meinen Todt. Mir sterb' ich täglich ab.
Der Leib, mein Irdnes Theil, der ist der Seelen Grab.
Er lebt nur auff den schein. Wer ewig nicht wil sterben.
Der muss hier in der Zeit verwesen und verderben,
Weil er noch sterben kan. Der Todt, der Geistlich heisst,
Der ist als denn zu spät, wann uns sein Freund hinreisst,
Der unsern Leib bringt um. HERR, gieb mir die Genade,
Dass dieses Leibes-Brauch nicht meiner Seelen schade.
Mein Alles und mein Nichts, mein Leben, meinen Todt,
Das hab' ich bey mir selbst. Hilffst du, so hats nicht noth.
Ich wil, ich mag, ich sol, ich kan mir selbst nicht rahten,
Dich wil ichs lassen thun; du hast bey dir die Thaten.
Die Wünsche thu ich nur. Ich lasse mich gantz dir.
Ich wil nicht meine seyn. Nim mich nur, gieb dich mir.

Not too tender, not too hard,
Now together, now apart.
Not too fast, and not too slow,
Mind you where you pleasures sow.

Half a whisper, half a bite,
Half immersed, the lips unite.
Mind you keep the times in view,
Most alone, 'midst people few.

Kiss indeed let every man,
As he knows, wants, ought, and can.
Only my belov'd and I
Know the kissing we would try.

Harold B. Segel

Devotion

I live; yet 'tis not I. He lives in me,
Who through his death my life did fast decree.
My life to him was death, his death my life,
Now give I him again what once he gave.
Through the death of me he lives. I die each day,
The grave of my body shuts my soul away;
It only seems to live. Who will not die
Must here in time decay and waste and sigh,
While yet he can, die. The spirit's death
Comes then too late, when his friend has robb'd our breath
And laid our body low. Lord, give me grace,
That my body's use may not my soul disgrace.
My Everything, my Nought, my Death, my Life
I have in me. If thou help'st I am safe.
Nor will, nor may, nor can I judge my needs;
That leave I thee, for thou alone hast deeds;
But wishes I. To thee then give I me.
I will not be mine. Only take me; give me thee.

F. Warnke

Es ist umsonst, das Klagen

Es ist umsonst, das Klagen,
Das du um mich
Und ich um dich,
Wir umeinander tragen.
Sie ist umsonst, die harte Pein,
Mit der wir itzt umfangen sein.

Laß das Verhängnis walten.
Was dich dort ziert
Und mich hier führt,
Das wird uns doch erhalten.
Dies, was uns itzt so sehr betrübt,
Ist's dennoch, das uns Freude gibt.

Sei unterdessen meine,
Mein mehr als ich,
Und schau auf mich,
Daß ich bin ewig deine.
Vertraute Liebe weichet nicht,
Hält allzeit, was sie einmal spricht.

Auf alle meine Treue
Sag ich dir's zu:
Du bist es, du,
Der ich mich einzig freue.
Mein Herze, das sich itzt so quält,
Hat dich und keine sonst erwählt.

Bleib, wie ich dich verlassen,
Daß ich dich einst,
Die du itzt weinst,
Mit Lachen mag umfassen.
Dies soll für diese kurze Pein
Uns ewig unsre Freude sein.

Eilt, lauft, ihr trüben Tage,
Eilt, lauft vorbei!

It is in Vain, the Sorrow

It is in vain, the sorrow,
that you with tears
and I with fears
for one another borrow;
and idle is the bitter pain
with which we now our love profane.

Care not though fate assail us.
What makes you dear
and leads me here
will surely never fail us.
And this, which now is sore distress,
is still our source of happiness.

Be mine, and faithless never;
more mine than I,
so you may tie
me to your heart forever.
A love as ours is firm and fast
and keeps its promise to the last.

I swear by all I treasure
that this is true:
it's you, it's you
who gives me peace and pleasure.
My heart, today a heavy stone,
has chosen you, and you alone.

Be as you were hereafter,
that we may reap—
though now you weep—
rewards of love and laughter;
that for this passing time of pain
eternal joy shall be our gain.

Depart, you dreary hours!
Depart from me

Eilt, macht mich frei
Von aller meiner Plage!
Eilt, kommt, ihr hellen Stunden ihr,
Die mir gewähren alle Zier.

Andreas Gryphius

Über die Geburt Jesu

Nacht, mehr denn lichte nacht! nacht, lichter als der tag!
  Nacht, heller als die sonn'! in der das licht geboren,
Das Gott, der licht in licht wohnhafftig, ihm erkohren!
  O nacht, die alle nacht und tage trotzen mag!
  O freudenreiche nacht, in welcher ach und klag
Und finsternis, und was sich auf die welt verschworen,
Und furcht und höllen-angst und schrecken war verlohren!
  Der himmel bricht; doch fällt nunmehr kein donnerschlag.
Der zeit und nächt schuff, ist diese nacht ankommen
Und hat das recht der zeit und fleisch an sich genommen
  Und unser fleisch und zeit der ewigkeit vermacht.
Die jammer trübe nacht, die schwartze nacht der sünden,
Des grabes dunckelheit muss durch die nacht verschwinden.
  Nacht, lichter als der tag! nacht, mehr denn lichte nacht!

Menschliches Elende

Was sind wir menschen doch! ein wohnhaus grimmer schmertzen,
  Ein ball des falschen glücks, ein irrlicht dieser zeit,
  Ein schauplatz herber angst, besetzt mit scharffem leid,
Ein bald verschmeltzter schnee und abgebrannte kertzen.

and set him free
whom yearning grief devours.
But oh, make haste, you sunny days
when beauty fills my heart with praise.

J. W. Thomas

Andreas Gryphius

On the Birth of Jesus

Night, lighter than day! Night, more than brilliant night,
  Night, brighter than the sun, in which the light's erected
That God, light dwelt in light, has for that light elected:
  Oh night, which to all nights, all days may give despite.
  Oh night, replete with joys, in which lament and fright
And gloom and what against the world a plot effected,
And fear and agony and terror were rejected.
  The heavens break, but now no thunderbolt may smite.
Who made time and the nights has on this night descended
And rights of time and flesh unto Himself extended,
  To timelessness our flesh and time has signed away.
  The night grown dull with woe, the night in sin defeated,
The darkness of the grave must by the night be cheated.
  Night, more than brilliant night! Night, lighter than the day!

George C. Schoolfield

Human Misery

What are we men indeed? Grim torment's habitation,
  A toy of fickle luck, wisp in time's wilderness,
  A scene of bitter fear and filled with keen distress,
And tapers burned to stubs, snow's quick evaporation.

Diss leben fleucht davon wie ein geschwätz und schertzen.
  Die vor uns abgelegt des schwachen leibes kleid
  Und in das todten-buch der grossen sterbligkeit
Längst eingeschrieben sind, sind uns aus sinn und hertzen.
  Gleich wie ein eitel traum leicht aus der acht hinfällt
  Und wie ein strom verscheusst, den keine macht auffhält,
So muss auch unser nahm, lob, ehr und ruhm verschwinden.
  Was itzund athem holt, muss mit der lufft entfliehn,
  Was nach uns kommen wird, wird uns ins grab nachziehn.
Was sag ich? wir vergehn, wie rauch von starcken winden.

Thränen des Vaterlandes, Anno 1636

Wir sind doch nunmehr gantz, ja mehr denn gantz verheeret.
  Der frechen völcker schaar, die rasende posaun,
  Das vom blut fette schwerdt, die donnernde carthaun
Hat aller schweiss und fleiss und vorrath auffgezehret.
Die thürme stehn in glut, die kirch ist umgekehret,
  Das rathaus liegt im graus, die starcken zind zerhaun,
  Die jungfern sind geschänd't, und wo wir hin nur schaun,
Ist feuer, pest und tod, der hertz und geist durchfähret.
  Hier durch die schantz und stadt rinnt allzeit frisches blut.
  Dreymal sind schon sechs jahr, als unser ströme flut
Von leichen fast verstopfft, sich langsam fort gedrungen.
  Doch schweig ich noch von dem, was ärger als der tod,
  Was grimmer denn die pest und glut und hungersnoth.
Dass auch der seelen-schatz so vielen abgezwungen.

This life does flee away like jest or conversation;
   Those who before us laid aside the body's dress
   And in the doomsday-book of monster mortalness
Old entry found, have left our mind's and heart's sensation.
   Just as an empty dream from notice lighty flees,
   And as a stream is lost whose course no might may cease,
So must our honor, fame, our praise and name be ended.
   What presently draws breath, must perish with the air,
   What after us will come, someday our grave will share.
What do I say? We pass as smoke on strong winds wended.

George C. Schoolfield

Tears of the Fatherland, Anno Domini 1636

Entire, more than entire have we been devastated!
   The maddened clarion, the bold invaders' horde,
   The mortar thunder-voiced, the blood-annointed sword
Have all men's sweat and work and store annihilated.
The towers stand in flames, the church is violated,
   The strong are massacred, a ruin our council board;
   Our maidens raped, and where my eyes have scarce explored
Fire, pestilence, and death my heart have dominated.
   Here through the moat and town runs always new-let blood,
   And for three-times-six years our very rivers' flood
With corpses choked has pressed ahead in tedious measure;
   I shall not speak of that which is still worse than death,
   And crueler than the plague and torch and hunger's breath:
From many has been forced even the spirit's treasure.

George C. Schoolfield

An die Sternen

Ihr lichter, die ich nicht auf erden satt kan schauen,
   Ihr fackeln, die ihr nacht und schwartze wolcken trennt,
   Als diamante spielt und ohn auffhören brennt;
Ihr blumen, die ihr schmückt des grossen himmels auen;
Ihr wächter, die, als gott die welt auff-wolte-bauen,
   Sein wort, die weisheit selbst, mit rechten namen nennt,
   Die Gott allein recht misst, die Gott allein recht kennt,
(Wir blinden sterblichen! was wollen wir uns trauen!)
   Ihr bürgen meiner lust! wie manche schöne nacht
   Hab ich, in dem ich euch betrachtete, gewacht?
Herolden dieser zeit! wenn wird es doch geschehen,
   Dass ich, der eurer nicht allhier vergessen kan,
   Euch, derer liebe mir steckt hertz und geister an,
Von andern sorgen frey werd unter mir besehen?

An sich selbst

Mir grauet vor-mir selbst; mir zittern alle glieder,
   Wenn ich die lipp' und nas' und beider augen klufft,
   Die blind vom wachen sind, des athems schwere lufft
Betracht' und die nun schon erstorbnen augen-lieder.
Die zunge, schwartz vom brand, fällt mit den worten nieder
   Und lallt, ich weiss nicht was; die müde seele rufft
   Dem grossen tröster zu, das fleisch reucht nach der grufft,
Die ärtzte lassen mich, die schmertzen kommen wieder.
   Mein cörper ist nicht mehr als adern, fell, und bein.
   Das sitzen ist mein tod, das liegen meine pein.
Die schenckel haben selbst nun träger wol vonnöthen.
   Was ist der hohe ruhm und jugend, ehr und kunst?
   Wenn diese stunde kommt, wird alles rauch und dunst,
Und eine noth muss uns mit allem vorsatz tödten.

To the Stars

You lights, for which on earth my sight's thirst ne'er is stilled,
  You torches, which the night and ebon clouds entame,
  Which glow like diamonds and without ceasing flame,
You flowers, which the fields of mighty Heaven gild,
You watchmen, who when God the orb of earth would build,
  His word, high wisdom, did by proper title name,
  You stars whose way and bounds great God alone can claim:
(Blind mortals! How can we to trust ourselves be willed?)
    You pledges of my joy! How many a wondrous night
    Have I held vigil while I pondered on your light?
Oh heralds of this time! When will it be my fare,
    That I, who here below can never you forget,
    You stars, whose love my heart and soul to fire does set,
Shall see you under me, all freed from alien care?

George C. Schoolfield

To Himself

I sicken of myself, my members all are shaking,
  When I my lip and nose, my breathing's heavy wave,
  My lids already numb, and next my two eyes' cave
Will contemplate, which last are blind from too long waking.
My tongue, with fever black and sense of words forsaking,
  Babbles I know not what, my spent soul can but crave
  The great consoler's aid, my flesh smells of the grave.
The doctors leave me now, whom pains again are taking.
  My body is no more than skin and bone and vein;
  To sit my certain death, and yet to lie my pain,
My thighs themselves are come into the need of bearers.
  Of what do lofty fame, youth, honor, art consist?
  When this hour has approached, all turns to smoke and mist,
One curse with all design must slay us through its terrors.

George C. Schoolfield

Abend

Der schnelle tag ist hin; die nacht schwingt ihre fahn
    Und führt die sternen auf. Der menschen müde scharen
Verlassen feld und werck; wo thier und vögel waren,
    Traurt itzt die einsamkeit. Wie ist die zeit verthan!
    Der port naht mehr und mehr sich zu der glieder kahn.
Gleich wie diss licht verfiel, so wird in wenig jahren
Ich, du, und was man hat, und was man sieht, hinfahren.
    Diss leben kömmt mir vor als eine renne-bahn.
Lass, höchster Gott! mich doch nicht auf dem lauffplatz gleiten!
Lass mich nicht ach, nicht pracht, nicht lust, nicht angst verleiten!
    Dein ewig-heller glantz sey vor und neben mir!
Lass, wenn der müde leib entschläfft, die seele wachen,
Und wenn der letzte tag wird mit mir abend machen,
    So reiss mich aus dem thal der finsternis zu dir!

Mitternacht

Schrecken und stille und dunckeles grausen, finstere kälte bedecket
    das land.
Itzt schläfft, was arbeit und schmertzen ermüdet; diss sind der
    traurigen einsamkeit stunden.
Nunmehr ist, was durch die lüffte sich reget, nunmehr sind
    menschen und thiere verschwunden.
    Ob zwar die immerdar schimmernde lichter der ewig
        schitternden sternen entbrant,
    Suchet ein fleissiger sinn noch zu wachen, der durch bemühung
        der künstlichen hand
Ihm die auch nach uns ankommende seelen, ihm, die anitzt sich
    hier finden, verbunden?
Wetzet ein blutiger mörder die klinge? wil er unschuldiger hertzen
    verwunden?
    Sorget ein ehren-begehrend gemüthe, wie zu erlangen ein
        höherer stand?

Evening

The rapid day is gone; her banner swings the night,
   And leads the stars aloft. Men's wearied hosts have wended
Away from field and work; where beast and bird attended,
   Now solitude laments. How vain has been time's flight!
   The vessel of our limbs draws nearer to the bight.
In but a little while, just as this light descended,
Will I, you, what we have, and what we see be ended.
   E'en as a runner's track seems life within my sight.
Great God, grant me that I in coursing do not blunder!
Nor joy trick me nor fear nor woe nor earthly wonder!
   Let Your unfailing light my comrade be and guide!
When my tired body sleeps, grant that my soul be waking,
And when the final day my eventide is making.
   Then take me from this vale of darkness to Your side!

George C. Schoolfield

Midnight

Terror and stillness and ebon-hued horror, night in its iciness
   covers the land.
These are the hours of sad isolation; sleeps soothes the victims of
   labor and pain.
Vanished are men now, and animals vanished, nor do the troublers
   of Heaven remain.
   Though the eternally shimmering lanterns of the e'er glittering
   stars fiery stand.
   Does an industrious mind keep its vigil, which through the
   efforts of talented hand,
Allies itself with the souls that succeed us, and with the folk of
   earth's present domain?
Do bloody murderers sharpen their daggers? Shall by them
   innocent spirits be slain?
   Does an ambitious heart wake in its worry, how higher rank it
   might think to command?

Sterbliche! Sterbliche! lasset diss dichten! Morgen, ach morgen,
    ach muss man hinziehn!
Ach wir verschwinden gleich als die gespenste, die um die stund
    uns erscheinen und fliehn!
Wenn uns die finstere gruben bedecket, wird, was wir wündschen
    und suchen, zu nichte.
Doch wie der gläntzende morgen eröffnet, was weder monde
    noch fackel bescheint,
So wenn der plötzliche tag wird anbrechen, wird was geredet,
    gewürcket, gemeynt,
Sonder vermänteln eröffnet sich finden vor des erschrecklichen
    Gottes gerichte.

Einsamkeit

In dieser einsamkeit der mehr denn öden wüsten,
    Gestreckt auf wildes kraut, an die bemooste see,
    Beschau ich jenes thal und dieser felsen höh',
Auf welchen eulen nur und stille vögel nisten.
Hier, fern von dem pallast, weit von des pöbels lüsten,
    Betracht ich, wie der mensch in eitelkeit vergeh',
    Wie auf nicht festem grund' all unser hoffen steh',
Wie die vor abend schmähn, die vor dem tag uns grüssten.
    Die höl', der rauhe wald, der todtenkopff, der stein,
    Den auch die zeit auffrisst, die abgezehrten bein
Entwerffen in dem muth unzehliche gedancken.
    Der mauren alter graus, diss ungebaute land
    Ist schön und fruchtbar mir, der eigentlich erkannt,
Dass alles, ohn ein geist, den Gott selbst hält, muss wancken.

Mortal men! mortal men! let this be written! Oh, with
    tomorrow, tomorrow, we die!
Oh, we must vanish e'en as the fey spirits, which at this hour
    surprise us and fly!
All that we wish for and seek for, is nothing, when by the gloom of
    the grave we're concealed;
Yet as the glittering morning lays open what neither moonlight
    nor torchlight could find,
So, when that sudden day enters upon us, all that was born of
    the tongue, hand, and mind,
Will in the terrible courtroom of Heaven, stripped of its cover stand
    bare and revealed!

George C. Schoolfield

Solitude

In this deep solitude of wastes more than forlorn,
    At rest on wild-grown grass, beside the mossy sea,
    I gaze upon that vale, these high cliffs' aery
On which the owls alone and silent birds do mourn.
Far from the rabble's joys and from the palace borne,
    I contemplate: how man must pass in vanity
    And how each solid ground our every hope must flee,
How welcomes at the dawn are changed to twilight's scorn.
    The cave, the barbarous wood, the death's-head and the stone,
    Which also time devours, the flesh-depleted bone
Have sketched within my soul of thoughts an endless chain.
    The ramparts' ancient wreck, this land without the plow
    Is rich alone to him who has determined now
That all must fail whose soul does not in God remain.

George C. Schoolfield

Eitelkeit der Welt

Du siehst, wohin du siehst, nur Eitelkeit auf Erden.
Was dieser heute baut, reißt jener morgen ein;
Wo jetzund Städte stehn, wird eine Wiese sein,
Auf der ein Schäferkind wird spielen mit den Herden.

Was jetzund prächtig blüht, soll bald zertreten werden;
Was jetzt so pocht und trotzt, ist morgen Asch' und Bein;
Nichts ist, das ewig sei, kein Erz, kein Marmorstein.
Jetzt lacht das Glück uns an, bald donnern die Beschwerden.

Der hohen Taten Ruhm muß wie ein Traum vergehn.
Soll denn das Spiel der Zeit der leichte Mensch bestehn?
Ach, was ist alles dies, was wir für köstlich achten,

Als schlechte Nichtigkeit, als Schatten, Staub und Wind,
Als eine Wiesenblum', die man nicht wieder findt!
Noch will, was ewig ist, kein einig Mensch betrachten.

Johann Klaj

Spazierlust

Hellglänzendes Silber, mit welchem sich gatten
der astigen Linden weitstreifende Schatten,
    deine sanftkühlend-geruhige Lust
      ist jedem bewusst!
Wie sollten kunst-ahmende Pinsel bemalen
die Blätter, die schirmen vor brennenden Strahlen?
    Keiner der Stämme, so grünlich beziert,
      die Ordnung verführt.
Es lispeln und wispeln die schlüpfrige Brunnen,

All Is Vanity

You see, where'er you look, on earth but vainness' hour.
Tomorrow will destroy that which was built today;
The meadow where the boy a-shepherding will play
Together with his flock, there now the cities tower.

That will be trampled soon which now is full in flower,
The morrow's ash and bone do now defiance inveigh;
No bronze nor marble stands that will not pass away.
Now fortune laughs, but we are soon in hardship's power.

The fame of noble deeds must like a dream desist,
Shall then the toy of time, inconstant man, persist?
Oh, what are all these things for which we long endeavor

But wretched nothingness, but wind and dust and shade,
A flower of the field from which our eyes have strayed!
Yet no man contemplates what will endure for ever.

George C. Schoolfield

Johann Klaj

Stroll-Joy

Oh bright-glancing Silver, who marriage has made
With branch-blessed linden's wide-wandering shade,
    Your gentle-cooling, your calm delight's fall
        Is known to us all.
How should then the art-aping brushes dare paint
The leaves which defend us from sun's hot constraint?
    None of the tree-trunks, so greenly adorned,
        Has order suborned.
They lisp and whisper, these slippery wells:

von ihnen ist diese Begrünung gerunnen.
Sie schauren, betrauren und fürchten bereit
die schneeichte Zeit.

AUF! güldenes Leben! glückliche Nacht!
Die Sonne hat sich zu Bette gemacht.
Ihr Gäste! Halt' feste die Früchte der Reben,
Ein jeder sei wieder zu trinken bedacht.
Nun heisset geschnittene Gläser hergeben.
Wie? Trauret ihr, wann die Fröhlichkeit wacht?
Auf güldenes Leben!

Der silberne Monde schimmert mit Macht,
Er führet auf die beflammete Wacht.
Die Zinken die winken, die Saiten die beben,
Man höret der Musik lieblichen Pracht.
Auf lasset die Becher fein reihenweis heben.
Dem Bräutigam haben wir dieses gebracht.
Auf güldenes Leben!

Philipp von Zesen

Abendlied

Es hat nun mehr das güldne Licht
Des Himmels seinen Lauf verricht',
Der Tag hat sich geneiget;
Der blasse Mond steht auf der Wacht,
Die Sterne leuchten durch die Nacht,
Der süße Schlaf sich zeiget.

From them all this greening, this growing all swells.
They shake, waking solemn, and already fear
The snow's time of year.

George C. Schoolfield

Oh golden life, waken! Fortunate night!
The sun's orb to bed had taken its flight!
You guests! Shall the best of the vine spill or shake?
Again to the cup each his promise must plight.
Now let the carved goblets their cupboards forsake!
What! Can you be saddened at merriment's sight!
Oh golden life, wake!

The moon in its silver shimmers with might,
Leading aloft the hot stars in their light.
The zincs as they wink and the strings as they quake
For sweet music's splendors our ears do excite.
Fair, row after row, we our beakers do take,
And now to the bridegroom this paeon recite!
Oh golden life, wake!

George C. Schoolfield

Philipp von Zesen

Evening Song

The golden light has presently
Its coursing through the sky let be;
The day its kingdom ends.
The pale moon keeps its sentry post,
Through darkness shines the starry host,
And gentle sleep descends.

Ei, nun will ich in sanfter Ruh
Die Nacht mit Schlafen bringen zu,
Ermüdet durch viel Schreiben,
Das durch den langen Tag ich trieb,
Bis mir die Nacht den Paß verhieb,
Die Sinnen fortzutreiben.

Indessen sei mein Glanz und Licht
Dein freudenreiches Angesicht,
O Sonne meiner Seelen,
Daß nicht der Nächte Schatten mich
Mit Frucht und Schrecken inniglich
Im Herzen möge quälen.

Nimm weg den schweren Sündenschwall,
So sich ereiget überall,
Aus meines Herzens Schranken.
Daß ich fein sanfte ruhen mag,
Und, wann nun kömmt der frühe Tag,
Dir, Höchster, freudig danken.

Hiermit will ich nun schlafen ein,
Und dir, o Gott, ergeben sein,
Du wirst mich wohl erretten.
Behüte mich für schnellem Tod,
Für aller Angst und Krieges Not
Und für des Teufels Ketten.

An die übermenschliche Adelmund/
als sie den geschehenen kus ungeschehen machen wolte

Es ist geschehn/ mein Lieb/ mein schatz/ mein tod/ mein Leben;
der schus ist loss-gebrand/ der kus ist auf den mund verstohlen
    abgegeben.
Was wil doch ihre hand
    der schon-getahnen taht noch lange widerstreben?

Oh, I shall now in sweet repose
See how the night in slumber goes,
Exhausted by my pen,
With which throughout the day I strove,
Until the fall of darkness drove
My senses from their ken.

But let my glow, my flame advance
From out your joyful countenance,
Oh sunlight of my soul,
That not the shadows of the night
With terror make and cozy fright
My heart a torture-hole.

Remove that heavy swell of sin,
Which everywhere has entered in,
From my heart's bounds away,
That I may sweetly sleep, and that
I thank you, Lord, all joyful at
The coming of the day.

Now I shall lay me down to sleep
And give my soul, God, to your keep,
Which surely you will save.
Protect me from a hasty death,
From terror and from war's cruel breath,
Nor make me Satan's slave.

George C. Schoolfield

To the Superhuman Adelmund, When She Would Undo the Kiss Already Done

Oh, it is done, my love, my death, my life, my prize,
The shot is fired away; my kiss unto your mouth was brought in
  thievish wise.
But why will then her hand
The deed already done still seek to fend away?

Das feuchte wasser-land/
darüber durch den tag die sonne pflegt zu schweben/
weis keinen wider-stand;
die strahlen ziehn es aus/ es lächzet mit dem munde
nach einem kühlen tau.   so hat auch durch den tag
ihr sonnen-augen-blitz/ den ich so heis entfunde/
mich feuchte-loss gemacht/ dass ich wohl seuftzen mag
nach ihrem lippen-tau/ der grossen gluht zu steuren/
die sie in mier entzündt mit ihren augen-feuren.

Sigmund von Birken

Hirtengedicht

Hier sitz' ich an dem Rand/ in deines Ufers Schatten/
   Du schlanker Pegnitzfluss/ hier nehm' ich meine Rast/
   Hier schau ich deiner Fluht nicht-ungestuemmen Brast/
   Hier seh ich neben dir die frischbegruenten Matten.

Du aber/ Vatterstrom in meinem Mutterland/
   Ist dein Geraeusche dann von Lust so weit entsessen/
   Dass deiner Ufer mich ein fremdes macht vergessen?
   Nein/Ungluekk Ungluekk hat dich mir/mich dir entwandt.

Es schwebet ueber dir ein schweres Himmelhassen/
   Der Weltgemeinde Sturm/ des Krieges Jammerglut.
   Kuertz'/ O du Wolkengott/ des starken Wetters Wut/

Lass ach! die Eger frey durchrauschen ihre Gassen/

The damp and watery land
O'er which the sun is wont to hang throughout the day,
Cannot its heat withstand;
The radiance sucks it dry, and for refreshing dew
Its poor mouth pants. And thus throughout the day there's freed
By her eyes' solar fire, which I so hotly knew,
A draught of damp in me, that I must sigh indeed
Toward her dewy lips, to check that mighty glow
Which she with torch of eye within my soul did sow.

George C. Schoolfield

Sigmund von Birken

Shepherd-Song

I sit here at your edge, in your embankment's screen,
　　You slender Pegnitz-tide;* here I do seek repose,
　　Here I see how your flight in hasteless vigor goes,
　　Here I beside you watch the meadows freshly green.

Oh father-flood which cuts my mother region through,
　　Is then your sound from joy at such great distance set
　　That on a foreign strand I must your strand forget?
　　No, mishap you from me did take and me from you.

There hovers over you a heavy Heaven's hate,
　　The world-troop's hurricane, the war's hot plunderage.
　　Make brief, oh welkin-god, the awful tempest's rage.

　　Oh let the Eger† free its paths negotiate

*The river Pegnitz.
†Birken was born in 1626 at Wildenstein near the town of Eger, through which flows the river of the same name. He came to Nuremberg, on the "slender Pegnitz-tide," in 1645; eleven years after the murder of Wallenstein in Eger's council hall had given the little northern Sudeten town a certain gruesome fame. Even in the final years of the Thirty Years' War the region saw heavy military activity on the part of both Lutheran and Imperial forces, and it is to this seemingly endless misery of his birthplace that Birken refers.

Die manches Thal durchwaescht. Dann soll mir ihre Lust
Staets eine Wollust seyn/ ein suesser Sinnenmust.

Hirtengedicht

Jener mag fluechtige Froelichkeit finden/
Kraentze von schaetzbaren Bluemelein binden.
Unsere Blumen/ so jedermann frey/
Bringen das Singen zur Schaefer-Schalmey.
    Die froelichen Lieder
    Erfreuen uns wieder.
Wir ruhen voll riechenden Dufftens allhier.

Blumen/ in niemahls-bepflantzeten Garten/
Blumen/von wilden/ doch lieblichen Arten.
Lentzen-beglaentzend-erneurender Lust
Hurtigen Hirten und Heerden bewust.
    Beschminket die Felder/
    Beschmukket die Waelder.
Wir leben voll loeblicher Liebesbegier.

Flora/ die sonder Bemuehung gebieret/
Unsere Wiesen und Fluesse bezieret/
Schliesset den schrofen truebkiesslichen Sand/
Mahlet die Ufer mit buntlicher Hand.
    Die Pegnitz Najaden
    Sich neben ihr baden/
Wir sehen die nakkicht/ entweichet mit mir!

And water many dales. Then will its joy for me
Sweet cider of the sense, and endless pleasure be.

George C. Schoolfield

Shepherd-Song

All men may hasty-gone happiness find,
Wreaths out of gold-worthy blossoms may bind;
Flowers which everyone picks to his need
Bring us sweet singing to shepherd-boy's reed.
     These high-hearted lays
     Make merry our days.
We rest full of fragrancy's sweet company.

Flowers from gardens that never knew spade,
Flowers in wild and yet lovely parade,
Sparkle-spring's gladness renewing its shine,
Known to the swift-footed shepherds and kine.
     Embellish the field,
     Emblazon the weald.
We live full of laudable love-lechery.

Flora, who fleeing each labor can bear,
Gives stream and meadow adornments to wear,
Closes the cruel, the sad-graveled sand,
Patterns the banks with a many-hued hand.
     The Pegnitz-sprites ride
     The waves at her side.
We see them all naked; come, vanish with me!

George C. Schoolfield

Christian Hofmann von Hofmannswaldau

Er liebt vergebens

Ich finde keinen Rat, die Liebe wächst alleine
Und wenig neben mir, es sei denn meine Not,
Die Brunst bestricket mich, warum nicht auch der Tod?
Frisst jene Mark und Fleisch, so fresse der die Beine.
Was aber hilft mein Wunsch, was hilfts mich, dass ich weine?
Der Tod hört nicht viel mehr, als sonst der Liebesgott,
Wo sollte meine Qual und meines Lebens Spott
Nun besser sein bedeckt als unter einem Steine?
Und bin ich endlich tot, vergraben und verscharrt,
So schwatzt die Grabschrift noch, dass dieser Mensch genarrt,
Und sagt: Hier liegt ein Narr und lässt nicht wenig Erben.
Ach! dass den schwarzen Leib das erste Wasserbad,
So mir die Mutter gab, nicht bald ersäufet hat,
So dürft ich jetzt allhier nicht wie ein Narr verderben.

Vergänglichkeit der Schönheit

Es wird der bleiche Tod mit seiner kalten Hand
Dir endlich mit der Zeit um deine Brüste streichen,
Der liebliche Corall der Lippen wird verbleichen:
Der Schultern warmer Schnee wird werden kalter Sand,

Der Augen süsser Blitz, die Kräfte deiner Hand,
Für welchen solches fällt, die werden zeitlich weichen.
Das Haar, das itzund kann des Goldes Glanz erreichen,
Tilgt endlich Tag und Jahr als ein gemeines Band.

Der wohlgesetzte Fuss, die lieblichen Gebärden,
Die werden teils zu Staub, teils nichts und nichtig werden,
Denn opfert keiner mehr der Gottheit deiner Pracht.

Christian Hofmann von Hofmannswaldau

He Loves in Vain

Love grows alone (though I my brain for counsel harrow),
And little's at my side unless it be despair.
If lust entangles me, why not a deathly snare?
Let death have then my bones, if lust eats flesh and marrow.
But death heeds me no more than does the god with arrow:
What profit that I weep? What profit my desire?
Where should my parody of life, my pain require
A better hiding place then 'neath the stony barrow.
And when I'm finally dead and buried and decayed,
My epitaph will boast that I a fool was made,
And say: "Here lies a fool, who many leaves successor."
Oh! if that newborn bath which me my mother gave
Had drowned my blackened self straightway into the grave,
I were not presently but foolish ruin's possessor.

George C. Schoolfield

Beauty's Transitoriness

Then pallid death at last will with his icy hand,
Where time hides in the palm, your lovely breasts contain;
The coral of your lips will from its beauty wane,
Your shoulder's warmth of snow will change to icy sand.

Sweet lightning of your eyes, the powers of your hand,
That do such conquests make, will but brief hours remain.
Your locks, which presently the glance of gold attain,
The day and year at last will ruin in common band.

Your well-placed foot will then, your movements in their grace,
To naught and nothing part, and part to dust give place.
Before your splendor's god no offering more is laid.

Diss und noch mehr als diss muss endlich untergehen.
Dein Herze kann allein zu aller Zeit bestehen,
Dieweil es die Natur aus Diamant gemacht.

Beschreibung vollkommener Schönheit

Ein haar, so kühnlich trotz der Berenice spricht,
Ein mund, der rosen führt und perlen in sich heget,
Ein zünglein, so ein gifft vor tausend hertzen träget,
   Zwo brüste, wo rubin durch alabaster bricht.
Ein hals, der schwanen-schnee weit weit zurücke sticht.
Zwey wangen, wo die pracht der Flora sich beweget,
Ein blick, der blitze führt und männer niederleget,
   Zwey armen, derer krafft offt leuen hingericht,
Ein hertz, aus welchem nichts als mein verderben quillet,
   Ein wort, so himmlisch ist, und mich verdammen kan,
   Zwey hände, derer grimm mich in den bann gethan,
Und durch ein süsses gifft die seele selbst umhüllet,
   Ein zierrath, wie es scheint, im paradiess gemacht,
   Hat mich um meinen witz und meine freyheit bracht.

    Wo sind die Stunden
    Der süßen Zeit,
    Da ich zuerst empfunden,
    Wie deine Lieblichkeit
    Mich dir verbunden?
    Sie sind verrauscht. Es bleibet doch dabei,
    Daß alle Lust vergänglich sei.

This and still more than this at last must pass away.
Your heart alone has strength its constant self to stay,
Since nature this same heart of diamond has made.

George C. Schoolfield

Description of Perfect Beauty

A hair which boldly speaks in Bernice's* despite,
A mouth which starts with rose and pearls within it hides,
A tonguelet where a bane for thousand hearts resides,
    Two breasts where ruby breaks through alabaster's white,
    A throat which snow of swans has put to distant flight,
Two cheeks within whose veins the pomp of Flora glides,
A glance which conquers men and lightning's weapon guides,
    Two arms whose power has oft wild lions slain in flight,
A heart from which alone my ruination flows,
    A word which both can damn and yet from Heaven stem,
    Two hands, whose awful rage can me to death condemn
And through sweet bane a cloak about the spirit throws:
    An ornament, it seems, born out of Paradise,
    Has made me both my sense and freedom sacrifice.

George C. Schoolfield

So sweet, so golden,
Where is the time
When I came first to bolden
And own your beauty's prime
Had me beholden?
It pearled away, as though again to show
That earthly joys which come, must go.

---

*Hofmannswalsdau is probably referring to Berenice (Bernice), the daughter of Agrippa I, whose beauty caused such confusion in the heart of Titus, Roman emperor-to-be.

Das reine Scherzen,
So mich ergetzt
Und in dem tiefen Herzen
Sein Merkmal eingesetzt,
Läßt mich in Schmerzen.
Du hast mir mehr als deutlich kundgetan,
Daß Freundlichkeit nicht ankern kann.

Empfangene Küsse,
Ambrierter Saft,
Verbleibt nicht lange süße
Und kommt von aller Kraft;
Verrauschte Flüsse
Erquicken nicht. Was unsern Geist erfreut
Entspringt aus Gegenwärtigkeit.

Ich schwamm in Freude,
Der Liebe Hand
Spann mir ein Kleid von Seide;
Das Blatt hat sich gewandt,
Ich geh im Leide,
Ich wein itzund, daß Lieb und Sonnenschein
Stets voller Angst und Wolken sein.

Angelus Silesius (Johannes Scheffler)

Aus dem Cherubinischen Wandersmann

1. Man weiss nicht, was man ist
Ich weiss nicht, was ich bin; ich bin nicht, was ich weiss;
Ein Ding und nicht ein Ding; ein Tüpfchen und ein Kreis.
2. Ich bin wie Gott, und Gott wie ich
Ich bin so gross als Gott, er ist als ich so klein;
Er kann nicht über mich, ich unter ihm nicht sein.

Your pleasantnesses,
So arch, so fleet,
Which in my heart's recesses
Found permanent retreat
Have brought distresses.
You more than clearly made me understand
That friendliness is drifting sand.

A kiss's flavor,
Its perfumed taste,
Keeps not for long its savor
And quickly goes to waste.
An emptied quaver
Is little use. For hearts to gather force,
A presentness must be the source.

I swam in pleasure;
The hand of love
Dressed me in silk to measure.
But pain, decreed above,
Fills now my leisure:
And I bewail that love and sunny skies
Prepare for heavy clouds and sighs.

Alexander Gode

Angelus Silesius (Johann Scheffler)

From the Cherubical Wanderer

    1. One Knows Not What One Is
I know not what I am, and what I know, I'm not:
A thing and not a thing, a circle and a dot.
    2. I Am As God And God As I
I am as large as God, and God as small as I;
He cannot over me, nor I beneath Him lie.

3. Leib, Seele, und Gottheit
Die Seel ist ein Kristall, die Gottheit ist ihr Schein;
Der Leib, in dem du lebst, ist ihrer beider Schrein.

4. Ein jedes in dem Seinigen
Der Vogel in der Luft, der Stein ruht auf dem Land;
Im Wasser lebt der Fisch, mein Geist in Gottes Hand.

5. Im Eckstein liegt der Schatz
Was marterst du das Erz? der Eckstein ist's allein,
In dem Gesundheit, Gold, und alle Künste sein.

6. Wer ganz vergöttet ist
Wer ist, als wär er nicht und wär er nie geworden,
Der ist, o Seligkeit, zu lauter Gotte worden.

7. Die geistliche Goldmachung
Ich selbst bin das Metall, der Geist ist Feu'r und Herd,
Messias die Tinktur, die Leib und Seel verklärt.

8. Die Rose
Die Rose, welche hier dein äuss'res Auge sieht,
Die hat von Ewigkeit in Gott also geblüht.

9. Bei Gott ist nur sein Sohn
Mensch, werd aus Gott gebor'n: bei seiner Gottheit Thron
Steht niemand anders als der eingebor'ne Sohn.

10. Die geheime Jungfrauschaft
Wer lauter wie das Licht, rein wie der Ursprung ist,
Derselbe wird von Gott für Jungfrau auserkiest.

11. Gott ist mir, was ich will
Gott ist mein Stab, mein Licht, mein Pfad, mein Ziel, mein Spiel,
 Mein Vater, Bruder, Kind, und alles, was ich will.

12. Das Licht besteht im Feuer
Das Licht gibt allem Kraft: Gott selber lebt im Lichte,
Doch wär er nicht das Feu'r, so würd es bald zu nichte.

13. Die geistliche Arch' und's Manna-Krügelein
Mensch, ist dein Herze Gold und deine Seele rein,
So kannst du auch die Arch' und's Manna-Krüglein sein.

14. Gott ist nichts (Kreatürliches)
Gott ist wahrhaftig nichts, und so er etwas ist,
So ist er's nur in mir, wie er mich ihm erkiest.

15. Der Mensch ist's höchste Ding
Nichts dünkt mich hoch zu sein: ich bin das höchste Ding,
Weil auch Gott ohne mich ihm selber ist gering.

3. Body, Soul, And Godhead
The soul a crystal is, the Godhead is its shine,
The flesh in which you live is of them both the shrine.

4. Each In His Own
The bird rests in the air, the stone rests on the land,
In water lives the fish, my spirit in God's hand.

5. The Treasure Lies In The Cornerstone
Why do you rack the ore? The cornerstone alone
Does call good health and gold and every art its own.

6. Whoever Has Become All Divine
Who is, as if he weren't and ne'er had even come,
He is, oh blessedness, a purest God become.

7. The Spiritual Alchemy
The metal I, the soul the hearth, the blaze that warms.
Messiah is the dye, that flesh and blood transforms.

8. The Rose
The rose, regarded here by your external eyes,
In God eternally has blossomed on this wise.

9. Only His Son Is With God
Oh man, be born of God: for at His Godhead's throne
None other than His Son, there born, a place may own.

10. The Secret Virginity
Who pure as light and chaste as origin has stayed,
That man has been by God elected as His maid.

11. God Is To Me What I Desire
God is my staff, my path, my goal, my game, my fire,
My father, brother, child, and all that I desire.

12. The Light Exists In The Fire
To all things light gives force; God dwells Himself in light,
Yet were He not the fire, then it would soon be night.

13. The Spiritual Ark And The Manna-Vessel
Man, if your heart is gold, and if your soul is pure,
Then you can be the ark and manna hold secure.

14. God Is Nothing (Physical)
Now God is truly naught, and if He aught may be,
He's it in me alone, as He for Him takes me.

15. Man Is The Highest Thing
I think naught great: I am the highest thing of all,
Since lacking me e'en God before Himself is small.

16. Je aufgegebener, je göttlicher

Die Heiligen sind so viel von Gottes Gottheit trunken,
So viel sie sind in ihm verloren und versunken.

17. Die Sünde

Der Durst ist nicht ein Ding und doch kann er dich plagen;
Wie soll denn nicht die Sünd den Bösen ewig nagen.

18. Der Glaube

Der Glaube, Senfkorn gross, versetzt den Berg ins Meer:
Denkt, was er könnte tun, wenn er ein Kürbis wär.

19. Die Abscheulichkeit der Bösheit

Mensch, solltest du in dir das Ungeziefer schauen,
Es würde dir für dir als für dem Teufel grauen.

20. Zufall und Wesen

Mensch, werde wesentlich; denn wenn die Welt vergeht,
So fällt der Zufall weg, das Wesen, das besteht.

21. Die geistliche Schwängerung

Ist deine Seele Magd und wie Maria rein,
So muss sie augenblicks von Gotte schwanger sein.

22. Nimm also, dass du hast.

Mensch, nimm du Gott als Trost, als Süssigkeit und Licht,
Was hast du dann, wenn Trost, Licht, Süssigkeit gebricht?

23. Der Tugend Ziel ist Gott

Gott ist der Tugend Ziel, ihr Antrieb, ihre Kron,
Ihr einziges Warum und ist auch all ihr Lohn.

24. An St. Augustin

Halt an, mein Augustin, eh du wirst Gott ergründen,
Wird man das ganze Meer in einem Grüblein finden.

25. Die Liebe

Die Lieb ist wie der Tod, sie tötet meine Sinnen,
Sie brichet mir das Herz und führt den Geist von hinnen.

16. The More Abandoned, The More Divine
The saints are in such wise from God's own godhead drunk,
As they in Him are lost, as they in Him are sunk.

17. Sin
Thirst is no thing and yet it cruel can torment you:
Should then eternally sin not on evil chew?

18. Belief
Belief, great mustard seed, sends mountains to the sea:
But think what it could do, could it a pumpkin be.

19. The Abomination Of Evil
Man, could you in yourself the vermin all behold,
Then, as 'twere Satan, you would at this sight grow cold.

20. Chance And Essence
Become essential, man, for if the world should flee,
The chance will know decay, the essence constancy.

21. The Spiritual Impregnation
If maiden is your soul, like Mary undefiled,
Then it will instantly from God have got a child.

22. Take Therefore That You May Have
Man, if you God as balm, as light, and sweetness take,
What have you then when balm, light, sweetness you forsake?

23. Virtue's Goal Is God
God does for virtue goal and urge and crown afford,
He is its single cause and is its whole reward.

24. To St. Augustine
Stop, my Augustine, stop: ere you will God explain,
A little dimple will the mighty sea contain.

25. Love
Love is a twin to death; it makes my senses dead;
By it my heart is broke, my soul from hence is led.

George C. Schoolfield

Hans Jakob Christoffel von Grimmelshausen

Komm Trost der Nacht, o Nachtigal,
Lass deine Stimm mit Freudenschall,
Auffs lieblichste erklingen;
Komm, komm, und lob den Schöpffer dein,
Weil andre Vöglein schlaffen seyn,
Und nicht mehr mögen singen!
   Lass dein Stimmlein,
      Laut erschallen, dan vor allen
        Kanstu loben
Gott im Himmel hoch dort oben.

Obschon ist hin der Sonnenschein,
Und wir im Finstern müssen seyn,
So können wir doch singen;
Von Gottes Güt und seiner Macht,
Weil uns kan hindern keine Macht,
Sein Lob zu vollenbringen.
   Drum dein Stimmlein,
      Lass erschallen, dan vor allen
        Kanstu loben
Gott im Himmel hoch dort oben.

Echo, der wilde Widerhall
Will seyn bey diesem Freudenschall,
Und lässet sich auch hören;
Verweist uns alle Müdigkeit,
Der wir ergeben allezeit,
Lehrt uns den Schlaff bethören.
   Drum dein Stimmlein,
      Lass erschallen, dan vor allen
        Kanstu loben
Gott im Himmel hoch dort oben.

Hans Jakob Christoffel von Grimmelshausen

Come, balm of night, oh nightingale,
And let your voice with joyful tale
Ring out in fairest ways.
Come, come, your Maker's praise essay,
Since other birds in slumber stay,
Nor will their voices raise.
   Let your faint lay
      Loudly call, since you 'fore all
         Can glorify
God Who reigns in Heaven on high.

Although the sun has gone away
And we must in the darkness stay,
Yet we our voice can raise:
Of God's benevolence and might,
Since there can hinder us no might
In making full His praise.
   Bid your faint lay
      Thus to call, since you 'fore all
         Can glorify
God Who reigns in Heaven on high.

Echo, the wild response's sound,
This joyful pealing will compound,
Nor will her silence keep:
She chides us for our weariness
To which we'd fain ourselves address,
And tells us tricks 'gainst sleep.
   Bid your faint lay
      Thus to call, since you 'fore all
         Can glorify
God Who reigns in Heaven on high.

Die Sterne, so am Himmel stehn,
Sich lassen zum Lob Gottes sehn,
Und Ehre ihm beweisen,
Die Eul auch die nicht singen kan,
Zeigt doch mit ihrem Heulen an,
Dass sie Gott auch thu preisen.
    Drum dein Stimmlien,
        Lass erschallen, dan vor allen
            Kanstu loben
Gott im Himmel hoch dort oben.

Nur her, mein liebstes Vögelein,
Wir wollen nicht die fäulste seyn,
Und schlaffend ligen bleiben,
Vielmehr biss dass die Morgenröth,
Erfreuet diese Wälder öd,
In Gottes Lob vertreiben.
    Lass dein Stimmlein,
        Laut erschallen, dan vor allen
            Kanstu loben
Gott im Himmel hoch dort oben.

Sibylla Schwarz

Sonett

        Ist Lieben keusch? wo kompt denn Ehbruch her?
Ist Lieben guht/ nichts böses drinn zu finden/
Wie kan sein Feur dan so gahr viel entzünden?
Ist Lieben Lust/ wer bringt dan das Beschwär?
        Wer Lieben liebt/ fährt auff der Wollust Meer/
Und lässet sich ins Todes Netze binden/
Das nicht zerreist/ er lebet nuhr den Sünden/
Liebt Eitelkeit/ und ist der Tugend leer.

The stars which stand along the skies
Will by their light God eulogize,
And Him will honor show.
The owl, which knows not how to sing
Would by its hoot a warrant bring
That it God's praise does know.
  Bid your faint lay
    Thus to call, since you 'fore all
      Can glorify
God who reigns in Heaven on high.

My sweetest bird, come but this way,
For we will not the sluggard play,
And sleep the night to end,
But rather till the ruddy dawn
Rejoicing through these woods has gone,
In praise the darkness spend.
  Let your faint lay
    Loudly call, since you 'fore all
      Can glorify
God who reigns in Heaven on high.

George C. Schoolfield

Sibylla Schwarz

Sonnet

    If love is chaste, what bears adultery?
If love is good, and does no evil own,
How can its fire so many flames propone?
If love is joy, why's it called cruelty?
    Who love adores, sails on a lustful sea,
And lets himself into death's net be sewn,
Which does not tear; he lives for sin alone,
Is stripped of virtue, worships vanity.

Das ewig lebt/ dem stirbt er gäntzlich ab/
Sieht seine Noht erst/ wan er siht sein Grab.
Wer dan nuhn wird in Liebes Brunst gefunden/
Der fliehe bald/ und hasse/ die er liebt;
Ist Lieb ihm süss? so werd er drümb betrübt;
Ist sie sein Brodt? so geb er sie den Hunden.

David Schirmer

Er liebet

Mein liebster Freund ist wund/ mit mir hats nun Gefahr/
weil meine Marnia so plötzlich sich erwecket/
und ümb mein Hertz herümb ihr Bildnis aufgestecket.
Mein liebster Freund ist wund/ ich brenne gantz und gar.
Wo bistu Freiheit nun/ die mein so zartes Haar
mit ihres Goldes Glantz hielt allezeit verdecket?
Wo bistu Phöbus hin? Wer hat dich so erschrecket?
Bleib hier/ verlass mich nicht/ bleib hier mit deiner Schaar.
Apollo/ ja du bleibst auf meinem Helicon.
So kom und setze dich zu Venus kleinem Sohn/
und meiner Marnien/ die meine Feder reitzen.
Auf! Schönste von der Welt/ dir geb ich einzig mich/
Apollo bleibt mir hold/ mein Vers steigt über sich.
Nun mag ich Eulen nicht/ ich kan mit Falcken beitzen.

For life eternal totally he dies,
And sees his grief but when his grave he spies.
  Whoever has been found in loving's fit,
Let him hate love and flee it in all haste.
Does love taste sweet? Let him despise its taste.
Is love his bread? Let him feed dogs with it.

George C. Schoolfield

David Schirmer

He Loves

  My dearest friend is struck, and I must stern beware,
Since she, my Marnia, does suddenly awaken,
Her image round my heart has guardian service taken.
My dearest friend is struck, and I am flame and flare.
  Where, freedom, have you fled, whose shine my tender hair
Once with its gold concealed and now has me forsaken?
Where, Phoebus,* do you go? And with what terror shaken?
Stay here with all your troupe, nor leave me in despair.
  Apollo, you will stay upon my Helicon.
So come and sit you down by Venus' little son
And by my Marnia: they've roused my writing feather.
  Come! Fairest of the world, you are my queen alone;
My verse outdoes itself, Apollo stays my own.
Now I'm no friend of owls but hunt with hawks at tether.

George C. Schoolfield

*Apollo.

Kaspar Stieler

Nacht-Glücke

Willkommen, Fürstin aller Nächte!
Prinz der Silber-Knechte,
     Willkommen, Mond, aus düstrer Bahn
     Vom Ozean!
Dies ist die Nacht, die tausend Tagen
Trotz kann sagen
     Weil mein Schatz
     Hier in Priapus' Platz
Erscheinen wird, zu stillen meine Pein.
Wer wird wie ich wohl so beglücket sein?

Beneidet, himmlische Laternen,
Weißgeflammte Sternen,
     Mit einem scheelen Angesicht,
     Ach, mich nur nicht!
Kein Mensch als ihr nur möget wissen,
Wie wir küssen.
     Alle Welt
     Hat seine Ruh bestellt,
Wir beide nur, ich und mein Kind, sind wach
Und Flammen, ihr, an Bronteus' Wolkendach.

Es säuselt Zephir aus dem Weste
Durch Pomonen Äste,
     Es seufzet sein verliebter Wind
     Nach meinem Kind.
Ich seh es gerne, daß er spielet
Und sie kühlet,
     Weil sie mir
     Folgt durch die Gartentür

Kaspar Stieler

Night's Delights

Princess of the nights, be welcome,
Prince of silver-thralldom,
    Welcome, moon, on paths of shadow
    From oceans' billow!
Behold the night, that challenge lays
To myriad days:
    For my delight,
    Here, in Priapus'* sight
Will soon appear, love's ecstasy to ease,
How more than this could ever fortune please?

Begrudge not heavenly light,
Stars flaming white,
    Aglow with eye of envious hate,
    Begrudge me not my lover's state.
No eye but yours, no mortal's gaze,
May behold our kisses' blaze.
    All mankind
    Blind rest will find;
From sleep my love and I, alone, remain aloof,
And you, too, flames on Bronte's thunderous roof.

Zephyr† sighs his westward hymns
Rustling through Pomona's‡ limbs.
    The wind cries out—a lover's moan
    For my love's own.
I like to watch him at his game,
He plays to cool her flame,
    Because she cannot wait—
    Runs after me through garden gate,

---

*Ancient god of fertility whose symbol was the erect phallus.
†God of the west wind.
‡Roman goddess of fruits and fruit-bearing trees.

Und doppelt den geschwinden Liebestritt.
Bringt, West, sie bald und tausend Küsse mit!

Was werd ich, wenn sie kömmt gegangen,
An- doch erstlichst -fangen?
        Küß ich die Hand, die Brust, den Mund
        Zur selben Stund?
Ich werd, ich weiß, kein Wort nicht machen!
So viel Sachen,
        Die an Zier
        Den Göttern gehen für
Und auf dies Schönchen sein gewendet an,
Erstaunen mich, daß ich nicht reden kann.

Komm, Flora, streue dein Vermügen
Darhin, wo wir liegen!
        Es soll ein bunter Rosenhauf
        Uns nehmen auf
Und, Venus, du sollst in den Myrten
Uns bewirten,
        Bis das Blut
        Der Röt herfür sich tut!
Was Schein ist das? Die Schatten werden klar.
Still, Lautenklang! Mein Liebchen ist schon dar.

Der Hass küsset ja nicht

1

Die ernstliche Strenge steht endlich versüsset,
    die qweelende Seele wird einsten gesund.
Ich habe gewonnen, ich werde geküsset,
    es schallet und knallet ihr zärtlicher Mund.

And quickens her swift lover's pace.
O Westwind, bring her soon with thousandfold embrace!

But how shall I, when she comes in,
Choose first—ere I begin?
    Kissing hand, breast, mouth sublime
    At selfsame time?
I shall—I know—no words express,
Such fair richesse—
    In grace so rare,
    No gods compare—
Is lavished on this beauteous one,
It does astonish me and strikes me dumb.

Flora,* come! Your bounty spread,
Make for us a lover's bed
    Roses gay will be our mattress,
    Heaping petals to receive us,
And Venus, you will host love's frays
Neath myrtles' sprays.
    Until the blood
    Of reddening day the sky will flood.
What light is that? The shadows slowly clear,
Lute, hush! My love is here.

Ingrid Walsøe-Engel

Hatred Surely Does Not Kiss

1

At last earnest sternness is transformed to sweet,
    The pain-spitted spirit must some day turn sound.
Now I have my triumph, I kisses do meet,
    Her delicate mouth does reecho, resound:

---

*Roman goddess of flowering plants, she was held in high regard by courtesans and prostitutes.

Die Dornen entweichen,
die Lippen verbleichen,
indehm sie die ihren den meinen auffdrükkt.
Ich werd' auss der Erde zun Göttern verschikkt.

2

Ihr klagende Plagen steht jetzo von fernen,
es fliehe der ächzende krächzende Neid!
Mein Gang ist gegründet auch über die Sternen,
ich fühle der Seeligen spielende Freud'.
Es flammen die Lippen.
Die rösslichte Klippen
die blühen und ziehen mich lieblich an sich.
Was acht' ich dich Honig! was Nektar-wein dich.

3

Durch dieses erwiess es ihr süsses Gemühte,
sie wolle, sie solle die Meinige sein.
Nu höhn' ich der Könige Zepter und Blüte,
mich nimmet der Vorraht Eufrates nicht ein.
Kan ich sie nur haben:
was acht' ich der Gaben
der siegenden Krieger im Kapitolin,
die durch die bekränzeten Pforten einziehn!

4

Ich habe die Schöne mit nichten gewonnen
mit Solde von Golde, mit Perlenem Wehrt,
und scheinenden Steinen in Bergen geronnen,
den Tyrischen Purpur hat sie nie begehrt.
Die Zeilen, die süssen
aus Pegasus Flüssen
die haben ihr härtliches Hertze gerührt:
Nu stehet mein Lorber mit Myrten geziert.

Her thorns, they do fail,
Her lips, they grow pale,
In that she her lips' fit on mine does essay,
I'm sent to the gods from this planet away.

2

You plagues with your nagging must presently fly,
Let envy's moans, groaning, to exile be pressed.
My coursing ascends o'er the stars of the sky,
I feel now the dallying joy of the blest.
Her lips' flaming coals,
Those rosy-hued shoals,
They bloom and their blooming does fair me entwine:
What care I for honey, for you, nectar-wine!

3

Her sweet mood did prove I had wooed me her bond,
She would be, she should be my mistress alone,
I mock at the monarchs, their glory and wand.
I would not Euphrates' reserves make my own.
If I her but hold,
What care I for gold
Of conquering troops on the Capitol's height,
Who march through the wreath-covered arches their might.

4

Nor did I with prizes her loveliness win:
Gold's weight in full holding, pearl's worth in full fire,
Nor glittering jewels, to mountains poured in;
The Tyrian purple she ne'er did desire.
The sweet lines that course
From Pegasus' source,
These lines have her heart in its hardness suborned:
My laurel stands now with the myrtle adorned.

George C. Schoolfield

Anton Ulrich (Herzog von Braunschweig-Wolfenbüttel)

Sterblied

Es ist genug! Mein matter Sinn
Sehnt sich dahin, wo meine Väter schlafen.
Ich hab es endlich guten Fug,
Es ist genug! Ich muss mir Rast verschaffen.

Ich bin ermüdt, ich hab geführt
Die Tages Bürd: Es muss einst Abend werden.
Erlös mich, Herr, spann aus den Pflug,
Es ist genug! Nimm von mir die Beschwerden.

Die grosse Last hat mich gedrückt,
Ja schier erstickt so viele lange Jahre.
Ach lass mich finden, was ich such.
Es ist genug! Mit solcher Kreuzes-Ware.

Nun gute Nacht, ihr meine Freund,
Ihr meine Feind, ihr Guten und ihr Bösen!
Euch folg die Treu, euch folg der Trug.
Es ist genug! Mein Gott will mich auflösen.

So nimm nun, Herr, hin meine Seel,
Die ich befehl in deine Händ und Pflege.
Schreib sie ein in dein Lebens Buch,
Es ist genug! Dass ich mich schlafen lege.

Nicht besser soll es mir ergehn,
Als wie geschehn den Vätern, die erworben
Durch ihren Tod des Lebens Ruch.
Es ist genug! Es sei also gestorben!

Anton Ulrich (Duke of Brunswick-Wolfenbüttel)

Dying Song

It is enough! My feeble sense
Yearns to that place my fathers slumber in.
At last I have good legacy;
It is enough! I must my Sabbath win.

For I am tired; I long have borne
The charge of day; sometime must darkness fall.
Unspan the plow, Lord, set me free;
It is enough! Take from me trouble's thrall.

This mighty weight has pressed me down,
Yea, near has throttled me these many years:
Oh, what I seek, that let me see;
It is enough! Put end to cross and tears.

And now good night, my faithful friends,
And you, my foes, you good men and you ill!
May you have troth, you treachery;
It is enough! My Lord will make me still.

So take then, Lord, my soul away,
Which I commend into Your hands and keep.
Into Your life-book enter me;
It is enough! That I may go to sleep.

No better shall it fare with me
Than with my fathers, who themselves have won
By very death life's remedy;
It is enough! Be now my dying done!

George C. Schoolfield

Catharina Regina von Greiffenberg

Eiferige Lobes Vermahnung

Ach lobe/ lobe/ lob'/ ohn unterlass und ziel/
den/ den zu loben du/ O meine Seel/ gebohren!
zu diesen Engel-werk bist du von Gott erkohren/
dass du ihm dienen solst im wunderpreisungs spiel.
  Das kleine scherflein ihm von jenem Weib gefiel:
dein' einfalt klinget wol in seinen Demut-Ohren.
Er geht sanfftmütig um mit den zubrochnen Rohren.
Wie schwach und bebend' auch/ beliebt ihm doch dein kiel
  Rühm/ weil du Othem hast; dieweil du ihn entfangen/
allein zu diesem ziel. dess Lebens unwehrt ist/
aus dessen Mund so viel nicht Lob/ als lufft gegangen.
  Weil du der Gottes Güt ein wunderspiegel bist/
so lass den Strahl zu ruck in deine Sonn gelangen.
weil du dazu/ so sey es auch von dir/ erkiest!

Auf die Fruchtbringende Herbst-Zeit

Freud'-erfüller/ Früchte-bringer/ vielbeglückter Jahres-Koch/
Grünung-Blüh und Zeitung-Ziel/ Werkbeseeltes Lustverlangen!
lange Hoffnung/ ist in dir in die That-Erweisung gangen.
Ohne dich/ wird nur beschauet/ aber nichts genossen noch.
  Du Vollkommenheit der Zeiten! mache bald vollkommen doch/
was von Blüh' und Wachstums-Krafft halbes Leben schon
  empfangen.
Deine Würkung kan allein mit der Werk-Vollziehung prangen.
Wehrter Zeiten-Schatz! ach bringe jenes blühen auch so hoch/

Catharina Regina von Greiffenberg

Zealous Admonition to Praise

Oh praise Him, praise Him, praise without an end or aim
Him for Whose praise, my soul, your birth was granted you.
For God does you elect this angel-work to do,
That you shall serve Him in the wonder-praising's game.
    That widow's tiny mite to Him a joy became,
Your plainsong His meek-ears will bring sweet revenue.
How soft He does His way midst broken reeds pursue.
Your quill-pen gives Him joy though it be weak and lame.
    Adore, since you have breath: you have been given it
But to this end alone. That man no life does earn
Whose mouth will more of air than of His praise transmit.
    Since you as wonder-glass of Heaven's goodness burn,
Then backwards let the beam into your sun-ball hit;
Since you are chosen for this, then make your choice return.

George C. Schoolfield

Concerning the Fruit-bringing Autumn Season

Glee-fulfiller, fruit-producer, cook who glad the year can feed,
Greening's bloom, time's terminus, wish-for-pleasure worker-
    weaved!
Long desiring has in you proof by means of act achieved.
From your lack would contemplation, not experience, proceed.
    You perfection of the ages, perfect make all that in deed
Which from bloom and burgeon-might half a life ere now received.
Only by your wonderwork can work's ending be conceived.
Worthy treasure of time's passage! Now thus high that blooming
    lead,

schütt' aus deinem reichen Horn hochverhoffte Freuden Früchte.
Lieblich süsser Mund-Ergetzer! lab' auch unsern Geist zugleich:
so erhebt mit jenen er deiner Früchte Ruhm-Gerüchte.
zeitig die verlangten Zeiten/ in dem Oberherrschungs-Reich.
Lass die Anlas-Kerne schwarz Schickungs-Aepffel safftig werden:
dass man Gottes Gnaden-Frücht froh geniest und isst auf Erden.

Gott Lobende Frühlingslust

Himmel voll Zimbel/ voll Lauten und Geigen/
Bisem- und Amber'-erfüllete Luft/
Rosen- und Lilgen-verlieblichter Tuft!
Wollest/ den Höchsten zu loben/ nit schweigen!

Himmel an wolle die Süssheit aufsteigen/
Herrlich Gott ehrend aus tiefester Kluft.
Seine Genaden und Wunder ausruft/
Wie sie sich mächtig und prächtig erzeigen.

Leset/ in weisslichen Blättern der Blüh/
Göttlicher Allmacht ungleichliche Werke.
Sehet/ in Traidern/ die himmlische Stärke/

Die das Blüh-Härlein bewahret ohn Müh.
Göttliche Wunder in allem man siehet/
Wann man den Vorhang der Faulheit aufziehet.

Shake from out your copious horn highly hoped rejoicing's fruit.
Sweet and lovely mouth-delighter! Make our spirit too expand,
That it raise up with the others this your harvest's famous bruit.
　Bring to time the times desired in the super-sovereign-land.
Let the causal-kernels black, let fate-apples juicy grow:
That the gracious fruit of God we on earth glad eat and know.

George C. Schoolfield

Spring Joy Praising God

Sky full of cymbals, of fiddles and lutes,
Air that the musk and the ambergris fill,
Rose-scent and lily-breath lovelier still,
Cease not your praise of the Lord's attributes!

Sweetness, ascend on the heavenly routes,
Giving God honor from earth's deepest kill.
Cry out his grace, his miraculous will,
Showing how mighty, how bright are their fruits.

Read in the white-tinted leaves of the bloom
Godly omnipotence-works without peer.
See strength divine in the corn and the ear,

Easily guarding the bloom's tiny plume.
Heavenly wonders in all things one finds,
If he but raises his slothfulness' blinds.

George C. Schoolfield

Daniel Casper von Lohenstein

Die Augen

Lasst Archimeden viel von seinen Spiegeln sagen,
Da durch geschliffen Glas der heissen Sonne Rad
Der Römer Schiff und Mast in Brand gestecket hat,
Die in der Doris Schoss für Syracuse lagen:
Den Ruhm verdienet mehr der güldnen Sonne Wagen,
Als Archimedens Kunst und seines Spiegels Blatt.
Denn dies sein Meisterstück hat nur an Dingen statt,
Mit denen jede Glut pflegt leichtlich anzuschlagen.
In deinen Augen steckt mehr Nachdruck, Schwefel, Tag,
Als hohler Gläser Kunst der Sonnen-Strahl vermag,
Ja ihr geschwinder Blitz hat viel mehr Macht zu brennen:
Sie zünden übers Meer entfernte Seelen an
Und Herzen, denen sich kein Eis vergleichen kann.
Soll man die Augen nun nicht Brenne-Spiegel nennen?

Nacht-Gedancken über einen Traum

GOtt ewig guter GOtt! ich falle dir zu Füssen/
Halb stum/ halb todt/ nun ich des Traumes Bild verliehr/
Ach GOtt was stellst du denn mir im Gesichte für?
Ich irre lange Zeit mit Schertze/ Tantz und Küssen
Durch Lust-Gemächer durch doch als solch Lust-Genüssen/
Zum höchsten Gipffel kam/ so stürtzt mich die Begier
In einen Pful/ wo Schlang und Natter nagt an mir:
Biss nach viel Qual ich ward an ersten Ort gerissen.
Ach GOtt! ich fühle mich die Lust-Gemächer sind

Daniel Casper von Lohenstein

Her Eyes

Let Archimedes* loud his glasses' glory roar,
Since hot Apollo's wheel, through polished mirror passed,
Did make a holocaust of Roman ship and mast
That lay in Doris's† arms off Syracusa's shore.
The sun's gold chariot deserves these praises more
Than Archimedes' art, his pane in crystal cast:
For this his masterwork but to such things holds fast,
In which each glow is wont all easily to bore.
Within your eyes there do more strength, light, sulphur dwell
Than sunbeams from the art of hollow glass compel.
Indeed, their hasty bolt owns much more force of flame:
Their fire across the seas has distant spirits won,
And hearts, with which no ice can bear comparison.
Now shall men not these eyes their burning-glasses name?

George C. Schoolfield

Night Thoughts Concerning a Dream

God, ever gracious God! Here I myself debase,
Half-mute, half-dead, when now the dreamer's world grows small.
Oh God, what did you then into my vision call?
With jest and dance and kiss I made an endless chase
Through pleasure-palaces, yet when I would embrace
These pleasures' highest peak, my lusting let me fall
Into a pit where snakes and gnawing adders crawl;
Until, long-tortured, I must meet my starting place.
Oh God! I think those rooms of joy where I'd begun

*Greek scientist of Syracuse, the greatest mathematician of the ancient world.
†The daughter of Oceanus and Thetis, the wife of her brother Nereus, and the mother of the Nereides: Doris's name is sometimes used to mean the sea itself.

Der Wollust Irrebahn; der Pful ist das Gewissen/
Das durch bewust der Schuld von Würmen wird zerbissen/
Und gleichwohl kehr ich um und renne so gar blind
Ins erst Sünden-Garn. GOtt zäume mein Beginnen/
Wo du nich hilffst/ werd ich der Höllen nicht entrinnen.

Sonette aus Arminius

1

Komm Sonne/ Brunn des Lichts/ zu unsern Hochzeit-Freuden!
Bring' uns den güldnen Tag; und gieb nicht nach: dass wir
Und unser Fackeln-Glantz kommt deinen Stralen für!
Was hemmet deinen Lauff?   kanstu/ O Riese/ leiden:
Dass Zwerg-Gestirne dir so Preiss als Lust abschneiden?
Weil der gestirnte Bär/ der faule Schwan und Stier/
Der blasse Mohnde sich aus Eyversucht von dir
Nicht lassen dringen weg/ den Tag die Nachte neiden?
Treib so viel schneller um dein Rad/ O Angelstern?
Als du's zu langsam triebst zu Liebe Jupitern/
Wie er Alciden zeigt'. Erzwinge diss Verlangen/
O Sonne/ weil die Nacht zu schlecht ist für diss Fest/
Seit Hermann eben diss/ was Jupiter gewest/
Und einen Hercules Thussnelde soll empfangen.

2

Hier liegt der weiseste der Sterblichen begraben/
Der grosse Socrates.   Diss glaubt ganz Griechenland/
Streut Blumen auff sein Grab/ und Weyrauch in den Brand/
Weil ein solch Zeugnüss ihm die Götter selber gaben.
Gott/ den die Griechen nie vorhin erkennet haben/
Den kein Verstand begreifft/ war ihm allein bekand.

Where lust's deceiving path; the conscience is the pit,
Which, pondering its guilt, by worms is cruelly bit;
And yet I turn my course, and like a blind man run
Into sin's starting net. Dear God, my yearnings stay;
Without your help I shall not come from Hell away.

George C. Schoolfield

Sonnets from Arminius*

1

Light-spring, oh sun, in light our wedding joys immure.
Bring us the golden day, and do not fail, lest we
(Our torches' shine) may take your beams' ascendancy:
What has restrained your course? Can you, oh giant, endure
That midget-stars your fame and joy as well obscure?
Since now the starry bear, the swan so lazily,
The steer, the pallid moon, for very jealousy
Will not depart your side, shall night the day abjure?
So much the quicker now, oh arch-star, turn your wheel,
As once for Jupiter you did that speed repeal
When he Alcides made. Oh sun, your wish relieve,
Since for our festival the night has grown too mean,
Since Herman is this hour what Jupiter has been,
And since Thusnelda now will Hercules conceive.

2

The wisest of all men lies buried on this spot,
The mighty Socrates. All Greece this fact will own
And has the grave with blooms, the flame with incense sown,
Since from the very gods he such a witness got.
True God, of Whom the Greeks before this time knew not,
And Whom no wit perceives, appeared to him alone:

*The sonnet celebrates the marriage of Arminius (Herman), the hero of Lohen-
stein's gigantic courtly novel, with his beloved Thusnelda.

Denn ihm war ein gut Geist vom Himmel zugesand/
Im Leben ihn zu lehr'n/ im Sterben ihn zu laben.
Athen/ das ihn bracht' um/ beseelt nun seinen Ruhm/
Vergöttert seinen Geist durch dieses Heiligthum/
Verdammt den Urtels-Spruch/ der ihn zwang zu erblassen;
Und machet sich hierdurch von Schmach und Unrecht frey.
Denn wer will nicht gestehn/ dass irren menschlich sey/
Was über-menschliches den alten Irrthum hassen?

3

Allhier ist Spartacus der edle Knecht geblieben/
Der seiner Fessel Stahl brach als ein Löw entzwey/
Und hundert tausend sprach von ihren Halsherrn frey.
Rom zehlt die Todten kaum die er hat aufgerieben/
Durch derer Blut er ihm den Frey-Brieff selbst geschrieben.
Die güldne Freyheit legt ihm selbst diss Zeugniss bey:
Dass gar nichts knechtisches an ihm gewesen sey.
Ja Feind und Adel muss den Helden-Sclaven lieben.
War sein zerfleischter Leib gleich hier nicht zu erkennen;
So wird sein Nahme doch unendlich kennbar seyn.
Rom gräbt zugleich sein Lob in dieses Siegs-Mal ein/
Das man nun erst kan Frau und Freygelass'ne nennen.
Denn hätte nicht der Todt ihn untern Fuss gebracht,
So hätt' er endlich Rom noch gar zur Magd gemacht.

Christian Weise

Auf die Geburt eines jungen und hoch-verlangten Sohnes

Das ist der beste Schatz/ der Kern von allen Gaben/
Die wir aus Gottes Hand hier zu geniessen haben;
    Wenn ein geliebtes Weib/ als ein Oliven-Baum/
    Mit steter Fruchtbarkeit den all zu weiten Raum

From Heaven a spirit came by whose help he has known
Instruction during life, at death a kinder lot.
Athens, his murderer, encourages his fame,
And through this holy place his godhead will acclaim,
Condemning that decree which forced him to depart;
It thus inequity and shame seeks to allay:
For who will not confess: to do wrong is man's way,
To hate the ancient wrong demands an angel's heart.

3

Here lies the noble flesh of Spartacus the knave
Who like a lion broke his fetters' steel array,
Who hundred-thousands taught to put their lords away.
Rome scarce can count the dead for whom he dug the grave,
And through whose blood to Rome he freeman's patent gave.
E'en golden freedom will this statement's truth display:
That nothing of the knave within his nature lay.
Nobility and foe must love the hero-slave.
Were his maimed body here not presently to see,
Life nonetheless would cling forever to his name.
Into this monument Rome has inscribed his fame,
Rome, which but now one may call mistress and set free:
For had he not by death been brought beneath the loam,
He would at last have made a serving-girl of Rome.

George C. Schoolfield

Christian Weise

Upon the Birth of a Young and Highly Desired Son

This treasure is the best, of all those gifts the grain
Which we from Heaven's hand do to our pleasure gain;
   When a beloved wife, all in the olive's ways,
    With constant fruitfulness, the yawning space allays

Am Tische kleiner macht. Denn die bewehrten Früchte
Sind unser Ebenbild; des Vaters Angesichte
   Steht in der zarten Reih so klärlich abgemahlt/
   Dass sein Gedächtnüs auch den blassen Todt bestrahlt/
Und in der Nach-Welt lebt. Das sind dieselben Stützen/
Die Kirch und Regiment mit neuer Krafft beschützen/
   Wenn wir verblichen sind: Ja das ist unser Geld
   Und unser höchstes Gut/ das auch in jener Welt
Die volle Währung hat. Hingegen andre Schätze/
Geld/ Acker/ Hauss und Hoff/ sind alle dem Gesetze
   Der Eitelkeit verknüpfft/ und können nicht bestehn/
   Wenn dieses gantze Rund durchs letzte Feuer gehn
Und sich verzehren wird. Ein Baum verliert die Blätter/
So bald ein rauher Nord das kalte Winter-Wetter
   In unsre Gräntzen bläst: Jedennoch in der Frucht
   Da lebt des Samens Krafft/ dadurch man solche Zucht
Noch weiter bringen kan. Wolan des Höchsten Güte
Hat diesen Stamm bissher mit einer schönen Blüte
   Belieblich angesehn: Nun kömt die beste Zeit/
   Und krönet solchen Glantz mit voller Fruchtbarkeit.
Willkommen kleiner Sohn/ du/ deines Vaters Leben;
Der dir das Leben giebt/ dem solt du künfftig geben/
   Dass er nicht sterben kan; du bist das Ebenbild
   Darein er ietzo zwar sein Angesicht verhüllt:
Doch künfftig wird sein Geist durch deine Seele dringen/
Da wirstu neben ihm den Gipfel höher schwingen/
   Als keine Ceder thut: worinn er uns gefällt/
   Da wirstu mit der Zeit der künfftig-klugen Welt/
Nicht minder kostbar seyn. Schau wie die Musen lachen/
Und dir in ihrer Schoss ein süsses Lager machen;
   Schau wie der Sternen Licht auff deinen Wirbel blickt/
   Und einen stillen Fluss biss in das Hertze schickt/
Das uns erfreuen sol.   Ja Gott der allen Samen
Am liebsten fruchtbar macht/ wenn er in seinem Nahmen
   Hinaus gestreuet wird/ der giebt den Willen drein/
   Du solst in allem Thun ein andrer Vater seyn.

Around the family board. For proven heritage
Are our small likenesses: the father's countenance
   Stands in the tender row designed with such clear brush
   That memory of him brings pallid death to blush,
And fills posterity. These pillars are the same
Which guard (with might renewed) both church and ruler's fame
   When we have passed away. Yes, these our moneys are
   And highest properties, which on that distant star
Their proper value keep. For other treasures: gold,
Fields, mansion, and estate, are subject to the hold
   Of vanity's decree, and can no longer last
   Than when this rounded globe through final fire has passed,
And has devoured itself. A tree its bareness shows
As soon as Boreas cold winter-weather blows
   Rough 'cross our boundaries: and yet the force of seed
   Still lives within the fruit, and through this force the breed
Can still be carried on. Now, Heaven's kindliness
Has deigned until this day with handsome bloom to bless
   Our family tree: at last there comes the finest time
   And crowns such splendor with its full and fertile prime.
Oh welcome, little son, who are your father's spark:
Who gives that spark to you, you'll rescue from the dark
   Of death by future gift: his image you reveal,
   Since in you recently his face he did conceal.
Yet henceforth will his soul your spirit penetrate:
Then you (next him) will lift your height to higher state
   Than any cedar might; the world does deem him dear,
   And you, with time's course, will to wisdom's world appear
No less desirable. See how the Muses smile
And in their lap prepare your couch of gracious style.
   See how the starry light upon your crown descends
   And deep into your heart a silent river sends,
Which carries our delight. Yes, God, Who seed does make
Most gladly fruitful when that seed for His name's sake
   Is in the furrow sown, will with this aim agree:
   You shall in every act another father be.

George C. Schoolfield

Quirinus Kuhlmann

Aus tiefster Not

Aus tiefster Not schrei, abgemergelt Herz!
Lass mich noch einst die matte Hand aufheben!
Es harnischt mich und panzert recht der Schmerz!
Die Zunge klebt! Angst hat mich rings umgeben!
Mein Gott, mein Gott! Du zentnerst stete Last!
Hör auf, hör auf, eh ich bin ganz verdrücket.
Gib endlich, gib um Jesu Kreuz mir Rast!
Wie lange soll dein Werk sein ganz entschmücket?
Was ist der Mensch, der ewigst wird gepresst?
Halt innen, halt, eh Geist und Seel ausbläst.

Beschwerst du mich als deinen ärgsten Feind?
Es hat mich Schmach nach aller Wunsch getroffen.
Sie schaun mehr Lust als sie zu schaun vermeint:
Verloren wird mehr täglich mir mein Hoffen.
Dein Wort scheint nichts als nur ein leerer Traum:
Dein Führen wird ein lauteres Verführen.
Sie zweigen sich gleich einem Eichenbaum:
Du aber lässt mich mehr und mehr verlieren.
Du mästest sie und nimmst mir alles hin:
Verirrest mich, gibst Schaden zum Gewinn.

Christ Gott und Mensch! Schau her, ich bin dein Glied!
Soll Harmung, Frost und Armut mich aufzehren?
Ich liege hier, stimm an dies Trauerlied,
Voll Elend, Ach, und tausender Beschweren!
Voll Kummer, Sorg, und was mein Stand erweckt!
Muss Herzenleid unhörlich in mich fressen!
Bin höchst bedrängt und überall befleckt,
Als hättest du schon deines Knechts vergessen!
Mein Gaumen klebt vor Durst an meine Lipp
Und werde ich lebendig zum Geripp.

Quirinus Kuhlmann

From Deepest Need

From deepest need cry out, oh hungered heart!
Let me but once again my tired hand raise!
Pain armors me and does good plate impart!
My tongue sticks fast! Fear round about me stays!
My God! my God! You hundredweighted load!
Desist, desist, ere whole it crushes me!
For Jesus' cross in peace give me abode!
How long shall then your creature naked be?
What's man, 'neath most eternal burden cast?
Stop, stop, ere mind and spirit breathe their last.

Do you oppress me as Your basest foe?
Disgrace to suit each taste does strike me sore.
(Men know more joy than they had thought to know.)
Each day my hoping vanishes the more.
Your word seems to be naught but empty dream,
Pathfinder, you a path of error choose.
(Men's branches like unto the oak tree's seem.)
But yet the more and more you let me lose.
You fatten them and take my all away:
For gain you give me hurt, lead me astray.

Christ, God, and Man! I am your arm, look hence!
Shall want and frost and sorrow me consume?
I lie here and my song of woe commence,
Of misery, a thousand kinds of doom!
Pain, care, and all the rest my work must bear,
I must to heart-wound endless food allot,
I'm cruelly grieved and tainted everywhere,
As though You had Your vassal all forgot.
From thirst my palate to my tongue is caught,
And living I to skeleton am brought.

Die Jugend fleucht! Verging als wie das Laub!
Ihr Süsses ist mir bitter weggeflossen.
Ich träne hier: Heut etwas, morgen Staub.
Die Tage sind mit Jammern mir entschossen.
Bin ich, mein Gott, zu lauter Schand gemacht?
Sollt ich allein unendlich mich abquälen?
Mein Leben war nur eine Trauernacht:
Es ist zu viel, mein Elend zu erzählen.
Doch traue ich, mein Gott, dir felsenstark:
Hilf gnädigst, eh vertrocknet Blut und Mark!

Der 15. Kühlpsalm.

Triumffunfzig betittelt über das herrliche Jesusreich, dessen Anfang
das Kühlmannsthum; fortgang das 7. Jahrtausend; Ausgang di
Ewikeit, gesungen den 28. Sept. 1677.

Triumf! Mein Jesus hat! Triumf! sein Reich bekommen!
Triumf! das Paradis! Triumf! ist eingenommen!
Triumf! drum singt mein Geist! Triumf! mit hohem schall!
Triumf! der sig verbleibt! Triumf! mein widerhall!

Triumf! wir sehen schon! Triumf! di Heilgen eilen!
Triumf! die Braut des Lamms! Triumf! beginnt zu pfeilen!
Triumf! in voller Lib! Triumf! in voller Pracht!
Triumf! weil Jesus si! Triumf! so herrlich macht!

Triumf! Ein Feur entzünd! Triumf! mir Leib und Glider!
Triumf! Ich stimme an! Triumf! di Hochzeitlider!
Triumf! zu ehren Gott! Triumf! und Gottes Sohn!
Triumf! dem Heilgen Geist! Triumf! im Himmels Thron!

Triumf! di Engel sind! Triumf! im triumffiren!
Triumf! weil widerbracht! Triumf! mit groessern ziren!

Youth flees away! Just as the leafage must!
Its sweetness bitterly from me is gone.
I weep here: present's something, morrow's dust.
My days have with loud mourning darted on.
Am I made, oh my God, for sheerest bane?
Should I alone in endless torment dwell?
My life was but a single night of pain,
My wretchedness did grow too great to tell.
Yet stone-strong, God, I on Your aid rely:
Help graciously, ere blood and marrow dry!

George C. Schoolfield

The 15th Kühl-Psalm

Triumphal Pentecost Entitled: Concerning the Splendid Realm of
Jesus, Whose Beginning Is Kuhlmann-dom; Whose Progression Is
the Seventh Millenium; Whose Exit Is Eternity; Sung on the
28th of September, 1677.

Triumph! My Jesus has! Triumph! His empire gained!
Triumph! and Paradise! Triumph! at last attained!
Triumph! thus sings my soul! Triumph! in Jubilee!
Triumph! my echo is! Triumph! His victory!

Triumph! we see forthwith! Triumph! the saints make haste!
Triumph! and full of love! Triumph! and splendor chaste!
Triumph! she hastens too! Triumph! the lamb's sweet bride!
Triumph! since Jesus her! Triumph! has glorified!

Triumph! set me afire! Triumph! in flesh and limbs!
Triumph! I shall entone! Triumph! the bridal hymns!
Triumph! to honor God! Triumph! His Son, His Own!
Triumph! and Holy Ghost! Triumph! on Heaven's throne!

Triumph! the angels now! Triumph! triumphant are!
Triumph! since there's returned! Triumph! and fairer far!

Triumf! dem Jesuel! Triumf! der Koenigstuhl!
Triumf! weil Lucifer! Triumf! im Schwefelpfuhl!

Triumf! das heilge Licht! Triumf! hat sich belichtet!
Triumf! di heilige Stadt! Triumf! ist angerichtet!
Triumf! Gott wird gesehn! Triumf! zur unser Sonn!
Triumf! wir sind verfüllt! Triumf! mit lauter wonn!

Triumf! der Erdkristall! Triumf! traegt heilge Früchte!
Triumf! unsehbar sind! Triumf! di Lichtgesichte!
Triumf! O Freudenfreud! Triumf! so gar behend!
Triumf! Triumf! Triumf! Triumf! der sonder
End.

Johann Christian Günther

Trostaria

Endlich bleibt nicht ewig aus,
Endlich wird der Trost erscheinen;
  Endlich grünt der Hofnungsstrauss,
Endlich hört man auf zu weinen,
  Endlich bricht der Thränenkrug,
  Endlich spricht der Tod: Genug!

Endlich wird aus Wasser Wein,
Endlich kommt die rechte Stunde,
  Endlich fällt der Kercker ein,
Endlich heilt die tiefe Wunde.
  Endlich macht die Sclaverey
  Den gefangnen Joseph frey.

Endlich, endlich kan der Neid,
Endlich auch Herodes sterben;

Triumph! to Jesus Lord! Triumph! the royal chair!
Triumph! since Lucifer! Triumph! knows sulphur's snare!

Triumph! the holy light! Triumph! itself has lit!
Triumph! the holy town! Triumph! will welcome it!
Triumph! God is elect! Triumph! to be our sun!
Triumph! by very bliss! Triumph! we are undone!

Triumph! earth's crystal orb! Triumph! bears holy fruit!
Triumph! the sights of light! Triumph! our sight confute!
Triumph! oh joy of joys! Triumph! that swift ascends!
Triumph! Triumph! Triumph! Triumph! that never
                  Ends!

George C. Schoolfield

Johann Christian Günther

Consolation Aria

Finally stays no more away,
Finally balm its pledge will keep,
   Finally burgeons hope's bouquet,
Finally men will cease to weep,
   Finally will the tear-jug break,
   Finally death its share forsake.

Finally water turns to wine,
Finally will the right hour peal,
   Finally falls the vault's confine,
Finally gaping wounds will heal,
   Finally will that slavery
   Turn imprisoned Joseph free.

Finally can e'en jealousness,
Finally can e'en Herod end,

Endlich Davids Hirtenkleid
Seinen Saum in Purpur färben.
Endlich macht die Zeit den Saul
Zur Verfolgung schwach und faul.

Endlich nimmt der Lebenslauf
Unsers Elends auch ein Ende;
Endlich steht ein Heiland auf,
Der das Joch der Knechtschaft wende;
Endlich machen vierzig Jahr
Die Verheissung zeitig wahr.

Endlich blüht die Aloe,
Endlich trägt der Palmbaum Früchte;
Endlich schwindet Furcht und Weh,
Endlich wird der Schmerz zu nichte;
Endlich sieht man Freudenthal;
Endlich, Endlich kommt einmahl.

Abschiedsaria

Schweig du doch nur, du Hälfte meiner Brust;
    Denn was du weinst, ist Blut aus meinem Herzen;
Ich taumle so und hab' an nichts mehr Lust
    Als an der Angst und den getreuen Schmerzen,
Womit der Stern, der unsre Liebe trennt,
                    Die Augen brennt.

Die Zärtligkeit der innerlichen Qual
    Erlaubt mir kaum, ein ganzes Wort zu machen.
Was dem geschieht, um welchen Keil und Strahl
    Bei heisser Luft in weitem Felde krachen,
Geschieht auch mir durch dieses Donnerwort:
                    Nun muss ich fort.

Finally David's shepherd-dress
Can its hem to purple lend.
  Finally Saul, by time made weak,
  Will no more his quarry seek.

  Finally will the lifelong sum
Of our woes an ending take,
  Finally will that Savior come
Who our serfdom's yoke can break,
    Finally forty years' accrue
    Timely makes the promise true.

  Finally will the aloe bloom,
Finally will the palm bear fruit,
  Finally fear must pass, and gloom,
Finally pain is destitute,
    Finally joy's demesne we see,
    Finally will some morrow be.

George C. Schoolfield

Departure Aria

Oh, be but still, you half-part of my breast!
  For what you weep is blood tapped from my heart.
I stumble and for nothing else have zest
  Than for my fear and for that faithful smart
Wherewith the star, which our love's end conspires,
                    My eye-light fires.

The tenderness of torment's inner ways
  Scarce gives me leave a single word to yield;
What him befalls, who's stunned by bolt and blaze
  In sultry weather on the open field,
Befalls me through this thunder-word's cruel blow:
                    Now I must go.

Ach harter Schluss, der unsre Musen zwingt,
　　Des Fleisses Ruhm in fremder Luft zu gründen,
Und der auch mich mit Furcht und Angst umringt!
　　Welch Pflaster kan den tiefen Riss verbinden,
Den tiefen Riss, der mich und dich zuletzt
　　　　　　In Kummer setzt?

Der Abschiedskuss verschliest mein Paradies,
　　Aus welchem mich Zeit und Verhängnüss treiben;
So viel bisher dein Antliz Sonnen wies,
　　So mancher Blitz jezt wird mein Schröcken bleiben.
Der Zweifel wacht und spricht von deiner Treu:
　　　　　　Sie ist vorbey.

Verzeih mir doch den Argwohn gegen dich,
　　Wer brünstig liebt, dem macht die Furcht stets bange.
Der Menschen Herz verändert wunderlich,
　　Wer weis, wie bald mein Geist die Post empfange,
Dass die, so mich in Gegenwart geküst,
　　　　　　Entfernt vergisst!

Gedenck einmal, wie schön wir vor gelebt,
　　Und wie geheim wir unsre Lust genossen.
Da hat kein Neid der Reizung widerstrebt,
　　Womit du mich an Hals und Brust geschlossen,
Da sah uns auch bey selbst erwüntschter Ruh
　　　　　　Kein Wächter zu.

Genung! Ich muss; die Marterglocke schlägt!
　　Hier liegt mein Herz, da nimm es aus dem Munde
Und heb es auf, die Früchte, so es trägt,
　　Sind Ruh und Trost bei mancher bösen Stunde,
Und lis, so oft dein Gram die Leute flieht,
　　　　　　Mein Abschiedslied.

Wohin ich geh, begleitet mich dein Bild,
　　Kein fremder Zug wird mir den Schaz entreissen;
Es macht mich treu und ist ein Hofnungsschild,

Hard end, by which our Muses' quire is bound
    To build our labor's fame in foreign air,
And which does me with fear and woe surround:
    What bandage can the gaping wound repair,
The gaping wound, which you and me at last
                                In woe makes fast.

The parting kiss my Paradise shuts tight,
    From which both time and fate have driven me,
So many suns your face till now did light,
    So many a bolt will now my terror be.
Doubt grows apace, and of your faith takes store:
                                Faith is no more.

And yet forgive the way my surmise goes.
    Who loves with fire, for fear is easy prey.
The heart of man strange transformation knows.
    Who'll tell when my soul's messenger will say:
That she, who me with present kisses pets,
                                Far off forgets.

Reflect again, how fair we once did live,
    And how with secret joy we once were blest.
No envy then that charm made fugitive
    With which you gathered me to throat and breast.
Nor did our self-desired repose fall prize
                                To sentry's eyes.

Enough! I go, the death-bell breaks the air.
    Here lies my heart, it from my mouth remove
And keep it safe: the fruits, which it will bear,
    In evil hours will rest and comfort prove;
And read, whene'er your grief would flee the throng,
                                My farewell-song.

Where'er I go, your image follows too,
    A treasure proof 'gainst every foreign blast;
It is a shield of hope, and makes me true,

Wenn Neid und Noth Verfolgungssteine schmeissen,
Bis dass die Hand, die uns hier Dörner flicht,
Die Myrthen bricht.

Erinnre dich zum öftern meiner Huld
Und nähre sie mit süssem Angedencken;
Du wirst betrübt, diess ist des Abschieds Schuld,
So muss ich dich zum ersten Mahle kräncken,
Und fordert mich der erste Gang von hier,
So sterb ich dir.

Ich sterbe dir, und soll ein fremder Sand
Den oft durch dich ergözten Leib bedecken,
So gönne mir das lezte Liebespfand
Und las ein Kreuz mit dieser Grabschrift stecken:
Wo ist ein Mensch der treulich lieben kann?
Hier liegt der Mann.

Friedrich von Hagedorn

Anakreon

In Tejos und in Samos
Und in der Stadt Minervens
Sang ich von Wein und Liebe,
Von Rosen und vom Frühling,
Von Freundschaft und von Tänzen,
Doch höhnt ich nicht die Götter,
Auch nicht der Götter Diener,
Auch nicht der Götter Tempel,
Wie hieß ich sonst der Weise?

When need and envy nagging cobbles cast,
Until the hand, which here our thorn-wreath makes,
           The myrtle breaks.

Think often how my love did you exalt,
   And feed it with sweet memory's dessert;
Now you are saddened: this is parting's fault,
   That I must for the first time do you hurt.
When from this place my infant steps I try,
           For you I die.

I die for you, and if some foreign sand
   That body hides which you oft pleasure gave,
Then put our love's last pledge within my hand,
   And let a cross, thus written, grace my grave:
Where is a man, who true love does revere?
           That man lies here.

George C. Schoolfield

Friedrich von Hagedorn

Anacreon

In Teos and in Samos
And in Minerva's city
I sang of wine and loving,
Of roses and of springtime,
Of friendship and of dances;
But never did I mock at
Gods, nor their servants,
Nor make sport of their temples.
Else, who'd call me the Sage One?

Ihr Dichter voller Jugend,
Wollt ihr bei froher Muße
Anakreontisch singen,
So singt von milden Reben,
Von rosenreichen Hecken,
Vom Frühling und von Tänzen,
Von Freundschaft und von Liebe,
Doch höhnet nicht die Gottheit,

Auch nicht der Gottheit Diener,
Auch nicht der Gottheit Tempel.
Verdienet, selbst im Scherzen,
Den Namen echter Weisen.

Ewald von Kleist

Grab-Lied

Weh dir! daß du gestorben bist.
Du wirst nicht mehr Auroren sehn
Wenn sie vom Morgen Himmel blickt
In rother Tracht, mit güldnem Haar;
Und die bethauten Wiesen nicht,
Auch nicht im melancholschen Hayn
Die Sonn im Spiegel grüner Fluth.
Der Veilchen Duft wird dich nicht mehr
Erfreun, und das Gemurmel nicht
Des Bachs, der Rosen-Büsche tränckt,
Auf dem vor Zephirs sanftem Hauch
Die kleinen krausen Wellen fliehn.
Auch wird dich Philomele nicht
Mehr rühren, durch der Töne Macht,

Brim-full of youth, you poets,
If you, in happy leisure,
Would sing Anacreon's measures,
Then sing of wine, mild-flavored,
Of hedges rich in roses,
Of springtime and of dances,
Of friendship and of loving;
But do not mock the godhead,

Nor mock the godhead's servants,
Nor mock the godhead's temples.
But, even jesting, merit
The title of true sages.

George C. Schoolfield

Ewald von Kleist

Song at Graveside

Unhappy fate: that you have died.
Aurora you will see no more
When she peers from the morning sky
All dressed in scarlet, golden haired,
Nor will you see the meadows' dew
Nor in the melancholy grove
Behold the sunlight on the greenish pond.
The smell of violets will no more
Delight you, nor the murmuring of
The brook that gives the roses drink,
The brook whose curling wavelets flee
Before the zephyr's gentle breath.
Philomele* will no more stir
You through the power of song,

---

*The nightingale.

Auch meines Krausens Laute nicht
Die Philomelen ähnlich seufzt.

Allein, du wirst auch nicht mehr sehn,
Daß sich der Tugendhaffte qvält,
Sich seiner Blöse schämt und darbt
Und seine Lebenszeit verweint;
Indeßen daß in Seid und Gold
Der Bösewicht stolzirt und lacht.
Du wirst nicht sehn, daß ein Tyrann
Die Ferse, freygebohrnem Volck
In den gebognen Nacken setzt,
Das ihm Tribut und Steur bezahlt,
Nicht für den Schutz, nein, für die Luft.
Kein Narr, kein Höfling wird dich mehr
Mit dummer Falschheit peinigen,
Und keine Rachsucht sieht auf dich
Mit scheelen Blicken eines Wolfs.
Nicht Ungewitter, Pestilenz
Und Erderschütterung und Krieg
Erschreckt dich mehr. Der Erde Punckt
(Samt Pestilenz und Krieg und Noth)
Flieht unter deinen Füßen fort,
In Dunst und Blitz gewickelt. Sturm
Und Donner ruft weit unter dir,
Und Ruh und Freude labt dein Herz
In Gegenden voll Heiterkeit.
Wohl dir, daß du gestorben bist!

Nor will the lute in Krause's* hands,
Which sighs like to Philomele.

And yet you will no more behold
How virtuous men are racked by tail,
Go almost bare in rags, and starve,
And weep away their time on earth,
While, proudly decked in silk and gold,
The scoundrel brags and preens and laughs.
You will not see how tyrants grind
Their heel into the servile neck
Of people free born, paying now
Their tributes and their taxes, not
For shelter but for very air.
No jester and no courtier now
Will twit you with dull perfidy,
Vengeance will follow you no more
With vulpine glances, eyes asquint.
No more will storm and pestilence
And quakings of the earth† and war
Fill you with fear. Earth's little dot
(And pestilence and war and want)
Now flee away beneath your feet,
Shrouded in mists and lightning. Storms
And thunder bellow far below,
And peace and gladness salve your heart
In regions of serenity.
Oh happy fate: that you have died!

George C. Schoolfield

---

*Christian Gottfried Krause (1729–70), lawyer by profession, was a friend of Kleist, Gleim, and Ramler. Kleist's own note to the poem describes Krause's other and very distinguished accomplishments: "Author of the treatise on musical poetry, a consummate musician both in practice and theory."

†The Lisbon earthquake of 1755 attracted horrified attention throughout Europe: see Voltaire's *Poème sur le déstastre de Lisbonne* and Johann Peter Uz's "Das Erdbeben" (The earthquake).

Johann Wilhelm Ludwig Gleim

An den Tod

Tod, kannst du dich auch verlieben?
Warum holst du denn mein Mädchen?
Kannst du nicht die Mutter holen?
Denn die sieht dir doch noch ähnlich.
Frische rosenrote Wangen,
Die mein Wunsch so schön gefärbet,
Blühen nicht für blasse Knochen,
Blühen nicht für deine Lippen.
Tod, was willst du mit dem Mädchen?
Mit den Zähnen ohne Lippen
Kannst du es ja doch nicht küssen.

Anakreon

Anakreon, mein Lehrer,
Singt nur von Wein und Liebe;
Er salbt den Bart mit Salben,
Und singt von Wein und Liebe;
Er krönt sein Haupt mit Rosen,
Und singt von Wein und Liebe;
Er paaret sich im Garten,
Und singt von Wein und Liebe;
Er wird beim Trunk ein König,
Und singt von Wein und Liebe;
Er spielt mit seinen Göttern,
Er lacht mit seinen Freunden,
Vertreibt sich Gram und Sorgen,
Verschmäht den reichen Pöbel,
Verwirft das Lob der Helden,

Johann Wilhelm Ludwig Gleim

To Death

Death, can you too be enamored?
Why then must you fetch my sweetheart?
Can't you fetch, instead, her mother?
After all, *she* looks quite like you.
Fresh-hued cheeks, as red as roses,
Which my wish made blush so nicely,
For pale bones will never blossom,
For your lips will never blossom.
Death! what good's to you my sweetheart?
With your lipless teeth you surely
Cannot mean to give her kisses.

> *George C. Schoolfield*

Anacreon

Anacreon, my teacher,
Sings but of wine and loving;
Anoints his beard with ointments,
And sings of wine and loving;
Enwreathes his head with roses,
And sings of wine and loving;
He couples in the garden,
And sings of wine and loving;
Becomes in drink a monarch,
And sings of wine and loving;
He plays games with his godheads,
He leads his friends in laughter,
Disperses care and worry,
Disdains the rich and vulgar,
Dismisses praise of heroes,

Und singt von Wein und Liebe:
Soll denn sein treuer Schüler
Von Hass und Wasser singen?

Johann Nikolaus Götz

Erstes Rondeau:
nach einem französischen Dichter aus dem 14. Jahrhundert

Des schönen Frühlings Hoffurier
Bereitet wieder das Quartier
Und spreitet über unser Gosen
Tapeten von beliebter Zier,
Durchstickt mit Veilchen und mit Rosen.
Des schönen Frühlings Hoffurier
Bereitet wieder das Quartier.

　Cupido lag als wie erstarrt
Im Schnee des Februar verscharrt;
Itzt tanzt er unter Aprikosen,
Und alles ist in ihn vernarrt.
Ein jedes Herz, ihm liebzukosen,
Ruft: „Rauher Winter, fleuch von hier";
Des schönen Frühlings Hoffurier
Bereitet wieder das Quartier.

And sings of wine and loving:
Shall then his faithful pupil
Sing songs of hate and water?

George C. Schoolfield

Johann Nikolaus Götz

First Rondeau:
after a French Poet of the Fourteenth Century

The quartermaster of the spring,
Once more his billet's readying
And on our Goshen's meadow throws
A carpet of sweet coloring,
Worked through with violet and rose.
The quartermaster of the spring.
Once more his billet's readying

Cupid, who as if frozen, lay
In February snowed away,
'Midst apricots now dancing goes,
For love of him, all's mad today,
And each heart its hotness shows,
With shouts: "Cruel winter, no lingering."
The quartermaster of the spring.
Once more his billet's readying.

George C. Schoolfield

Zweites Rondeau

Den Rock von Regen, Wind und Schnee
Hat nun die Jahrszeit ausgezogen.
Ihr ist ein schönerer von Klee
Und Sonnenstrahlen angeflogen.
Myrtill singt mit der Galathee:*
Den Rock von Regen, Wind und Schnee
Hat nun die Jahrszeit ausgezogen.

Das junge Tal, die lichte Höh
Stehn glänzender als Regenbogen.
Demanten trägt auch selbst der Schlee;
Es funkeln alle Wasserwogen
In prächtig-silberner Livree.
Den Rock von Regen, Wind und Schnee
Hat nun die Jahrszeit ausgezogen.

Karl Wilhelm Ramler

Sehnsucht nach dem Winter
1744

Die Stürme befahren die Luft, verhüllen den Himmel in Wolken,
     Und jagen donnernde Ströme durchs Land;
Die Wälder stehen entblöst: das Laub der geselligen Linde
     Wird weit umher in die Thäler geführt.

---

*"Galatea" is the name of the sea nymph to whom the shepherd Moeris sings in Virgil, *Eclogue* IX:39–43—"Come hither, oh Galatea; for what fun is there in the waves? Shining spring is here; here, hear the rivers, the earth brings forth all sorts of flowers."

Second Rondeau

Its skirt of rain and wind and snow
The season now has put aside,
And, to her, fairer garments go
Where shamrocks and the sun abide.
The nymph and shepherd sing in twain:
"Its skirt of rain and wind and snow
The season now has put aside."

The youthful vales, the hills' bright row
Outshine the rainbow in its pride,
And diamonds even deck the sloe,
While all the waves at waterside
In splendid-silver vestments flow.
Its skirt of rain and wind and snow
The season now has put aside.

George C. Schoolfield

Karl Wilhelm Ramler

Yearning for Winter
1744*

The tempests pass through the air, as they pile up cloudbank on
        cloudbank,
    And chase the thundering streams through the land;
The forests stand stripped all bare, and the leaves of the sociable
        lindens
    Are harried far and away in the dales.

*Like Klopstock, Ramler in this poem uses a "Horatian" strophic form, an altered
version (with anacrusis) of the First Archilochian:

u/-uu/-uu-//uu/-uu/-uu/-u
u/-uu/-uu/-

Also, the poem is a partial imitation of Horace, *Odes,* I: 9. Ramler's text used here is
that of his first version of 1744; he later revised (and weakened) some lines.

Der Weinstock, ein dürres Gestrauch—Was klag ich den göttlichen
    Weinstock?
    Auf! Freunde, trinket sein schäumendes Blut,
Und lasst den Autumnus entfliehn mit ausgeleeretem Füllhorn,
    Und ruft den Winter im Tannenkranz her.

Er deckt den donnernden Strom mit diamantenem Schilde,
    Der alle Pfeile der Sonne verhöhnt,
Und füllt mit Blüthe den Wald, daß alle Thiere sich wundern,
    Und säet Lilien über das Thal.

Dann zittern die Bräute nicht mehr in wankender Gondel; sie
    fliegen
    Beherzt auf gleitenden Wagen dahin:
Der Liebling wärmet sich falsch im Hermeline der Nymphe,
    Die Nymphe lächelt und wehret ihm falsch.

Dann baden die Knaben nicht mehr, und schwimmen nicht unter
    den Fischen;
    Sie gehn auf harten Gewässern einher,
Und haben Schuhe von Stal: der Mann der freundlichen Venus
    Verbarg der Blitze Geschwindigkeit drein.

O Winter! eile voll Zorn, und nimm den kältesten Ostwind,
    Und treib die Krieger aus Böhmen zurück,
Und meinen erstarrten Kleist. Noch hab' ich ihm seine Lykoris,
    Und Wein von mürrischem Alter bewahrt.

The grapevine's a withered bush—yet do I mourn for the
    grapevine?
    Come, friends, and drink of its high-frothing blood.
Now let Autumnus escape, his horn of plenty exhausted.
    And summon Winter, fir-crowned, to our midst!

He covers the thundering stream with a breastplate as hard as a
    diamond,
    Which mocks each arrow the sun may dispatch,
He fills the forests with blooms that make animals stop in
    amazement,
    And strews his lilies out over the dale.

Now maidens need tremble no more at the gondola's bob: they go
    soaring,
    Stout-hearted, safe in the swift-gliding sleigh,
A pretense, the lover seeks warmth in his nymph's soft wrapping of
    ermine,
    The nymph but smiles and, a pretense, resists.

No more do the boys go to bathe, go swimming no more with the
    fishes,
    Instead, they stride over waters grown stiff,
And have footwear forged out of steel: the husband of amiable
    Venus
    Concealed the lightning-bolts' speed in their last.

Oh Winter, advance in your rage, enlisting the iciest eastwinds,
    And drive the troops in Bohemia home,
And with them my Kleist!* since for him I have kept his Lycoris†
    well-sheltered,
    And wine too, guarded from grumpy old age.

George C. Schoolfield

---

*Ewald von Kleist, Ramler's close friend.
†The name of a girl, "with a low forehead" and probably fickle, in Horace, *Odes,*
I:33.

Friedrich Gottlob Klopstock

Das Rosenband

Im Frühlingsschatten fand ich sie;
Da band ich sie mit Rosenbändern:
Sie fühlt' es nicht und schlummerte.

Ich sah sie an; mein Leben hing
Mit diesem Blick an ihrem Leben:
Ich fühlt' es wohl und wußt es nicht.

Doch lispelt' ich ihr sprachlos zu
Und rauschte mit den Rosenbändern:
Da wachte sie vom Schlummer auf.

Sie sah mich an; ihr Leben hing
Mit diesem Blick an meinem Leben,
Und um uns ward's Elysium.

Die Frühen Gräber

Willkommen, o silberner Mond,
Schöner, stiller Gefährt der Nacht!
Du entfliehst? Eile nicht, bleib, Gedankenfreund!
Sehet, er bleibt, das Gewölk wallte nur hin.

Des Maies Erwachen ist nur
Schöner noch wie die Sommernacht,
Wenn ihm Tau, hell wie Licht, aus der Locke träuft,
Und zu dem Hügel herauf rötlich er kömmt.

Friedrich Gottlob Klopstock

The Rose Wreaths

I found her in the shade of spring
and bound her then with wreaths of roses;
she felt it not and slumbered on.

I looked at her, and in this glance
my life was joined to hers forever;
I felt it, though I knew it not.

I stammered several broken words
and made the leaves and petals rustle;
then from her slumber she awoke.

She looked at me, and in this glance
her life was joined to mine forever,
and round us was Elysium.

J. W. Thomas

The Early Graves

I welcome you, silvery moon,
lovely, silent compeer of night.
Must you go? Hasten not, stay, O friend of thought.
See, she remains, only clouds wandered their way.

The waking of May is alone
fairer still than the summer night,
when the dew, bright as light, from her ringlets falls
and, cheeks aglow, she ascends over the hill.

Ihr Edleren, ach, es bewächst
Eure Male schon ernstes Moos!
O wie war glücklich ich, als ich noch mit euch
Sahe sich röten den Tag, schimmern die Nacht!

Die Sommernacht

Wenn der Schimmer von dem Monde nun herab
  In die Wälder sich ergießt, und Gerüche
    Mit den Düften von der Linde
    In den Kühlungen wehn;

So umschatten mich Gedanken an das Grab
  Der Geliebten, und ich seh in dem Walde
    Nur es dämmern, und es weht mir
    Von der Blüte nicht her.

Ich genoß einst, o ihr Toten, es mit euch!
  Wie umwehten uns der Duft und die Kühlung,
    Wie verschönt warst von dem Monde,
    Du o schöne Natur!

You noble ones, now the dark moss
grows on stones which were carved for you.
O how glad was I then, when I shared with you
reddening gleams of the dawn, shimmering nights.

J. W. Thomas

The Summer Night*

When the shimmer of the moonlight now descends
On the forests, and there comes now a sweetness
With the breezes from the linden
In the cool of the glade;

Then, as shadows, thoughts surround me of the grave
Of my loved ones, and I see in the forests
But *its* looming, and the blossoms
Come no more to me here.

Once I knew joy in it with you, oh you dead!
Oh how sweet then came to us smell and coolness,
Oh how fair then from the moonlight
You, fair nature, did grow!

George C. Schoolfield

---

*The strophic form is 'quasi-Horatian', of Klopstock's own devising; in his musical setting, Christoph Willibald Gluck perfectly captured the flowing metrical scheme:

```
uu-u/uu-u/uu-
uu-u/uu- /uu-u
uu-u/uu-u
uu-/uu-
```

Friedensburg

Selbst der Engel entschwebt Wonnegefilden, läßt
Seine Krone voll Glanz unter den Himmlischen,
  Wandelt, unter den Menschen
    Mensch, in Jünglingsgestalt umher.

Laß denn, Muse, den Hain, wo du das Weltgericht,
Und die Könige singst, welche verworfen sind!
  Komm, hier winken dich Täler
    In ihr Tempe zur Erd' herab.

Komm, es hoffet ihr Wink! Wo du der Zeder Haupt
Durch den steigenden Schall deines Gesangs bewegst,
  Nicht nur jene Gefilde
    Sind mit lachendem Reiz bekränzt;

Auch hier stand die Natur, da sie aus reicher Hand
Über Hügel und Tal lebende Schönheit goß,
  Mit verweilendem Tritte,
    Diese Täler zu schmücken, still.

Sieh den ruhenden See, wie sein Gestade sich,
Dicht vom Walde bedeckt, sanfter erhoben hat,
  Und den schimmernden Abend
    In der grünlichen Dämmrung birgt.

Sieh des schattenden Walds Wipfel. Sie neigen sich.
Vor dem kommenden Hauch lauterer Lüfte? Nein,
  Friedrich kömmt in den Schatten!
    Darum neigen die Wipfel sich.

Fredensborg*

From the meadows of bliss even the angel goes,
Leaving among the blest, in all its light, his crown,
Wanders, human 'midst humans,
In the form of a youth on earth.

Come, oh Muse, from that grove where of the final day
You have sung, and of kings who shall be set aside!†
Come, the valleys here call you,
Come to earth, to this Tempe's vale.

Come, their call springs from hope! There you have moved the tops
Of the cedars‡ with song, rising in splendor high,
—Not those regions alone are
Crowned with wreaths wrought of blessedness.

Here too nature did stand, pouring out freely
Over valleys and hills beauty that lived and breathed,
Still, with tarrying footstep,
It made lovely these valleys too.

See the lake in its rest, see how its edges rise,
Thickly covered with woods, all the more gently here,
And, in greening of twilight,
Hide the shimmer of eventide.

See the treetops bow down in the shadowing woodlands;
Does the sweet air that blows give them this movement? No,
Frederick comes in the shadows,
Thus the tops of the trees bow down.

---

*In 1751, Klopstock was the guest of his Maecenas, Fredrik V of Denmark (1723–66), at the latter's summer residence, Fredensborg, on the shore of Lake Estrom in northeastern Sjelland. As a patron of the arts and sciences, Fredrik deserved Klopstock's praise; unfortunately, the monarch had a taste for drink, and other pleasures of the flesh, which contributed substantially to his early death.
†The muse of Klopstock's biblical epic *The Messiah*.
‡*The Messiah* mentions the cedars of Lebanon in its eighteenth canto.

Warum lächelt dein Blick? warum ergießet sich
Diese Freude, der Reiz, heller vom Aug' herab?
   Wird sein festlicher Name
     Schon genannt, wo die Palme weht?

»Glaubest du, daß auf das, so auf der Erd' ihr tut,
Wir mit forschendem Blick wachsam nicht niedersehn?
   Und die Edlen nicht kennen,
     Die so einsam hier unten sind?

Da wir, wenn er kaum reift, schon den Gedanken sehn,
Und die werdende Tat, eh sie hinübertritt
   Vor das Auge des Schauers,
     Und nun andre Gebärden hat!

Kann was heiliger uns, als ein Gebieter sein,
Der zwar feurig und jung, dennoch ein Weiser ist,
   Und, die höchste der Würden,
     Durch sich selber, noch mehr erhöht?

Heil dem König! er hört, rufet die Stund' ihm einst,
Die auch Kronen vom Haupt, wenn sie ertönet, wirft,
   Unerschrocken ihr Rufen,
     Lächelt, schlummert zu Glücklichen

Still hinüber! Um ihn stehn in Versammlungen
Seine Taten umher, jede mit Licht gekrönt,
   Jede bis zu dem Richter
     Seine sanfte Begleiterin.«

Why, Muse, does your glance smile? Why does a tear descend,
Brighter, sprung from this joy, out of your eye entranced?
Is his name in its splendor
Named already where palmtrees grow?*

"Do you think we do not, ever with searching glance,
Look in our vigilance down at your deeds on earth?
That we know not those noble
Hearts which, lonely, reside below?

Almost ere it is born, we can perceive the thought,
See the deed as it grows, ere it crosses, to pass
To the eyes of earth's watchers,
And now takes other movements there.

What's more sacred to us than such a king as this,
Truly, fiery and young, and yet a sage at heart,
Who, that highest of virtues,
Through himself rises higher still.

To this monarch, all hail! When someday that hour comes
Which, at its call, will take crowns of the earth away,
Unafraid he will listen,
Smile, and go, quietly slumbering,

To the land of the blest. There, each crowned with a light,
All in their serried rows, marshalled his deeds will stand,
Each, his gentle handmaiden,
Will walk with him before his judge."

George C. Schoolfield

---

*That is, Heaven itself, invested by Klopstock with the vegetation of the Holy Land. (The strophic form of this encomiastic ode is the same as that employed in "The Lake of Zurich," the Fourth Asclepiadean.)

Der Zürchersee

Schön ist, Mutter Natur, deiner Erfindung Pracht
Auf die Fluren verstreut, schöner ein froh Gesicht,
    Das den großen Gedanken
      Deiner Schöpfung noch *einmal* denkt.

Von des schimmernden Sees Traubengestaden her,
Oder, flohest du schon wieder zum Himmel auf,
    Komm in rötendem Strahle
      Auf dem Flügel der Abendluft,

Komm, und lehre mein Lied jugendlich heiter sein,
Süße Freude, wie du! gleich dem beseelteren
    Schnellen Jauchzen des Jünglings,
      Sanft, der fühlenden Fanny gleich.

Schon lag hinter uns weit Uto, an dessen Fuß
Zürch in ruhigem Tal freie Bewohner nährt;
    Schon war manches Gebirge
      Voll von Reben vorbeigeflohn.

Jetzt entwölkte sich fern silberner Alpen Höh,
Und der Jünglinge Herz schlug schon empfindender,
    Schon verriet es beredter
      Sich der schönen Begleiterin.

»Hallers Doris«, die sang, selber des Liedes wert,
Hirzels Daphne, den Kleist innig wie Gleimen liebt;

The Lake of Zurich*

Mother Nature, how fair has your invention's grace
Been strewn over the world. Fairer's a happy face,
Which the mighty designing
Of creation once more has thought.

Leave the shimmering lake's vine-shrouded shores and come,
Or, if already you've flown up to the heavens now,
Come then, in the red beamings,
On the wings of the evening air.

Come, instructing my song how to be young and glad,
Gladness, even as you! Like the more vigorous,
Quick rejoicing of young men,
Like to Fanny, the gentle one.†

Uto lay far behind, Uto,‡ at whose foot Zürich feeds
Free-born citizens there, safe in the vale of peace,
Many hills had already
Hastened past with their vinyardings.

Now the silvery Alps came from their clouds on high,
And the heart of these youths beat more mightily now,
Now it spoke the more freely
To the fair one who came with us.

Haller's Doris was sung by Hirzel's Daphne there,
She worthy of her song, he Gleim's dear friend and Kleist's,

---

*Klopstock's excursion on the Lake of Zurich took place on July 30, 1750. The poem, like the "Fredensborg" ode, is written in a so-called Horatian meter, the Fourth Asclepiadean.

$$-\upsilon/-\upsilon\upsilon/-//-/\upsilon\upsilon-/\upsilon\upsilon$$
$$-\upsilon/-\upsilon\upsilon/-//-/\upsilon\upsilon-/\upsilon\upsilon$$
$$-\upsilon/-\upsilon\upsilon/-\upsilon$$
$$-\upsilon/-\upsilon\upsilon/-\upsilon-$$

†"Fanny" is Klopstock's cousin, Maria Sophie Schmidt, to whom the poet addressed his early amatory odes.
‡The Utlisberg.

Und wir Jünglinge sangen
Und empfanden wie Hagedorn.

Jetzo nahm uns die Au in die beschattenden
Kühlen Arme des Walds, welcher die Insel krönt;
   Da, da kamest du, Freude!
     Volles Maßes auf uns herab!

Göttin Freude, du selbst! dich, wir empfanden dich!
Ja, du warest es selbst, Schwester der Menschlichkeit,
   Deiner Unschuld Gespielin,
     Die sich über uns ganz ergoß!

Süß ist, fröhlicher Lenz, deiner Bergeistrung Hauch,
Wenn die Flur dich gebiert, wenn sich dein Odem sanft
   In der Jünglinge Herzen,
     Und die Herzen der Mädchen gießt.

Ach du machst das Gefühl siegend, es steigt durch dich
Jede blühende Brust schöner, und bebender,
   Lauter redet der Liebe
     Nun entzauberter Mund durch dich!

Lieblich winket der Wein, wenn er Empfindungen,
Beßre sanftere Lust, wenn er Gedanken winkt,
   Im sokratischen Becher
     Von der tauenden Ros' umkränzt;

Wenn er dringt bis ins Herz, und zu Entschließungen,
Die der Säufer verkennt, jeden Gedanken weckt,
   Wenn er lehret verachten,
     Was nicht würdig des Weisen ist.

Reizvoll klinget des Ruhms lockender Silberton
In das schlagende Herz, und die Unsterblichkeit

And we youths raised our voices
And our hearts were as Hagedorn's.*

Now the welcoming Au† took us, and led the way
To that woodland's cool shade, which is the island's crown.
Then, then, joy, you did greet us,
Come down full in your measuring!

Joy, oh goddess, you came, and we perceived you there!
Surely now, it was you, sister of humankind,
Your sweet purity's playmate,
You who entered us wholly there!

Happy springtime, how sweet is your high-hearted breath,
When you're born of the fields, when your gentle breath flows
To the hearts of the youths there,
Flows to the hearts of the maidens there.

Oh, to feeling you give triumph, and in your grasp
Breasts grow fairer and bloom, grow more sensitive still,
Stronger, loving's own mouth is
Freed from spells by your strength, and speaks.

Lovely sparkles the wine, when it calls feelings forth,
Better, quieter joy, when it can summon thoughts
Out of Socrates' goblet,
Wreathed with roses the dew's made wet.

When it goes to the heart, and can awake each thought
To decisions which are never the drunkard's own.
When it tells us to shun
All that wise men call shamefulness.

Fame's seductive-sweet tone, silvery luring us,
Strikes the heart with its charm, for mighty is the thought,

*The strophe contains references both to Klopstock's Swiss admirers and German poets of his time. "Doris" is a poem by Albrecht von Haller, "Hirzel's Daphne" is the wife of the Swiss physician, Johann Kaspar Hirzel.
†"Die Au" is an island in the Lake of Zurich.

Ist ein großer Gedanke,
    Ist des Schweißes der Edlen wert!

Durch der Lieder Gewalt, bei der Urenkelin
Sohn und Tochter noch sein; mit der Entzückung Ton
    Oft beim Namen genennet,
        Oft gerufen vom Grabe her,

Dann ihr sanfteres Herz bilden, und, Liebe, dich,
Fromme Tugend, dich auch gießen ins sanfte Herz,
    Ist, beim Himmel! nicht wenig!
        Ist des Schweißes der Edlen wert!

Aber süßer ist noch, schöner und reizender,
In dem Arme des Freunds wissen ein Freund zu sein!
    So das Leben genießen,
        Nicht unwürdig der Ewigkeit!

Treuer Zärtlichkeit voll, in den Umschattungen,
In den Lüften des Walds, und mit gesenktem Blick
    Auf die silberne Welle,
        Tat ich schweigend den frommen Wunsch:

Wäret ihr auch bei uns, die ihr mich ferne liebt,
In des Vaterlands Schoß einsam von mir verstreut,
    Die in seligen Stunden
        Meine suchende Seele fand;

O so bauten wir hier Hütten der Freundschaft uns!
Ewig wohnten wir hier, ewig! Der Schattenwald
    Wandelt' uns sich in Tempe,
        Jenes Tal in Elysium!

That we may be immortal,
Worth a noble man's laboring.

Through the power of song still to find dwelling-place,
In the daughters and sons of some descendant: there
With the tone of entrancement
Named and called from the grave to them,

Song shapes their gentler heart, pours in that gentle heart
You, love, joining to you virtue, all pious, there:
This, in truth, is not small!
Worthy of noble laboring!

Yet it's sweeter by far, fairer and lovelier,
This: to know you're a friend held in a friend's sure arm!
Thus to taste of existence
Is a way worth eternity!

With true tenderness full, hidden in shadowed glades,
In the winds of the wood, with my gaze downward turned,
Back to waves all of silver,
I, in silence, went wishing there:

Were you also with us, you who love me afar,
You in the homeland's womb, lonely and far from me,
Who in blissfulness' hours
Found my soul as it sought for you,

Oh, then, know we would build friendship's fair dwellings* here,
Here forever we'd dwell, and this fair, shaded wood
Would be changed into Tempe,†
And that vale to Elysium.

George C. Schoolfield

*Klopstock alludes to Mark 9:5, "And Peter answered and said to Jesus: 'Master, it is good for us to be here; and let us make three tabernacles; one for thee, and one for Moses, and one for Elias.' "
†Tempe is the vale in Thessaly, often praised in antiquity for its beauty.

The Authors

HEINRICH ALBERT (1604–51) was born in Lobenstein in Thuringia. He studied law at Leipzig, but abandoned that career to devote himself to music, spending the greater part of his life as the cathedral organist in Königsberg, where he was prominent in the Königsberg circle of lyricists. He set the songs of his friends to music as well as writing verse of his own.

ALBRECHT VON JOHANNSDORF (late twelfth century) was a minor nobleman from East Bavaria who was employed in the service of the bishops of Passau. His life is documented between 1185 and 1209. It is possible that he may have been acquainted with Walther von der Vogelweide. As did Friedrich von Hausen, Albrecht participated in the third crusade.

ANGELUS SILESIUS (Johannes Scheffler) (1624–77) was born in Breslau and raised in the Protestant faith. Scheffler, who wrote under the pseudonym of Angelus Silesius (The Silesian Messenger), studied medicine at Strasbourg, Leyden (where he read Böhme and Ruysbroeck) and Padua, entering the service of Duke Sylvius Nimrod of Württemberg-Oels in 1648 as court physician. Here he got to know Abraham von Frankenberg and further pursued his interest in mysticism. After a dispute over a religious tractate, he returned to Breslau, where in 1653 he converted to Catholicism. Ordained in 1661, he devoted himself to the cause of the Counter-Reformation, spending his last years as a recluse in the St. Matthew cloister in Breslau. In 1657 his *Geistreiche Sinn- und Schlußreime (Ingenious Rhymes of Wit and Conclusion)* appeared, and, of all his writings, earned him enduring fame, after being augmented by a sixth book, reissued and retitled *Der cherubinische Wandersmann (The Cherubical Wanderer)* in 1675. The work contains over 1,600 brief poems, most of which are mystical and paradoxical epigrams set in pairs of Alexandrines.

ANTON ULRICH (HERZOG VON BRAUNSCHWEIG-WOLFENBÜTTEL) (1633–1714), the second son of duke Ernst August, was given an excellent education by Siegmund von Birken and J. G. Schottel. After his father's death, he was named stadholder by his brother in 1667, and, in 1685, co-regent. He succeeded to power after his brother's death, returning to Brunswick after a brief punitive eviction (at the order of Leopold I) for his pro-French and pro-Hanoverian stance during the War of the Spanish Succession. He converted to Roman Catholicism in 1710, having first safeguarded the rights of his Protestant citizens. A patron of both the arts and the sciences, Anton was an artist himself, and was made a member of the Fruit-bringing Society in 1659. Beginning his literary career by writing Protestant odes, he wrote two very long and highly complex courtly novels, *Die Durchleuchtige Syrerin Aramena* (The Illustrious Syrian Aramena, 1669–73) and *Octavia, Römische Geschichte* (Octavia, a Roman story, 1677), later revised as *Die römische Octavia* (The Roman Octavia, 1711 and 1712).

SIGMUND VON BIRKEN (1626–81) was sent as a child to Nuremberg by his father, a Protestant pastor, to escape the dangers of the war. Birken returned briefly to Nuremberg after studying in Jena, and, in 1646, joined the Hirten-und Blumenorden an der Pegnitz (the Shepherd-and-Flower-Order on the Pegnitz). He returned again to Nuremberg in 1648, after having tutored the Brunswick princes in Wolfenbüttel and in 1662, became the head of the Flower-Order. A versatile writer, his elaborate compositions include dramas, odes, and pastoral novels, but his genius is most evident in his lyric works.

SIMON DACH (1605–59) was born in Memel on the Baltic. He became schoolmaster in Königsberg in 1633 and professor of poetry at the university in 1639, swelling his slender earnings with the diligent publication of occasional verse. By nature a melancholy and retiring lyricist, Dach was nevertheless a congenial member, with Heinrich Albert and Robert Roberthin, of the "Pumpkin-Hut" group, and figured prominently in the Königsberg circle of poets.

DIETMAR VON EIST (?–1171?) was a member of a noble Upper-Austrian family. He wrote in the middle of the twelfth century and may be identical with a Dietmar von Aist who died in 1171. It is believed that he lived too early to have written many of the stanzas attributed to him.

PAUL FLEMING (1609–40) was one of the greatest lyric poets of the baroque. He left his village of Hartenstein to attend the Thomasschule at Leipzig, and later, to study medicine there. In 1633 he traveled across Germany to take part in a commercial expedition that Friedrich III of Holstein-Gottorp was planning to send to Russia and Persia. The intrepid ambassadors reached Moscow and returned in 1634, while Fleming waited in Reval for the second stage of the journey. He set out for Persia in 1636, returning to Reval the following year, where he married Anna Niehus, who, unlike her sister, Elsabe, had been able to wait, unwed, for his return. He completed his medical studies in 1639, setting up a practice in Hamburg, only to die of an illness shortly after his arrival. The loss was an enormous one to German literature. His *Teutsche Poemata* were published posthumously in 1642.

FRIEDRICH VON HAUSEN (?–1190) belonged to a well-known noble family from Kreuznach near Mainz. He was part of the most intimate circle around Friedrich I and served in two campaigns in Italy in 1186 and 1187. During the latter, his commander was Heinrich VI. He died on Friedrich's crusade in 1190. Provençal influence dominates in his early work. His three crusaders' songs, in which *minne* and God are in conflict, are his finest achievement.

PAUL GERHARDT (1607–76) was son of the mayor of the little Saxon town of Gräfenhainichen. He became the most notable Protestant hymn writer of the Baroque. Educated at the Prince's School at Grimma and at Wittenberg University, where he studied theology, he was eventually given one of the most important pastoral appointments in Berlin, the St. Nicholas Church, in 1651. A staunch and uncompromising Lutheran, Gerhardt became embroiled in a dispute with the Calvinistic Elector of Brandenburg during which he was dismissed. Although the Electoral order for his dismissal was rescinded, Gerhardt bowed to the higher demands of his conscience and insisted on resigning from his post in 1667. He was supported by friends and parishioners for two years before being appointed pastor at Lübben, where he lived out the rest of his years. Gerhardt's verse, almost all of which is intended to be sung, is steadfastly devout and unsentimental, testifying to a powerful, unwavering faith. It is still included in hymnals and anthologies.

JOHANN WILHELM LUDWIG GLEIM (1719–1803), a student at Halle, where he and his friends Uz and Götz developed a stylized, almost asensual poetry in praise of wine, women, and song, modeled on Anacreon. Gleim published an acclaimed volume of patriotic poetry during the Seven Years' War.

JOHANN NIKOLAUS GÖTZ (1721–81) was a chaplain in the French army in 1751. Götz spent his later life first as a pastor and then a town official in the Palatinate. He wrote anacreontic poems and was a friend of Uz and Gleim during his student days at Halle.

CATHARINA REGINA VON GREIFFENBERG (1633–94) was born to a noble Protestant family at Seysenegg in Lower Austria. She was thirty-one when she married her uncle, Hans Rudolf von Greiffenberg (who had directed her excellent education) in Nuremberg, the city in which she finally settled in 1679, after her husband's death and long years of tribulation over her property rights in Catholic Austria. Her finely crafted, emotionally intense work, consisting principally of complex religious sonnets, was encouraged by S. von Birken and P. von Zesen. She was a member of Zesen's German-Minded Company. She also wrote a book of devotional meditations, a mixture of both prose and poems, the second volume of which appeared just before her death.

HANS JAKOB CHRISTOFFEL VON GRIMMELSHAUSEN (1621–76) was the grandson of a Gelnhausen baker. The youth was carried off by Croat and Hessian soldiers in the Thirty Years' War in 1635, and served with various regiments until he became steward to Carl Bernhard von Schauenburg at Gaisbach in 1649. He transferred his duties as steward to Johannes Küffer on the Ullenberg near

Gaisbach, and between 1665–67 was a tavernkeeper in Gaisbach. He left this employment to enter the service of the Strasbourg bishop, Egon von Fürstenberg, having converted to Roman Catholicism some time before. He served as the mayor of Renchen in his last years. His *Der abenteurliche Simplicissimus* (1669) and its satellite novels are perhaps the greatest literary works inspired by and commenting on the Thirty Years' War.

ANDREAS GRYPHIUS (1616–64) was born at Glogau in Silesia where he studied at the Danzig grammar school and became tutor to the sons of the wealthy Georg Schönborn, who bequeathed him enough money to allow him to study and lecture at the university of Leyden. After traveling in Europe, he returned to Glogau, and, refusing appointments to the universities of Frankfurt/Oder, Heidelberg, and Uppsala, he became syndic of the diet of Glogau in 1650, a position he maintained until his death. A prolific dramatist, most of his plays were composed between 1646 and 1649, when the works of the Dutch dramatist, Vondel, still echoed powerfully in his memory. His dramas included, among others, *Peter Squenz, Leo Armenius, Catharina von Georgien, Carolus Stuardus,* and *Aemilius Paulus Papinianus.* His melancholy poetic spirit is best revealed in his religious lyric. His *Sonn- und Feiertags-Sonette* (Sunday and holiday sonnets) were published in 1639.

JOHANN CHRISTIAN GÜNTHER (1695–1723) was born in Striegau in Silesia. He was disowned by his physician father over a love affair, while studying medicine in Wittenberg. Moving to Leipzig, he continued his studies, yet drifted ever deeper into a dissolute life-style. Refused a position as Dresden court poet (arranged by J. B. Mencke), allegedly because he was drunk at the interview, it became clear that even his poetic genius could not save him from his own destruction. After an unsuccessful marriage to a pastor's daughter, he moved to Jena to resume his medical studies in 1722, but his health was already ruined. A writer of occasional poetry that often supplemented his income, he is most notable for his strikingly warm love poems.

FRIEDRICH VON HAGEDORN (1708–54) was a man of independent

means who devoted his years in Hamburg to his social life and his deft, charming poetry. Influenced by both English poetry and classical models, he was known in his time as "the German Horace."

HARTMANN VON AUE (1160–70–after 1210). Little is known of this great narrative poet who mourns the death of his feudal lord, whom he served somewhere in the Alemannic linguistic region. Writing between 1180 and 1205, his principal works include the Arthurian epic *Erec, Gregorius,* a legend of atonement, and *Der Arme Heinrich,* his best known and perhaps his finest work. *Minne* is usually seen as morally educative in his lyric verse. He wrote three moving crusaders' songs.

HEINRICH VON MORUNGEN (?–1222) was a nobleman whose family may have been settled in Sangerhausen in Thuringia. He was one of the most intense and lyrically powerful of the Minnesänger. Serving as an official for the Markgraf of Meissen, he may have been active at the Thuringian court. He is known to have died in 1222, possibly at the Thomaskloster in Leipzig. His poetry is visually striking, with images of light and fire; the beloved is sometimes given demonic, magical qualities. He soon became the stuff of legends, and he is the hero of the late medieval ballad *Vom edlen Möringer.*

HEINRICH VON VELDEKE (dates unknown). Writing in the second half of the twelfth century, Heinrich may have been born between 1140 and 1150, and is believed to have died before 1210. His home was near Maastricht, and he was active at the Thuringian court, the new literary center. His principal work is the narrative *Eneit,* an adaptation of the anonymous French novel, *Roman d'Eneas.* Begun in Maastricht in 1170, the manuscript was stolen and not returned to him until the eighties, whereupon he completed it. He was the first to bring the Greek gods into the purview of German literature.

CHRISTIAN HOFMANN VON HOFMANNSWALDAU (1617–79), the son of a nobleman, soon became a distinguished councillor of his native Breslau, after studying at Leyden and taking a grand tour of the Netherlands, England, France, and Italy. He was appointed president of the council in 1677. Technically skilled in poetic forms and a master of the Alexandrine, he was early influenced by Opitz, and is Marino's chief student in Germany. He is chiefly remembered for his erotic verse.

JOHANN KLAJ (1616–56) born in Meissen, studied at Wittenberg and in 1644 because a private tutor, then instructor, in Nuremberg. There he met and became fast friends with Georg Philipp Harsdörffer, with whom he founded the Löblicher Hirten-und Blumenorden an der Pegnitz (The Pegnitz society of shepherds and flower-order). He was appointed pastor at Kitzingen in 1650. Klaj wrote religious and pastoral poetry (under the pastoral name Clajus), including the volume *Pegnesisches Schäfergedicht* (1644) in which he collaborated with Harsdörffer.

EWALD CHRISTIAN VON KLEIST (1715–59), a Pomeranian nobleman who studied at the University of Königsberg, entered the Danish army in 1736, resigned and entered the Prussian army in 1740. Not enthusiastic about life in the regiment, his literary friends included Ramler, Gleim, and Nicolai. A major at the time of the Seven Years' War, he was stationed at Leipzig in 1758, there becoming a close friend of Lessing. He died of wounds inflicted at the Battle of Kunersdorf and was believed to have been the model for Major von Tellheim in Lessing's *Minna von Barnhelm*.

FRIEDRICH GOTTLOB KLOPSTOCK (1724–1803), a poet of intense lyric force, Klopstock was born in Quedlinburg and attended school at Schulpforta, where he was exposed to a classical education and the influence of Pietism. He studied briefly at Jena, moving then to Halle. In 1748 the first three cantos of his powerful religious epic, *Der Messias,* appeared and earned him a nationwide reputation as a poetic genius. He began to write odes, his most original poetic compositions, in 1747. Invited to Copenhagen in 1751 by King Frederick V, he received a pension that continued until his death. In 1754 he married Meta Moller, who died in childbirth in 1758. After the fall of his patron in 1770 he left Denmark for Hamburg, where the first publication of his odes gave him great influence over the poets of the younger generation. His *oeuvre* includes plays, patriotic historical dramas, and religious poems, but he is best remembered for his odes and *Der Messias*.

QUIRINUS KUHLMANN (1651–89) was a poet and religious fanatic, influenced by Jacob Böhme. He studied in Jena and Leyden, from where he was expelled for his unorthodox religious views. Failing to convert the Sultan on a trip to Constantinople (1678), and convinced that he was the Son of God, he eventually traveled to Moscow to proclaim the Kühlmonarchie, his own heavenly kingdom. He was condemned and burned at the stake as an enemy of religion and of the state. His first collection of religious poetry is *Himmlische Liebesküsse* (Heavenly kisses of love, 1671) but his most extravagant, bizarre, and best-known verse is found in *Der Kühlpsalter* (1684).

DER VON KÜRENBERG DER KÜRENBERGER (c. 1150–75), a nobleman who wrote around the middle of the twelfth century, was possibly the earliest Middle High German lyric poet. The name is common in the Austrian-Bavarian region. Almost all examples of his work depict the poignant dialogic exchange between man and woman. The strophic form he employs is virtually identical with that of the *Nibelungenlied*.

FRIEDRICH VON LOGAU (1604–55), an epigrammatist of noble descent from Brockhut in Silesia, obtained a position as councillor to Duke Ludwig of Brieg in 1644, and followed him to Liegnitz in 1654. Known only for his social and political epigrams, his first collection appeared in 1638 as *Zwei Hundert Teutscher Reimensprüche* (Two hundred German rhymes) under the pseudonym Salomon Golau. In 1654 he published *Salomons von Golau Deutsche Sinngedichte Drei Tausend* (Three-thousand German epigrams of Salomon von Golau). Witty and tolerant in his criticism, Logau, whose work was revived by Lessing, has achieved lasting popularity.

DANIEL CASPER VON LOHENSTEIN (1635–83) was educated in Breslau, Leipzig, and Tübingen. This tax-collector's son traveled abroad and settled down to the practice of law in Breslau, later becoming syndic of the city. He was raised to the nobility and given the name *Lohenstein* in 1670. Composing only in his leisure hours, he wrote the most important (and rhetorically bombastic) tragedies of the later baroque: *Ibrahim Bassa, Cleopatra, Agrippina, Epi-*

charis, Sophonisbe, and *Ibrahim Sultan.* Toward the end of his life he wrote the massive courtly novel *Grossmütiger Feldherr Arminius,* which was published after his death.

MARTIN LUTHER (1483–1546) is the major figure of the Reformation. He was born into a peasant family at Eisleben and studied at Erfurt University from 1501 to 1505, when he entered an Augustinian monastery. Ordained in 1507, he taught philosophy at the University of Wittenberg. Obtaining the degree of doctor of theology in 1512, he was appointed professor of biblical exegesis. On October 31, 1517, he nailed his 95 (Latin) theses, criticizing the Church's sale of indulgences, to the door of the castle church at Wittenberg. After a disputation with Johann Eck, in which he argued that the papacy was not a divine institution, he published the important tracts *An den christlichen Adel deutscher Nation, De Captivitate Babylonica,* and *Von der Freiheit eines Christenmenschen.* Refusing to renounce his beliefs, he publicly burned the papal bull demanding his recantation in 1520, and was excommunicated. Despite a courageous defense at the Diet of Worms in 1521 he was outlawed by the Edict of Worms, but was rushed to sanctuary at the Wartburg, where he spent 10 months translating the New Testament. He returned to Wittenberg in 1522, at great risk, to quell the excesses of the reforming party. In 1525 he married the runaway nun, Katharina von Bora. His entire translation of the Bible was published in 1534, but he continued to labor on it until his death. A prolific writer on matters doctrinal and theological, he is the author of many powerful, moving hymns.

MEINLOH VON SEVELINGEN (dates unknown). Writing around 1170–80 he is presumed to be the ancestor of the high steward of Graf Dillingen in Söfflingen near Ulm. He sings of mutual love and of courtly *minne* as service to a remote lady.

NEIDHART VON REUENTHAL (ca. 1185–ca. 1240) was a court poet of the lower nobility. He was active first in Bavaria, then in Austria (until c. 1237) at the court of Friedrich II. He revolutionized lyric verse, introducing, in rich parody, the peasant milieu to the courtly art form and writing most of his socially dissonant pieces as dance songs of either the summer or the winter.

MARTIN OPITZ (1597–1639). The son of a Bunzlau butcher, Opitz studied at Beuthen, Frankfurt/Oder, and Heidelberg. After the dissolution of the Heidelberg University, he fled to Holland, where he became a friend of Heinsius in 1620. Returning from a brief teaching appointment in Transylvania, he entered the service of the duke of Liegnitz, publishing *Das Buch von der deutschen Poeterey,* the poetic manual of the German baroque in 1624. This was soon followed by his collected poems, and he was crowned poet laureate by Ferdinand II. From 1626 until 1632 he was, although a Protestant, secretary to Burggraf Karl Hannibal von Dohna, who was in charge of the Counter-Reformation in Breslau. When Dohna was deposed, he entered the service of the dukes of Liegnitz-Brieg, eventually settling in Danzig where he died of the plague. He translated Heinsius, Grotius, Sophocles, Seneca, Barclay, and Rinuccini, among others, and although he was not the greatest lyric genius of the age, his work, particularly his poetic theories, left an indelible imprint on the German literary baroque.

OSWALD VON WOLKENSTEIN (1377–1445) is a well-documented personality. This dynamic and peripatetic poet was of noble birth. After extensive youthful wanderings in Southern and Eastern Europe, he inherited his father's estate and returned home in 1401, marrying Margarete of Schwangau in 1417. In February 1415 he entered the service of emperor Sigismund and undertook diplomatic missions to England, Scotland, Portugal, France, and Hungary. He was captured on several occasions (with the help of his former love Sabine Jäger) by duke Friedrich IV of Austria-Tirol. He continued to display a contentious nature well into his later years. Consisting of over 125 songs, his *oeuvre* is varied and includes dawn songs, Minnelieder, dance, travel, and religious songs. Many of his songs refer to his own life experiences, and are boldly original.

KARL WILHELM RAMLER (1725–98) completed his studies at Halle and Berlin and became a professor of logic at the Berlin military cadet school, where he was a friend of Gotthold Ephraim Lessing, Kleist, and F. Nicolai. He was co-director of the royal theater in Berlin (1786–96). Adept at classical forms, he translated, among others, Horace, Catullus, and Martial, and wrote in the anacreontic style.

REINMAR DER ALTE (dates unknown). Almost nothing is known of Reinmar's life, although he may have come from Hagenau in Alsace. He appears to have held a position akin to that of court poet at the Babenberg court in Vienna, where most of his poems were written between 1185 and 1205. Acknowledged master and classical representative of Minnesang, he was probably Walther von der Vogelweide's teacher, becoming involved in a lengthy (literary) disputation with him.

MARTIN RINCKHART (1586–1649) is the author of devout, moving hymns, including the still popular "Nun danket alle Gott," Rinckhart came from Eilenburg in Saxony. After studying in Leipzig, he was made cantor, then deacon at Eisleben, and, in 1617, was appointed principal pastor in his native town. When not working selflessly for his parish, he wrote spiritual comedies such as *Der Eislebische Ritter* (The knight of Eisle, 1613) where Luther triumphs over the Pope and Calvin.

JOHANN RIST (1607–67) was the son of the pastor at Ottensen near Hamburg. He studied theology at Rinteln and Rostock universities, and was appointed pastor at Wedel in 1635. Ten years later he was named *poeta laureatus* by emperor Ferdinand III and wrote two festival dramas concerning the end of the Thirty Years' War, *Das friedewünschende Teutschland* (Germany longing for peace, 1647) and *Das friedejauchzende Teutschland* (Germany rejoicing in peace, 1653). He was a member of the Fruit-bringing Society and the Society of Pegnitz Shepherds, and, in 1656, founded the Order of the Elbe Swan. Some of his simple, powerful poems, including "O Ewigkeit, du Donnerwort," have survived as hymns to the present day.

HANS SACHS (1494–1576) was a Nuremberg shoemaker and a prolific writer. He became a noted and very productive member of the Guild of Meistersinger, writing a large number of these complex songs. He celebrated Luther in *Die wittenbergisch Nachtigall* (The nightingale of Wittenberg, 1523) and, until dissuaded by the city council, penned prose dialogues to support the Protestant cause. He wrote large numbers of Meisterlieder, epigrams, fables, farces, and some 200 verse plays.

DAVID SCHIRMER (1623–83) studied at Leipzig and Wittenberg, and in 1674 was made a member of Zesen's German-minded Fellowship, becoming court poet at Dresden three years later. Appointed librarian to Johann Georg II in 1656, he was dismissed from his post in 1682 and died the following year. His charming verse includes many light and graceful love poems and was published in *Rosen-Gepüsche* (1650) and *Poetische Rautengepüsche* (1663).

SIBYLLA SCHWARZ (1621–38), sometimes known as "the Pommeranian Sappho," spent her seventeen short years in Greifswald, where her father was a member of the city government. Her poems, written in the manner of Opitz, were published in 1650 by Samuel Gerlach.

FRIEDRICH SPEE (1591–1635) was born to a noble family in Kaiserswert near Düsseldorf. He entered the Society of Jesus in 1610 and was ordained as a priest in 1622. In 1627–28 he served in Würzburg as father-confessor to those condemned to die, and among his desperate flock were over two-hundred unfortunates sentenced to be burnt for witchcraft. Convinced that many had been condemned unjustly, he published, anonymously, an attack on the judicial procedures he had observed (*Cautio Criminalis*, 1631). Spee died of the plague while nursing the sick and dying at Trier. The most considerable Roman Catholic vernacular poet of the early seventeenth century, his greatest work is his gently pious *Trutznachtigall* (Better than the nightingale), first published in 1649.

STEINMAR (dates unknown). Active in the second half of the thirteenth century, Steinmar was present at the siege of Vienna by Rudolf von Habsburg in 1276, and he participated in a campaign against Meissen between 1294 and 1296. He is best known for his songs of *niedere minne* and his parody of the dawn song.

KASPAR STIELER (1632–1707). After studying theology and medicine at Leipzig, Erfurt, Marburg, and Giessen, the quixotic son of Erfurt joined the military, later to become an administrator in princely service. He was ennobled in 1705. Stieler was the author of *Die geharnschte Venus* (Venus in armor, 1660), a collection of erotic poetry that appeared in Hamburg under the name of Filidor der

Dorfferer. He was a member of the Fruit-bringing Society from 1668.

ULRICH VON HUTTEN (1488–1523) was born near Fulda to an impoverished noble family. He ran away at seventeen and wandered from university to university. Having found favor at the court of Mainz, he seemed to have settled into a life of learning when, in 1516, his cousin was murdered by duke Ulrich of Württemberg, and the pugnacious Hutten penned a dialogue against the duke that became a denunciation of all tyrants. For a time, he was protected by Emperor Maximilian I, and was crowned poet by him in Augsburg. In 1519 he participated in a war that evicted Ulrich from his lands. In 1520 he wrote a dialogue against the Pope and went on to use the dialogue form to express his own personal discontents and desires. He translated some of his dialogues into trenchant, energetic German. Constantly involved in conflicts, he eventually took refuge in Switzerland with Zwingli and finally succumbed there to an old case of syphilis. A man of great energy, but considerably less judgment, his mottoes "Alea jacta est" and "Ich hab's gewagt" are characteristic. A fearsome satirist, he supported the Reformation but did not devote himself unswervingly to the cause.

WALTHER VON DER VOGELWEIDE (c. 1170–c. 1230) is the greatest Middle High German lyric poet, though nothing is known of his origins. At the Babenberg court in Vienna from 1190 to 1198, he was undoubtedly Reinmar's pupil. He later served at the courts of various lords, including Philipp von Schwaben, bishop Wolfger von Passau, and Landgraf Hermann of Thuringia. In 1220 he was granted a fief by Friedrich II. His *oeuvre*, over 100 poems, consists mainly of Minnelieder and political poems, his most original lyric expressions. His Minnelieder are usually divided into three periods: conventional depictions of *minne*, poems where these conventions are discarded and there is spontaneous and equal love between man and woman, and poems dealing with the spontaneity of *niedere minne* in the aristocratic world of *hohe minne*.

GEORG RUDOLPH WECKHERLIN (1584–1653), after completing studies in Tübingen, traveled throughout Germany, and visited Paris and London, where, in 1616, he married Elizabeth Raworth. Secre-

tary and court poet to the duke of Württemberg, he attempted to
address what he felt to be some of the ills and inadequacies of
German verse in his *Oden und Gesänge* (Odes and songs, 1618–
19). In 1620 he joined the administration of the exiled Elector
Palatine, Friedrich V, in London, which was to become his permanent home. He was soon appointed to the ranks of the English
administration, where he remained until Cromwell's accession to
power. He was named Secretary for Foreign Tongues in 1625 and
was succeeded in 1649 by John Milton, whom he later assisted from
1652 until his death. Weckherlin was geographically isolated and
avoided all Opitzian influence, never conforming his poetic meter to
the demands of natural word order. His work was rediscovered by
Herder in the eighteenth century.

CHRISTIAN WEISE (1642–1708) was a man of prodigious education.
After studying at the University of Leipzig and serving as secretary to
Count Leiningen of Halle, the Zittau native was appointed professor
at the newly founded gymnasium at Weissenfels in 1670. Eight years
later he returned to his home town as rector of the Zittau gymnasium, and during the thirty years of his leadership, the institution
became one of the best of its kind in Germany. He introduced
theatrical production into the curriculum and wrote about sixty
dramas for the students to perform. The best known of these are the
Trauerspiel von dem Neapolitanischen Rebellen Masaniello (1683)
and *Bäurischer Macchiavellus* (1979).

WOLFRAM VON ESCHENBACH (c. 1170/75–c. 1220) was an impoverished nobleman. He was born at Eschenbach in Bavaria and
may have been a professional poet, although he himself insisted that
his calling was arms. It is assumed that Landgraf Hermann of
Thuringia was one of his patrons. He was the author of three epic
poems, *Parzival, Willehalm,* and *Titurel* and of eight lyric poems,
five of which are moving dawn songs.

PHILIPP VON ZESEN (1619–89), born the son of a Lutheran pastor
in Dessau, was the most prolific of all the Baroque poets, having
discovered his talent as a child and fostered it at the University of
Wittenberg under the eye of August Buchner. For the most part, he
was able to live from the profits of his pen and the generosity of

various patrons. In 1643 Zesen founded the poetic society Die deutschgesinnete Genossenschaft (The German-minded fellowship) in Hamburg. He traversed Europe in his frequent travels and was eventually named poet laureate of Regensburg by Ferdinand III and raised into the nobility. He lived for many years in Holland and spent his last days in Hamburg. Obsessed with the purification and cultivation of the German tongue, Zesen's theories were extreme, and at times absurd, but he was a figure of enormous literary import. His poetry is ingenious and technically inventive.

ACKNOWLEDGMENTS

Every reasonable effort has been made to locate the owners of rights to previously published translations printed here. We gratefully acknowledge permission to reprint the following material:

Excerpts from *German and Italian Lyrics of the Middle Ages* by Frederick Golden, translation © 1973 by Frederick Golden. Used by permission of Doubleday, a division of Bantam, Doubleday, Dell Publishing Group, Inc.

Excerpts from *The German Lyric of the Baroque in English Translation* translated by George C. Schoolfield. Published for *Studies in Germanic Languages and Literatures,* no. 29. Copyright © 1961 The University of North Carolina Press. Reprinted by permission of the publisher.

Excerpts from *Medieval German Lyric Verse in English Translation* by J. W. Thomas. Copyright © 1968 by the University of North Carolina Press. Reprinted by permission of the publisher.

"A farmhand lay all hidden," with permission of James J. Wilhelm from his *Lyrics of the Middle Ages.* New York: Garland Publishing Inc., 1990.

Excerpts from *Lutheran Worship,* prepared by The Commission on Worship of The Lutheran Church—Missouri Synod, St. Louis. Text and setting Copyright © 1982 Concordia Publishing House.

Excerpts from *Old German Love Songs* edited by Frank C. Nicholson, M.A. Copyright © 1907 University of Chicago Press. Reprinted by permission of the publisher.

Excerpts from *European Metaphysical Poetry* edited by Frank J. Warnke. Copyright © 1961 by Yale University. Reprinted by permission of the publisher.

"Eternity, Thou Thundrous Word," from *The Texts to Johann Sebastian Bach's Church Cantatas* translated by Z. Philip Abrose. Kirchheim/Teck (Germany): Hänssler Musik Verlag, 1984.

Index of Titles and First Lines

German

English

THE GERMAN LIBRARY
in 100 Volumes

Wolfram von Eschenbach
Parzival
Edited by André Lefevere

Gottfried von Strassburg
Tristan and Isolde
Edited and Revised by Francis G. Gentry
Foreword by C. Stephen Jaeger

German Mystical Writings
Edited by Karen J. Campbell
Foreword by Carol Zaleski

German Medieval Tales
Edited by Francis G. Gentry
Foreword by Thomas Berger

German Humanism and Reformation
Edited by Reinhard P. Becker
Foreword by Roland Bainton

Immanuel Kant
Philosophical Writings
Edited by Ernst Behler
Foreword by René Wellek

Friedrich Schiller
Plays: Intrigue and Love and Don Carlos
Edited by Walter Hinderer
Foreword by Gordon Craig

Friedrich Schiller
Wallenstein and Mary Stuart
Edited by Walter Hinderer

Johann Wolfgang von Goethe
*The Sufferings of Young Werther
and Elective Affinities*
Edited by Victor Lange
Forewords by Thomas Mann

German Romantic Criticism
Edited by A. Leslie Willson
Foreword by Ernst Behler

Philosophy of German Idealism
Edited by Ernst Behler

Heinrich von Kleist
Plays
Edited by Walter Hinderer
Foreword by E. L. Doctorow

E. T. A. Hoffmann
Tales
Edited by Victor Lange

Georg Büchner
Complete Works and Letters
Edited by Walter Hinderer and Henry J. Schmidt

German Fairy Tales
Edited by Helmut Brackert and Volkmar Sander
Foreword by Bruno Bettelheim

German Literary Fairy Tales
Edited by Frank G. Ryder and Robert M. Browning
Introduction by Gordon Birrell
Foreword by John Gardner

Heinrich Heine
Poetry and Prose
Edited by Jost Hermand and Robert C. Holub
Foreword by Alfred Kazin

Heinrich von Kleist and Jean Paul
German Romantic Novellas
Edited by Frank G. Ryder and Robert M. Browning
Foreword by John Simon

German Romantic Stories
Edited by Frank G. Ryder
Introduction by Gordon Birrell

German Poetry from 1750 to 1900
Edited by Robert M. Browning
Foreword by Michael Hamburger

Gottfried Keller
Stories
Edited by Frank G. Ryder
Foreword by Max Frisch

Wilhelm Raabe
Novels
Edited by Volkmar Sander
Foreword by Joel Agee

Theodor Fontane
Short Novels and other Writings
Edited by Peter Demetz
Foreword by Peter Gay

Theodor Fontane
Delusions, Confusions and The Poggenpuhl Family
Edited by Peter Demetz
Foreword by J. P. Stern
Introduction by William L. Zwiebel

German Essays on History
Edited by Rolf Sältzer
Foreword by James J. Sheehan

Wilhelm Busch and others
German Satirical Writings
Edited by Dieter P. Lotze and Volkmar Sander
Foreword by John Simon

Writings of German Composers
Edited by Jost Hermand and James Steakley

German Lieder
Edited by Philip Lieson Miller
Foreword by Hermann Hesse

Arthur Schnitzler
Plays and Stories
Edited by Egon Schwarz
Foreword by Stanley Elkin

Rainer Maria Rilke
Prose and Poetry
Edited by Egon Schwarz
Foreword by Howard Nemerov

Robert Musil
Selected Writings
Edited by Burton Pike
Foreword by Joel Agee

Essays on German Theater
Edited by Margaret Herzfeld-Sander
Foreword by Martin Esslin

German Novellas of Realism I and II
Edited by Jeffrey L. Sammons

Friedrich Dürrenmatt
Plays and Essays
Edited by Volkmar Sander
Foreword by Martin Esslin

Hans Magnus Enzensberger
Critical Essays
Edited by Reinhold Grimm and Bruce Armstrong
Foreword by John Simon

Gottfried Benn
Prose, Essays, Poems
Edited by Volkmar Sander
Foreword by E. B. Ashton
Introduction by Reinhard Paul Becker

German Essays on Art History
Edited by Gert Schiff

Max Frisch
Novels, Plays, Essays
Edited by Rolf Kieser
Foreword by Peter Demetz

All volumes available in hardcover and paperback editions at your bookstore or from the publisher. For more information on The German Library write to: The Continuum Publishing Company, 370 Lexington Avenue, New York, NY 10017.